Praise for Op[

Jude and John are brave to write their book. Of particular use for others, and surely not easy to write about, are their descriptions of behaviors in their son that in retrospect were signs of his addiction that they wish they could have recognized and acted on, as well as occasions when they were given advice by people who knew addiction, advice which they didn't fully take.
–Jennifer P. Schneider M.D., Ph.D., Addiction and Pain Medicine

Like almost all parents, Jude and John were intentional in their parenting, trying their best to raise their kids with strong morals and a vision for their future. But the world that Millennial's have grown up in is a dangerous world. During normal adolescent experimentation, they are offered highly addictive and extremely potent drugs. Even when they want to stop using, they find it almost impossible. Read Jude and John's story and you will read the story that hundreds of thousands of American families could have written.
–John Leggio, MA, LISAC
Clinical Director, The Mark Youth & Family Care Campus, Inc., Tucson, AZ

We lost our only son when he chose to take his life at 25, the same age as John Leif when he died from an overdose. I knew little about the opioid disaster that was raging around the nation—I just knew Jude and John. That was enough. We were grieving our sons, both gone too soon. Reading "Opiate Nation" was deeply moving. I admire their willingness to give readers such an honest and transparent view of their broken hearts. This memoir helped me to address my own residual grief. You will be changed by reading this tribute to an amazing son. It changed me.
–Connie Kennemer, co-founder of Community Alliance for Healthy Minds (CAHM), a public service nonprofit in San Diego, CA

OPIATE NATION

A Memoir of Love, Loss & Acceptance

Jude DiMeglio Trang

with John M. Trang

Foreword by Johanna Trang Schumacher

Cover Design Concept: Jude DiMeglio Trang
Poppy Pods Cover Art: Michelle Hammer
Finalizing Cover Design: Noel Morado
Interior Layout: Chandrashekhar Yadav

First published in Australia 2019 by Gowor International Publishing

ISBN: 978-1-7355460-0-1

In remembrance of our son
Johnathan Leif Trang (March 10, 1989–August 2, 2014)
We offer this memoir to those who have lost loved ones to addiction,
and to those struggling with addiction.
May our story encourage you to never give up or give in.
There is hope and help if you search for it.

Table of Contents

A WORD BEFORE: Woefully Unprepared

My younger brother, John Leif, and I were very fortunate as kids to be given lots of opportunities by our parents for awesome experiences, whether it was horseback riding and pony club or rock climbing and dirt biking. Not the least of which were wonderful trips to Europe, which gave us invaluable time together as a family and exposure to other cultures and ways of thinking, as well as a connection to our own cultural roots and extended family. These trips definitely inspired a love of travel and other cultures and languages in me, and I'm sure they did for JL as well.

One of these trips in the summer of 2004 served as a chance for JL and me to get to know each other again. We had been quite close as young kids having been homeschooled together, but when I started going to high school, I naturally gravitated towards my peers and new friendships, without much time for the "little kid stuff" my brother was interested in. While I was still at home during high school, I then took a year off before I started college during which time I lived in Mexico. I then moved out of home for my second year of college, and we gradually grew further apart.

When we took this family trip, JL was now 15 (I was nearly 21), and it felt like we were finally living in the same world again. We had a great time hanging out together and catching up with friends in Paris and hanging out with our cousins and their friends on our great-grandparents' home island of Ischia in Italy. It was while we were on Ischia, hanging out one night, playing cards and drinking limoncello, that JL mentioned he'd been doing Oxy's (oxycodone) and that this trip was the first time he'd been off them for a while. I had only started party drinking earlier that year and had smoked weed a few times, depending on who I was around (I wouldn't have had a clue where to source it), and the worst I'd ever heard of anyone doing (but never witnessed) was cocaine. I knew that Oxy's were like Vicodin/painkillers, but I really had no idea what that meant, especially regarding addiction. I remember telling him, "You've gotta stop doing that stuff, it's bad news!" I had thought my brother and I were now living in the same world, but in reality, we were worlds apart—yet again.

It never once occurred to me to tell anyone, especially not our parents. It felt like we were finally connecting again and sharing little secrets was a form of sibling solidarity. Of course, in hindsight I would have, at a bare minimum, followed up on him after the trip to see how he was doing. And I don't doubt for a second that that year could have made a big difference in his recovery, perhaps even catching him before he started smoking BT (black tar heroin). But then again, the sober JL was extremely persuasive, let alone when his cravings were speaking for him. I'm sure even if I'd brought it up, he would have down-played it and convinced me not to tell anyone. In reality, we as a society were *woefully unprepared* for the beginnings of the opiate epidemic. As with all epidemics, we were not even "inoculated" with accurate information. This is the same way a virus becomes an epidemic, when not enough of the population has the defenses and immunity against it, it can take over with unsettling speed and power.

Interestingly, while we were on that trip to Italy in 2004, I happened to see the movie *Trainspotting* with our cousins. JL wasn't with us that night. The thing that stuck out to me the most was when the baby died because its parents were so high and strung-out. I had never been tempted by harder drugs or pills, but even though I was not yet a mother, seeing that baby die (and the mother's anguish when she came down and was lucid again) was enough to make me want to keep as far away as I could from those drugs. Perhaps that was a natural reaction for me, as someone who had always wanted to be a mom for as long as I could remember. I think I am naturally a nurturer, but I was also positively influenced by our upbringing and wanted to emulate the example I saw in my mom, who stayed-at-home and home-schooled us, and was supported and valued in this role by my dad.

I was studying in Mazatlán, Mexico in 2005 when my parents found JL passed out in his car and discovered he was using BT. I came back after my summer school program had finished, but I was largely removed from those years of his life and his initial sobriety, living my own life, partying, finishing up college, and even meeting my now-husband. I do vividly remember the day he fell off the parking garage on Thanksgiving 2007. I was recently married and my husband, Gerard, and I said to ourselves in the months following, "sober people don't just fall off buildings." We didn't know what he was struggling with, drugs or alcohol, but we knew it wasn't good. In May of 2008, we packed up all our belongings and moved to Gerard's home country of Australia. We started planning to expand our family soon after arriving, while changing careers and making new friends, and we were focused on our new life there. Once our first baby arrived, our lives changed completely yet again.

While it was a devastating shock, my brother's death was not entirely unexpected. I think when someone is addicted to heroin, the potential for an overdose is always looming in the back of your mind. Especially after hearing in the news about actor Philip Seymour Hoffman's accidental overdose and death in February of 2014. He had relapsed in 2013, but prior to that he had been 23 years sober since going to rehab after college. Somewhere in our minds was the dreaded knowledge that most heroin addicts do not survive; it is only a matter of time before they overdose, accidentally or otherwise.

I did experience some guilt after JL died, mostly surrounding not being more in contact with him, all those "I love you's" left unsaid. But I mostly felt a deep, deep sadness. Not only for my loss as a sibling, but naturally putting myself in my parents' shoes and being unable to even imagine the devastation of losing a child. I think it is something only other parents can begin to comprehend, as author Elizabeth Stone has said, "Making the decision to have a child—it is momentous. It is to decide forever to have your heart go walking around outside your body."

It has been a difficult journey for us all since JL died and therapy has been the most significant step in my path towards healing and letting go. Looking forward, I can only hope that my brother's story will be a warning to other current/potential addicts, but even more importantly, that my parents' story will be a source of hope and encouragement for other survivors and help break the pattern of silence and shame surrounding drug addiction. The only way to fight this epidemic is with transparency and life-saving knowledge, so that we and our children can be immunized from its devastation and destruction.

Johanna Trang Schumacher
2018 October

1

THE LETTER

The pain that comes from loving someone who's in trouble can be profound.

–Melody Beattie, *Codependent No More*

On a morning of intense emotional strain and internal dialogue with myself, I found a letter inside an already opened envelope, a letter that would suddenly change our lives—mine, my husband's, our son's. This is not an exaggeration. This was the letter I didn't know I was searching for while I was desperately searching for help—just a scrap of information that would begin to answer the questions about what was wrong with my teenage son that would cause him to say:

"Why do you keep frustrating me? Do you want me to become one of those kids that are so frustrated and angry with their parents that they end up shooting them?"

I can't begin to explain what went through my mind when these questions came out of our 16-year-old son's mouth. As teenagers, I think many of us told our parents—in moments of anger—that we hated them for withholding some privilege we felt was our right, but in the spring of 2005, when I heard these questions not just once, but twice, I knew something was dreadfully wrong with our son.

June 22, 2005, my husband John's birthday, is a date now indelibly stamped into our minds for reasons not of celebration.

The few months leading up to this particular day, we had noticed increasing agitation in our son John Leif (JL) during most of our interactions. He had become more easily irritated, frustrated, and expressed a lot of anger towards us, especially over having a midnight curfew. He had been arguing with us for over an hour about why he should not have a curfew at all. We told him he just needed to accept that midnight was going to be it for now, and that was when he asked those chilling questions. That night I began begging God to show me what was happening to him.

The next morning after JL had left for his summer job, and as I was walking around the house, my cries for help were answered when I went into his bedroom. I have never rifled through his personal belongings—it felt sneaky, invasive, dishonest, and it was, sadly, what my mother did when I was growing up. I had always wished she would have just asked me for whatever information she felt she needed, but direct communication was not her forte. John and I always felt it was best to be respectful to our kids and ask them directly. But this was different, and I knew JL's well-being was at stake. On his desk, I found the envelope enclosing a letter from his close friend James. I thought it was odd when it had arrived in the mail, as his friend lived in town and never wrote letters; was he out of town on vacation? In searching for clues, I pulled it out and read it. This letter was exactly what I needed to see.

James told JL about the detox ranch where he was staying, and how regimented it was, but that he was glad because now his life was going in a different direction, and he felt good about himself. He warned JL to "stay away from that BT stuff" because it had already ruined James' life, and he knew JL was headed down the wrong road. I was shocked and decided to get on the web and see if I could find out what BT was. I finally found a drug information web site from the UK with lots of drug street names, but nothing called BT—and the only one close was "Ball," short for Black Tar Mexican Heroin. Surely that wasn't what this was?

I immediately called James' mother. She answered the phone and asked if I was sitting down. I listened as she explained that BT is Black Tar Heroin, and that her son had been smoking it and was addicted. A month earlier, she placed him in a 6-month rehab program out of state. She asked me carefully, "Have you found any little balls of tin foil with black debris in them around JL's room?" "Yes," I replied. "I have, but I figured they were related to his making fireworks," (which we allowed, as a family of Italian pyromaniacs, and had loads of fun with together). She explained that BT was crudely refined heroin from Mexico that the kids liquefied by heating under the foil and then smoked the rising vapors.

I was shocked. "Why hadn't you told us that your son was sent away for using drugs, especially *this* drug, and especially since JL and James were close friends?" She said "I called all my son's friends' parents. I just never thought JL would have been using it because he was so responsible and smart." She also mentioned that JL was not a part of her son's circle of close friends. This didn't make sense to me since we thought JL was one of his *closest* friends. They were together before school many mornings and most weekends. Was there more to this story than I was hearing? Only after JL's death did we hear from another friend that there had been a drug bust at his high school that May of 2005 where several students had been caught using opiates. Why hadn't the school officials let the rest of us parents know and address it openly in a school-wide meeting? The kids were quietly sent away to long-term rehabilitation programs. Many of them were part of the close circle of friends that James, and JL, knew well.

I will never forget that summer day I found tight little balls of tinfoil in his closet. Never. The memory of rapidly unfolding several of them, finding black tarry debris inside in an odd spiral pattern, having to call John at work to give him the bone chilling details. It's burned into my brain, as is the anxiety that wracked my body as I waited for him to drive home. I vividly recall waiting together for JL to arrive after his shift at the restaurant—pacing from the kitchen window to the living room window—anxiously watching for our son to come home. We heard him drive up and nervously waited for him to come in. Minutes passed. What was he doing? I walked out the back door to check. JL was sitting in the truck, windows rolled up, engine off. The truck was absorbing the 110-degree heat with him inside, slumped over the steering wheel as if asleep. At that moment, my heart broke as I saw my broken son. I walked out and knocked on the window. Startled, he looked up at me. I didn't need to wait for him and walked back into the house.

He came inside. I said, "We need to talk." Sitting down in the living room, John and I told him we did not want to accuse him of something if we didn't have evidence to support it, but we felt that he was using drugs. We asked him to tell us the truth, as it would go better for him in the long run. "Are you using drugs?" we asked. He replied, "No." We asked him again. "Of course not," he said. So, we told him about our conversation with his friends' mom and the evidence we had found. He broke down, and wept heavy, heaving sobs, and told us all he was able to, I believe, at the time. His story changed as he went along, as we pressed him. He just couldn't admit to us, or to himself, how addicted he was.

We decided to take the next few days and keep JL with us at all times, and not allow him to drive or be with friends or go to work, as we searched out what we should do to help him keep his commitment to be drug free. The more we read about heroin, the scarier it became, because it is so addictive physically, not to mention the withdrawal symptoms are hard and dangerous according to how much you have done. We were unsure of how bad it would be with smoking as opposed to injecting it; was there even a difference? There was so little information available. I also began immediately reading the book I bought over a month before when I was concerned that he was doing drugs but never read: *Drug Proof Your Kids* by Stephen Arterburn and Jim Burns. I wish we had read it when JL was ten, when it would have helped "drug proof" him (or, more accurately, us) just as the very early "drown proofing" of our infants is really training parents on how to keep babies safe around water.

The book was just what we needed, giving us the help we needed for how to proceed at that point. First step: uncover it. Done. Second step: intervention with facts so they can't deny it. Done. Third step: decide on a treatment program. Difficult. There were few programs in town for teen boys—opiate addiction was historically found in older people. I spent hours on the phone and Internet trying to find out what to do, and finally connected with a counselor and scheduled an appointment. But by that evening, JL started having terrible aches all over, shakes, and total insomnia that even Restoril and Benadryl didn't help. He was also hit with relentless diarrhea as his guts let loose. We went to his pediatrician, who had never heard of BT. He had to search to find a physician who could tell him, and us, what to do for heroin withdrawal. Heroin withdrawal for a 16-yr. old.

Because of the stigma associated with having so many students with addiction problems, the high school JL was attending was not open or informative about what was happening. It seemed that the parents of many of his friends from school were not open either; my guess is that it was due to the shame and embarrassment parents feel when their child is exhibiting any behavior that carries stigma, especially drug use. Information seemed nowhere to be found, and we were only just beginning to experience the veil of secrecy that surrounds heroin addiction. Had we been involved in the social life of his school, we would have at least known about the drug bust. It wasn't until years later that we finally heard more of the details that filled in the blank spaces of this narrative.

Initially, we found options for long-term rehab programs, and while they were fairly easy to find, the price tags for them were astronomical, some upwards of $75,000 to $100,000. We knew we had to try something else. Even though we were paying high premiums for private health insurance, "mental health" services were not covered—every expense we would incur over the years of our son's rehab efforts came out of our pockets. After a few weeks of intense searching to find someone local who knew about heroin addiction and what to do to help our son, we finally found an adolescent recovery program that works with parents and their teens. The Mark Youth & Family Care, run by John Leggio here in Tucson, was a lifesaver for us all. Regrettably, we did not take the advice to have JL in the Intensive Outpatient Program, which he desperately needed. As a very persuasive young man, JL talked us into doing just the twice-a-week meetings, which did not give us—as his parents and codependents—the information we needed to be armed with fighting this life-threatening addiction, and what would become a life-long struggle. We truly did not know what we were up against, or what our son was up against, and we did not really know the truth about how long he had been using opiates or what amount he was currently addicted to. Neither John nor I were aware at that point of the changes that had already occurred in our son's brain, and we thought since he stopped, once he got through the physical withdrawal, he would be normal again. How wrong we were.

The depth of the love of parents for their children cannot be measured.
It is like no other relationship. It exceeds concern for life itself.
The love of a parent for a child is continuous
and transcends heartbreak and disappointment.
–James E. Faust

2

THE KNOCK AT THE DOOR

*There is just so much hurt, disappointment, and oppression
one can take...
The line between reason and madness grows thinner.*

–Rosa Parks

Fast forward to a hot summer morning on August 2, 2014, nine years later. The air is muggy and still, in anticipation of the gathering storms that will yield rain in the afternoon of our monsoon season. John is at his desk working, and I am hanging pictures when we hear a knock at the door. The pictures are lined up on the sofa while I decide how to group them—a long overdue project that has been waiting for a quiet Saturday since we moved in over a year before. With the sound of the knock, a strong, demanding rap on the door, Brutus' deep, insistent German Shepherd bark motivates us to respond. Our other dog Bella follows suit. Their job has always been to protect us; if only they could have protected us from what was coming. John calms the dogs, puts them behind their gate, and opens the door.

Curious, I set down my hammer and hooks and go to the entryway. I see John standing outside the open screen door with a sheriff. In an instant, I am in panic mode. My heart speeds up. I begin thinking immediately that JL has been in an accident. I step out on the threshold as the sheriff is saying, "Are you the parents of Johnathan Leif Trang? I'm sorry to have to inform you that your son is dead." John says, "There must be a mistake…" I hear myself cry out, loudly, "OH NO, Oh No, oh no…" My knees give way. I fall toward the ground. John catches me, repeating, "There must be a mistake." The entryway shrinks, as if the walls are squeezing the life out of both of us. I am unable to breathe. In that moment, my life disintegrates.

John supports me, and I moan like a wounded animal. He asks the sheriff to come in and sit down. The officer, maybe thirty years old, and just a few years older than our son, is understandably pained at having to deliver this worst of news to parents about their child. He is choosing how to tell us the details, as we are simultaneously choosing which questions to ask. He faces us from the sofa, and calmly tells us the few details he has been given when he was sent to our home. This traumatic news keeps replaying in my mind: *our son is dead*. It blocks out everything else. The moment never progresses beyond that. I am experiencing dissociative amnesia—the temporary loss of recall memory due to a traumatic event. It can occur abruptly and last for minutes or years—certain details are still so hard to recall.

I know my world through my eyes, like our wolf-dog Bella; sight guides me. I remember events as a visual snapshot, stop-action pictures frozen in time. Like the old-fashioned View-Master stereoscopes, I see myself in abrupt freeze frames embedded in my memory, jerking from one 3D scene to the next. Click. Click. Click. The sheriff at the door then sitting on the sofa—are the only memories I had—as if the scene was frozen, stuck on this one frame, not moving forward with the click.

Our son, John Leif, died of a heroin overdose in the early morning hours of August 2nd, 2014. He was twenty-five. Few heroin users live long. Our son had been hanging on for ten years, addicted since he was fifteen. Deep in the recesses of our minds we feared that unless a Lazarus-type miracle happened, he would become one of the statistics. He was among the new generation of heroin addicts: bright and promising teenagers and young adults, from towns and cities across the country. People who have been exposed to heroin before they have even reached the legal age to drink, or drive.

Together, John and I kept a daily journal for the year following our son's death. This was our way to express the overwhelming emotions that were too frightening, and too painful, to verbalize. We didn't realize at the time how cathartic it would be. It was also a way to help us remember our journey. Our overloaded psyches might rearrange and edit the memories of our feelings, or even worse, forget. We didn't want to forget our son. We had already lost him, separated by an invisible yet impenetrable veil. We didn't want to forget the emotions that were our only connection we had left to him. For decades, John and I have risen early, before our days begin with children, work, and life, to sit with our espresso and read, meditate, and pray; and for me, to write. I have journals going back 40 years. I now have one more.

We wrote the journal *to* our son. Conversations directly to him, as if he were still alive. We believe he is still alive, just in another realm. Through writing to him, it allowed us to ask him questions as we searched for some meaning to the chaos we felt. With his unexpected death, there was the feeling that our conversations were cut off mid-sentence. Frustration over wanting explanations that only he could give, and that now we could never hear. But we still needed to ask. So many questions with no answers. A sudden death does this to you. *"What happened between when we last spoke to you at 10 pm and when you were found dead at 10 am? What went wrong in those 12 hours? Why didn't you tell us you were struggling and relapsed? Or, why couldn't we tell there was something amiss?"*

Writing focuses my thoughts that tend to wander as I stand and gaze out my picture window every morning; my eyes lighting on the hummingbird zeroing in on a red blossom, the cactus wren squawking on top of the saguaro, the cerulean blue sky of a desert morning, and the strong, solid Catalina Mountains behind them all. So, I bring my focus back to the page, sometimes closing my eyes, forcing my mind to go back to places it wants to avoid. Since my memory is visual, writing helps me pull up scenes and create "pictures" that I can go back to and recall.

Saturday, August 2, 2014
Dear JL,
 Dad here. *Our world stopped today at 11:20 am. Mom and I were both working at home when a Sheriff's officer came to the door. That moment everything in our lives changed forever—and we changed—and we will remain changed for the rest of our lives. "There must be a mistake…" I said as I still thought—hoped unreasonably, illogically— surely there must be some mistake. The officer came in and told us that you had died earlier this morning from an accidental heroin overdose. He said that we did not need to go to your apartment, and we could see you next week at the Coroner's office. We said absolutely not—we must go—we must see you. Mom called Heather and she was at our house within a few minutes. As she walked in, all mom and I could do was cling to her and sob—we knew she would help hold us together as the pieces of our hearts started tearing away.*

No matter how often we wrote, our journal could not contain everything that happened, and neither did our memories. I turn around now and look back at the morning of August 2nd attempting to recall more details, but some are missing. I asked Heather what she remembers from that day. "I heard you cry out over the phone, 'JL's dead and they are telling me I can't go see him!'" Heather recognized my voice but was at first unable to comprehend what I was saying through my cries. I told her I must go and see him even though the sheriff said not to. I was verbally and mentally composed when Heather arrived, but too weak physically to walk to the car without her and John's support. "You were like a wet rag, drained of all life and energy," Heather remembered. I would not have been able to verbalize it at the time, but I was experiencing

Post Traumatic Stress Disorder (PTSD) and would continue to do so for many weeks. It is horror, frozen in time, that your psyche can't dislodge.

I also had moments of just staring blankly. This is something that John bought to my attention decades ago when we were first dating. He asked me one evening if I had *petit mal seizures?* "Not that I know of," I'd said. He was in Pharmacy school at the University of Arizona, and had studied epilepsy, explaining to me that they were a type of brief seizure that cause a lapse in awareness or blank staring. Now they are referred to as *Absence Seizures.* Yes, my unconscious self wanted to be—needed to be—absent from this seismic news.

Heather, a family therapist, told me that my normal process from feeling to thinking was unusual and extremely rapid, moving between the two like lightning. During this time, it was no different. I felt like I was in a trance, unresponsive to any external stimuli, while my mind was quickly clicking through thoughts—click, click, click—and trying to make some sense out of them. But shock is protection against what our psyche cannot handle and allows us to respond to selective bits, the ones we think we can absorb without being reduced to fragments and disintegrating. I am sure that's why I don't recall sections of these first hours and days.

Fifteen years ago, we had never heard of smoking "BT." From what we knew growing up in the 1960's and 70's, heroin was the drug of choice for a very few hard-core drug users, those who had been through all the experimental drugs and were "addicts." Addicts were loser people who came from loser families in loser parts of town. So how was it that we, as upper-middle-class, well-educated parents in the most affluent part of our city, were now faced with a son addicted to heroin?

"Heroin High." That is what our neighborhood public high school is called in the recovery community (along with every other affluent high school) and for good reason. Why? As our son told us a decade ago: it is easier to get drugs than alcohol as under-age kids—they are even delivered to school. We didn't know any parents who had a child using heroin or lost a child to drug addiction; not because there were none in our community, as we later realized, but because no one was speaking out about it. Many still aren't.

Without realizing it, we had joined thousands of other families in America with whom we shared common struggles and with whom we now shared a common grief. But it was like heading off on an arduous hike through a rocky wilderness with blindfolds on. Those who had already been on this journey were walking back, blindfolds removed, but holding a gag over their mouths.

When we experience grief, life slows down almost to a stop, becoming interminable at times. Moving forward is very slow, and sometimes life stalls like a car running out of gas. When I was young, my family had a 1958 Volkswagen Beetle and it had an "emergency" reserve gas tank. I remember the car begin to hesitate as the engine sputtered on the last drops of gas and the quick movement of my mother's foot as she flipped over the lever to infuse the tank with one gallon of gas, just enough to get us to the next gas station. John and I ran out of emotional fuel many, many times during the year following our son's death, and we truly wondered if we would find any reserve that would make it possible to go on.

August 2, 2014, continued

__Mom here.__ We called your sister Johanna. It was already Sunday morning in Melbourne, Australia. She can't believe it—can't speak for the tears—in shock, especially after being here in Tucson with you in April when you were clean, sober, healthy—your real self.

Nonna and Nunu came over for dinner this evening. We waited to tell them in person—they were, at that moment, stripped of all hope. Through the sobs, and with the tears trickling down the valleys on those wrinkled, aged faces, all your grandparents could say was

"Oh, my God, NO, No, no…" They have experienced so much loss—personal and close. First J.D. (my brother, who died of AIDS at forty), then Susan (my sister, who died of breast/brain cancer at fifty-six), now you. Children are not supposed to predecease their parents, let alone grandchildren dying before their grandparents. Nunu has told me over and over that he prays for you every night—how is this an answer to all his prayers—all our prayers? We wanted a "Yes"—we had a "Wait"—now we have a "No." I guess "No" is an answer.

That "No" that came with the knock on the door took us to a place of the deepest darkness and unbearable physical and emotional pain we, a father and a mother, have ever known. It was as if we had been sitting in our living room quietly reading when a sinkhole opened below our home and sucked half of it down and out of sight, while we suddenly jumped up and backed away as we stared into the darkness, hoping we, and what was left of our life, would survive.

To live is to suffer, to survive is to find some meaning in the suffering.
–Friedrich Nietzsche

3

GARAGE MAHAL AND THE BODY BAG

Very quietly, the world loses blood overnight—
without a fight
In the morning, the sickness will hide in the light—
out of sight

–Mark Heard, *I'm Cryin' Again*

You would have never guessed that our son had an opioid addiction. He was clean and neat, was never living on the streets or out of his car, and had a wide circle of friends, some who used drugs and most who didn't. While he was in high school during the early years of his increasing addiction to opiates, he maintained his friendships and was going to parties as often as he could (and as often as we approved). He also had parties at our house as we wanted to be as closely involved with him and his friends as was reasonable for a teenager. We knew he was drinking, but never saw him drunk, and he didn't drink and drive that we knew of. Our kids had a commitment to sober driving and would take turns being the designated driver, or just stay put overnight.

One of the places where many parties were held was fondly referred to by JL and his friends as "Garage-Mahal." It was two apartment-style bedrooms attached to a large industrial-type building, where his friend Cory's family works to restore cars, build motorcycles, and fabricate things—and where their group of high school friends spent many weekend nights together listening to music, fooling around, and drinking. It is where JL spent the first night living in a new apartment after 6 months in a sober living home, and where he spent his last night on this earth. John wrote:

August 2, 2014, continued

Mom, Heather, and I all drove to "Garage-Mahal". When we arrived, I understood immediately why you were excited about this move. What a cool place. Although you had described it to us before, we had never been here. The place that had become your new home just two days ago, had now become your last.

We met your roommate Cory and a friend—they were devastated. Like a pane of safety glass hit by a bullet, they were in a million jagged pieces still holding together, but only just. Cory told us that you, he and some friends were hanging out together drinking beer last night until 4 am. He heard your alarm going off repeatedly at 10:25 am for work, without even being turned off to snooze. "I knew something was wrong." He knocked, then banged on your door, and finally broke into your room and found you sitting on the edge of your bed, your head hanging down to your ankles, dead. He called 911 and was still crying at 11:45 when we arrived. We added our tears.

We wanted to go in immediately and see our son. The medical examiner said we should not. *"Why? Why not?"* we asked. We decided to ask Heather to listen to the description and decide. Minutes passed, minutes that seemed like hours, until she walked back to us and confirmed that we should not because of the condition of his face. He had been found slumped over with the needle still in his vein and all the blood had rushed to his head, which was now bruised, swollen, and disfigured. It was not the way to remember our son.

We sat down on metal folding chairs to wait for the medical examiner and his team to finish up their investigation. What were they looking for? What were they finding behind the wall that separated his apartment from the shop area? They didn't take long. Just one more young person dead from a drug overdose. While we waited, we talked with Cory and his parents, as we had not met them before this particular hot summer morning. His parents were stunned when they heard what had happened. They knew JL as one of Cory's good friends from many conversations and interactions over the years, as an intelligent and responsible young man. While we were struggling with our emotions, we felt sadness and empathy for them as well, knowing that JL's lack of disclosure had now put an entire family in an emotional free-fall. Their shock was compounded by the fact that they had no idea he was a recovering drug addict and was just leaving a sober living house that he had lived in for the previous six months. John and I did not think it was a good step for him, but it was his decision to make. We knew that Cory was not using drugs, and so we felt this would be a good solution given JL's determination.

The Medical Examiner and his team let us know they were finished, had placed our son in The Body Bag, and were ready to transport him to the coroner's. The time had come for us to say our goodbyes. JL was wheeled out of his room on a cold steel gurney in a thick black bag, zipped up the front. Heather's husband, Curt, had arrived, and as we stood in the sweltering August sun, we laid our hands on JL, feeling his arm that was laid across his chest. We wept and prayed for him; in reality, praying for ourselves.

In that moment, Heather turned to us and said, "I had an other-worldly experience a few weeks ago while I was praying for John Leif's recovery from oral surgery. I saw him in a glorious light and God assured me that JL was going to be Victorious." We caught our breath; Leif, his grandfather's name, means "Victorious One." She didn't know that.

"No parent should ever have to say goodbye to their child in a body bag. I never imagined that I would have to do that." These were my words at John Leif's memorial service. How many times have I seen someone zipped up in a body bag on TV? It had never affected me. It was just another part of a story and I was an onlooker, an outsider, an uninvolved spectator. How different an experience when the body inside the bag is someone you know, someone you love, someone who is a physical part of you. You are separated from them by those 10 millimeters of heavy black plastic. That big, heavy metal zipper. When it is pulled up, it tells you "This is it. You will never see or touch or hear or smell this person again."

John and I could only say goodbye to our son by putting our hands on that black plastic bag, trying to get a sense of what part of his body we were touching. Where was his arm? We didn't want to touch his face, since we knew that it was swollen, even though his face was the part of him that was most important to us. It would only increase the horror of what we were already picturing in our minds and give our senses a jolt from what had happened. This black plastic bag was not like a garbage bag, the ones you fill with leaves and yard debris or trash. It was something like the old raincoats we used to wear when we were kids. Thick and stiff—but black—not colorful. We wanted to unzip it and see our only son one last time. The sense of desperation was mounting inside us as we were forced to accept that this was our son, he was no longer alive, and we could not see him as we said goodbye.

I would never rub my fingers through his short, fuzzy hair again; it reminded me of a bear. He liked it buzzed and as I gave him his haircuts, I would see the scars from an accident he had in 2007, scars on his scalp and ear that had healed unevenly.

I would never sense the warmth radiate from him as I put my lips against his cheek or feel his body as we hug.

I would never again smell the anti-perspirant that he wore, much to my frustration, because of the chemicals that were residual in his T-shirts even after being washed, nor would I smell the cigarette smoke that lingered and had become a part of his person. How frustrating it was when we found out he was smoking as a fifteen-year-old.

I would never hear his voice again. The voice that I remember as a five-year-old calling the remote control for the TV the "remote control under the bridge," or the way he would refer to our friends' pool table as the "swimming pool table." From his earliest age, he made connections between things through the filter of what a young child hears: The Three Billy Goats Gruff and the Troll under the bridge to the TV remote con-Troll. The pool table to the swimming Pool.

That voice that could frustrate the heck out of me with his rapid, circular arguments for or against something he felt strongly about. Whose child was he anyway? Was that what I sounded like to others when I was younger, able to debate until my victim gave in or gave up? I have been told innumerable times that I should have been a lawyer. John Leif heard the same thing and studied political science as an undergraduate. He intended to go to law school.

Ultimately, through tears and body-wrenching sobs, I wondered what it would be like to be the person zipped into that bag, sealed off from life on this earth forever. But it wasn't me in that bag. It was my son, closed up in that dark, slick shroud, smothered in the heat of that August sun. We had layers and layers of emotions flooding our hearts, like a complex piece of beautiful music, the vibrations and sounds of so many instruments, all overlapping. To process and sink into each separate emotional note, we would need the luxury of time and a clear mind to fully distinguish them all. But in this moment, it was as if we were listening to a cacophony of discordant instruments, all playing different pieces at once.

After we said our goodbyes to JL, John and Curt went into his room. I didn't, couldn't, go in. I couldn't face seeing where JL had died. It would have made everything too vivid. The guys gathered up his belongings and loaded them into his car for John to drive back to our house. JL had just moved in, and his things were still neatly stored in bins and suitcases, not yet unpacked. His down pillow, bunched up as he liked it, sitting on his empty grey sheets, waiting for him to lie down and sleep. How was John able to do this? Couldn't this have waited? It was one of the many robotic actions we, like others, take after a death in order to have something to do in an attempt to divert our minds from the tragedy.

Tried as we might, there really was no way to divert our minds, regardless of what our bodies were doing, regardless of what our minds were supposedly occupied with. A month later, my journal entry gives proof of this duplicity. Apparently engaged with the activity we were involved in, while actually being completely consumed with thoughts of our son. I don't think we were intentionally pretending, it was just a built-in survival mechanism all of us humans have in order to manage the internal chaos of crisis.

September 3, 2014
   JL,
   Mom here. *When I drive to see clients, I have to go right past an intersection I never gave a second thought to before August 2nd. August 2nd, when we had to follow directions to Garage-Mahal to where you lay dead. Now, even when I'm listening to the radio or talking on my phone, I just don't look up that street. I purposefully focus my gaze straight ahead, away from where we turned that day. It has become a habit for the past weeks, automatic. I just can't think about that day, that place, or you. Otherwise I cannot function and do what I need to do.*

I remember this happening after my brother JD died in 2001. I couldn't look at his house for months when I would drive past it, as it brought up too many distressing memories of a life cut short, of the consequences of deadly choices and a dysfunctional family, all the layers from the past resurfacing. If I saw a black Toyota pickup truck, I would have to look twice and strain to see who was driving it, because sometimes I thought (or rather hoped) it was JD. Within seconds, however, my mind would jar itself back into knowing it wasn't him or his truck, that he was really gone.

About a year before JD died, I was in a near-fatal collision with a truck at the intersection of our daughter's high school. The airbag deployed, and in the instant after it smacked me in the face and threw my head back against the headrest, a fine dust filled the car, and I thought it was on fire. I frantically squeezed myself out of the partially open door to escape. After minutes sitting in the heat on the ground, an ambulance arrived, and I was taken to the emergency room. For many months following the accident, I drove out of my way in order to avoid the scene. I had nightmares and panic attacks, and was ultimately treated for PTSD, due to my failure to recover after experiencing this terrifying event. I had very disrupted sleep and jumped at the slightest unexpected sound. In 2014, with the death of our son, the vivid reality had struck once again that life on this earth is fragile and fleeting. PTSD has four major symptoms, and I think most people who experience any sudden or traumatic death will experience them: reliving the event with memories that trigger the same fear from the event, the need to avoid situations that remind you of the event, taking on negative feelings about yourself and others, and always being on the alert for danger.

Heather and Curt came home with us after we left JL's apartment. They knew we shouldn't be alone in our now shattered, empty world. We needed an emotionally safe environment with friends who knew us so well that we didn't have to cover up or control any emotions or explain anything we did or said. Heather recalls, "John was strong emotionally for you as he went through the process of going to JL's apartment and then packing up his belongings into the car to bring back home. But once he was home, John freely released his emotions with tears and heaving sobs," his entire body revealing the intensity of his feelings, sometimes falling to his knees on the floor. Through phrases broken by convulsive gasps, he voiced expressions of deep remorse and unmerited guilt that would plague him for many months to come.

During that first afternoon, we decided to write a Facebook post so that JL's friends and family could get the real story before rumors flew through cyberspace, creating confusion. There was never a question of trying to cover up the truth or hide the facts; John and I are just not wired to do that. We had long since passed the point where we were embarrassed to let people know our son was struggling with opiate addiction. We know so many other young people who have died from overdose or suicide, whose families kept the tragedy as secret as possible, feeling shame and embarrassment. That is understandable, given our society's moralistic view about addiction, but we felt then as we do now, that the stigma around addiction is unhealthy and counterproductive, and that it does such a disservice to the person struggling, as if there was something inherently wrong with *them* instead of their fighting a battle with a disease. (I prefer the term "Substance Use Disorder" (SUD) as opposed to "addiction." SUD describes a problematic pattern of using alcohol or another substance that results in impairment in daily life. But I will use "addiction" as the more commonly known term.) Our Facebook post for August 2, 2014 read:

We received terrible news today. Our son, John Leif, 25 years old, died of an accidental heroin overdose. He has been struggling with opiate addiction since early high school. He has been clean and sober for the past six months and was the same wonderful, loving, intelligent, responsible, caring guy that we knew and loved. He has been working two jobs, paying his way, buying a car, enjoying life and relationships again, and was optimistic about the future. He had just finished six months in a sober living house and had spent his first night in a new apartment with a friend. The recent hugs, "I love you mom, I love you dad, thank you for everything that you have done for me," are a great source of strength for us at this time. Our *only* solace is in the confidence that he is with the Lord and that we will see him again.

Just as the body goes into shock after a physical trauma, so does the human psyche go into shock after the impact of a major loss.
–Anne Grant

4

THE URN

O soft embalmer of the still midnight,
Shutting, with careful fingers and benign,
Our gloom-pleas'd eyes, embower'd from the light,
Enshaded in forgetfulness divine...

–John Keats, *"To Sleep"*

Sleep. "In forgetfulness divine." That's all I wanted to do but couldn't. To be asleep would mean I wouldn't remember what had just happened, I wouldn't know I was in pain, I wouldn't have to think. Sleep would be similar to what an opiate addict experiences after their high—nodding off—oblivious to anything except the all too fleeting sensation of pleasure. John expressed it well the morning after our son's death:

August 3, 2014
   JL,
   Dad here. *Mom and I had to take medication to get any sleep at all—then we did not want to wake up or put our feet on the floor because it might all be real. We are numb, as if we have been shot by a taser and our emotions stunned—there are no words—it simply can't be true. You can't really be gone. We don't want it to be true because we can't picture how we will live through this. We are exhausted in every way.*

I am chastising myself for what I have and have not done as your dad—the many ways I let you down. How my not-so-subtle disrespect for your decision to move out of sober living two days ago was perceived by you as rejection and not acceptance. I know all of the "I love you's" in the world could not hide the judgment that you must have sensed in my heart. I am so sorry for this—for hurting you—I feel so bad, but now, it is too late to change anything. I really do love you—more than life itself. But I loved so imperfectly. Aside from Heather's vision of you in "Victorious Light," the only comfort I have is in the knowledge that "Whoever the Son sets free, is free indeed"—completely, irrevocably, free.

To me, death is fear—fear that I won't make it. I'm afraid I won't survive the catastrophic tear in the earth that has separated me from the one I love. I'm afraid I will get sucked down into the chasm between us, and more than that, it's as if I'm in the chasm already and won't make it out. That fear caused me to feel catatonic, as though I were watching events from some remote location, unable to inject any opinion or cause anything to change. Depression in its fullest form. An inability to think clearly, speak cohesively, concentrate, or remember. John was depressed too, but it didn't show up as fear. His way to manage his feelings tended to focus outward, expressed by his need to interact with others and retell the story, to process it externally. I think he was more courageous than me in facing his feelings by his willingness to keep visiting photos and videos of JL, and repeatedly feeling the anguish of the separation. When I couldn't sleep, I felt a desperate need to be alone, to turn inward, to process this trauma in my inner world. I visualized being with JL in past events and interactions, where I thought I could change or control them and turn them off when I wanted some rest from the feelings—like shutting off a show on TV. I was wrong. I could not.

August 19, 2014

JL,

Mom here. *So many memories fill our thoughts day and night, so many "If only…" I have a recurring "video" of several conversations I had with you in July while you were on Percocet after your oral surgery, and you were being your other, drugged self and self-absorbed—not alive. It was very frustrating to me because I hated it when you were not your real, wonderful self. Addicts by definition and necessity are self-absorbed. It is a miserable way to exist. I wanted so much more for you. I regret not having found a way to talk about it with you without making you defensive, a way to get you to say you needed help before it was too late. Instead of sitting beside you and facing the problem with you, my normal approach was to stand in front of you and ask questions. In hindsight, more of an interrogation than a conversation.*

We made calls and answered emails, coordinated the arrival of our daughter and others, sat with friends who came by to offer love and support and meals. We swam our laps, to generate endorphins, to stay sane, to counter the overwhelming messages that continually urged us to do something, anything, to make this nightmare go away. A franticness haunted us. Although we wanted to, we couldn't escape what had happened and all the tasks that now needed our attention. All we could do was inch forward. The next inch was to make funeral arrangements for our son.

On Monday, Heather took me to several funeral homes to ask about services and compare prices. Funeral homes are strange places. Perhaps it is something physical about how they are designed: the pallid paint, the smell like a chem lab in high school, the commercial carpeting; something ubiquitous. Is it an industry standard or is it the very nature of being in the place where the one thing we don't want to face in this life is where we are forced to face it? They were quiet places with people speaking in hushed voices, expressing empathy for strangers as part of their daily job—a service industry at bottom line. At this point, I didn't know if we would have a memorial service at whichever funeral home we picked, so it was important that it not seem dreary or shabby and add to the discomfort that everyone, especially all of JL's friends, would be already feeling.

I had no tears. I just went through the motions like a robot, to take care of what must be done after death, things people have had to do for millennia. I was thankful that my friend offered to take me for this fact-finding duty, to help get the information John and I would need to make decisions. My defenses were on full alert as we went through the doors. I put up emotional walls like a force field around me. I would not absorb the full impact, nor reflect, what it meant to me to be checking out funeral homes and urns for my 25-year-old son.

In this business of death, I kept moving forward. How cold this sounds, how emotionally removed, but activity is the all-purpose, self-protective garment that those in shock must wear in order to survive. At least that is what my family has always done—and it's not too unusual. No room for self-indulgent behaviors like sitting and quietly weeping. I felt as though I had to stay busy, stay as distracted as possible, in order to not have to face what was looming before me. But decisions had to be made. We were the parents, after all.

John and I never thought twice about what to do with his body. Not that we ever pictured having to make this decision, but we knew that we would be cremated and so it was a logical decision. We do regret now that we didn't first offer his brain to science to help in research about the brains of addicts. Oh well. Heather and I looked at urns and saw a white marble one that we both felt was right for JL's ashes—it was smooth and heavy and the gravity of it somehow made it feel stable, weighted down to earth, able to keep him here near us. The simple urn reminded us of him—he didn't like to draw attention to himself. And it reminded us of Italy, a place we are genetically and emotionally attached to. Something you would see in Pompeii. Heather bought it for him.

More questions loomed: What kind of Memorial Service will we have, where will it be, who will speak? It was depressing to think of remembering our son in one of those little chapels that seemed more appropriate for a grandparents' memorial. We needed help so we called our friends Mark and Marcy, pastors of a local church with whom we have been friends over the decades, and who watched our kids grow up in youth group and loved them. They immediately made time for us to come over and walk us through the process they have had much experience with. In a crisis, people are almost like magnets; some people move in towards us and some people are repelled and move away. Mark & Marcy pulled us close, prayed with us, loved us, cried with us. We planned a private time for viewing JL's body for the family and then a time for friends before the memorial service. Both John and I knew that funerals make people uncomfortable and, knowing his friends were young adults, and being concerned that they might feel awkward, we wanted to make plans to minimize their discomforts about the unknowns: possible liturgical peculiarities, friends they hadn't been in contact with for years, and—if they chose to view JL's body—their unpredictable emotions. Mark & Marcy offered their church facility for the memorial, and shared ideas for what the service could be like and how to plan it. We set the date for the following Monday, not wanting to rush. It was a comfort knowing we were not carrying this weight alone, and the heaviness on our shoulders felt markedly lighter as we left.

We met with the mortician and discussed with her the gritty details. She needed a good photo of him so that her work on his face could mirror him as much as possible. She warned us that the hours that had elapsed between his death and when he was found, and much later when he was slid into the cold cubicle at the morgue, left bruises and swelling that would make it difficult to make him appear like "himself" before he died.

And what clothing would look natural for JL to be dressed in? A T-shirt and shorts. But we wanted to cover up the results of the autopsy, the incisions and huge sutures that went up to his neck. Going to the closet, we began looking through his clothes, each one bringing back a painful memory of the last time we saw him wear it, when there was a living soul inhabiting it. Tears hit us once again. Together, we chose one of his long sleeve dress shirts that he liked to wear, a pair of slacks, and his belt, the one he had used as a cinch. We didn't need to bring shoes because his feet wouldn't show. It was weird thinking of him all dressed up in the casket but without shoes. I think he was barefoot.

When we went with Johanna to view his body after the embalmer had done her work with makeup and clothing, we experienced a profound range of emotions. The very first feeling was the complete certainty, *a knowing*, that JL was not there. This was an empty shell, like the exoskeleton of a snail or a clam, what was left after the living being had exited. Yet, even knowing and sensing that so clearly, we wanted (and needed) to see and touch the physical body that once held the person we loved. His hair felt the same, but his face was puffy and inflexible with thick make-up. It was a pseudo JL. All we could do was hold his stiff, cold hand and weep.

I remember the first time that I was close to an embalmed body, after my brother JD died. It was like being in Madame Tussaud's Wax Museum. What I was seeing certainly wasn't him. It was just a representative of my younger brother, and not a good one at that. It vaguely resembled him, but there was definitely a *fake*, waxy aspect to his face. It was the same when my sister Susan and, more recently, my youngest brother Joseph died. It is so striking that when the *person* leaves their body, what is left is just not them. Yet, this shell is all we have, so we accept it as a stand-in for the person we love who is no longer with us on this earth.

By the day of John Leif's memorial service, it had been ten days after his death. The mortuary had kept him in cold storage, of course, but after several hours with his body in room temperature for the viewing, when they wheeled him into the back room of the church for us to say our last goodbye, he was starting to smell. One more unanticipated and abrupt transition. As we stood over our son's body, knowing this was the last time we would see him, we were startled, taken from the spiritual realm of immortality back to the physical realm of mortality, as if someone had yanked the chairs out from under us (where we had been quietly meditating), landing us on the floor in stunned dismay. Without JL's spirit and soul inside his body, it was decaying. It was time to let this last physical vestige of our son go. The lid on the casket was closed, as we took our last view of our son's body. He was wheeled into the hearse and back to the mortuary, where his body would be cremated. From the frailty of humanity, to the ashes of morbidity.

It was a few days after the memorial service that we received the call that JL's ashes were ready for us to pick up in The Urn. For some still unknown reason, John went to pick it up by himself.

August 15, 2014

JL,

Dad here. *I made the mistake of going to pick up your ashes yesterday afternoon alone. Everything seemed OK until I got back to the truck carrying The Urn with your ashes in it. Then it hit—I cried in a crumbling ball behind the steering wheel for what seemed like hours. It was horrible. I called your uncle Mike, sobbing unintelligibly. I asked him to pray.*

And then God, as He has always done throughout my life, met me and sent His light. I went to the church to pick up stuff and met with the worship leader. We talked for a bit, then he put on an album of worship tunes. I went up to the stage, plugged in the bass, and played along with the CD—I didn't know the songs, but they were expressing love to God, expressing what I couldn't put into words— very encouraging. Music reaches into our souls. Very much a spiritual experience for me. I love you and miss you more than I can describe. You will probably hear mom and me saying this a lot. I hope you heard it a lot from us when we were all still together...

After John brought The Urn home with our son's ashes in it, and we decided on a place to set it, I put my hands around it. It was still warm. I don't know what I was expecting, but I wasn't expecting that. Feeling that heat sent an immediate sensation through my fingers up through my heart to my mind's eye. A visual of my son's body, being glided into that oven—these ashes were his body, burned to a crisp. Tears, and more tears.

He who learns must suffer. And even in our sleep,
pain that cannot forget
falls drop by drop upon the heart, and in our own despair,
against our will,
comes wisdom to us by the awful grace of God.
—Aeschylus

5

DRUG OF CHOICE

I don't use drugs. My dreams are frightening enough.

—M. C. Escher

E ven amid all the planning and making decisions, the instant replays from the days and hours leading up to JL's death were haunting us. Why had he overdosed? Was there something mixed in unbeknownst to him? Why didn't we see warning signs that he was going to relapse; were there some we missed because we were on auto-pilot, thinking all was well? So many questions, and no answers, until John received a call:

August 4, 2014 continued
  JL,
  Dad here. *I just had a long call with the Pima County Medical Examiner. She confirmed that your death was due to acute heroin toxicity. She noted signs of acute, subacute, and chronic injection injury with evidence of recent use (several within the past 3–5 days) and the bent needle still in your arm. We were not expecting to hear that. She said your death was immediate unconsciousness, then cerebral and respiratory arrest, cessation of breathing, and death. No pain. No more pain.*

Part of the evidence found in JL's room that morning was one used syringe with BT residue, along with the syringe and the needle that was bent and still in the vein in his right arm as he fell forward. Of course, no one knows if the other syringe was used in those early morning hours or not, but it would seem so. And if that is the case, then what does that say about the amount of heroin he was using, aside from the unregulated strength of what he bought? It was only a month since he had started taking Percocet before his oral surgery. Had he started shooting up that long ago, while he had the "cover" of the Percocet in his system and, since they knew that, there was no reason to have drug tests at the sober living house? Once you start an opiate, it is like climbing on an "up" escalator that doesn't give you options for getting off and resting on a bench somewhere. It just keeps going up, like a treadmill into space, until you push the emergency stop—or go off the end.

Was he intoxicated from having been drinking all night? Even though Cory said he thought he only had four beers, we know that many times he would get away from the party and drink vodka alone. Addicts are almost always alcoholics. Recent statistics establish that more than half of all alcohol-related deaths occurred in combination with heroin. If he was drunk, and started shooting up, then he would have had worse judgment than normal. Somehow, I can put myself in his shoes, even though I never used drugs or get drunk, and I feel such pity for him. It is the visual image of him being all alone that just kills me, a jagged blade that stabs through my heart to the deepest part of my soul.

August 5, 2014

   JL,

   Dad here. *As I think about the weeks that led up to your death, once again I am kicking myself for not being more insistent with you about not taking the Percocet before and after your oral surgery— regardless of the pain. All addiction kills eventually. Heroin kills sooner than most. How could I be so stupid? Why did I not prevent you from getting the prescription? We were paying so we did have the final say, but we listened to you. I am way too selfish in wanting your*

love, yet so short sighted—so foolish, so unwise. I love you and I am
so sad that you went through much of your young adult life in such
continual struggle. I know that you fought hard—very hard—and I
am very thankful for your many victories.

John received the autopsy and toxicology report while I was
out on a job site, so we didn't discuss it until I got home. We didn't
understand what the numbers meant as to how much JL thought
he was using as opposed to what he actually got. How did the
overdose happen? It appeared that what he used was extremely
potent or there was something else mixed in. We decided to meet
with JL's addiction doctor to help understand. After handing him
JL's autopsy report he told us that, as medical director of a clinic
in Tucson, he had seven or eight of the same autopsy reports every
month on his desk since May 1, 2014. There had been unusually
strong heroin (and more of it) in Tucson the previous months, and
forty to fifty deaths from his clinic alone, which was unbelievable.
When John spoke with the sheriff later, he confirmed that "there
have been some extremely strong batches of heroin leading to a
greater than normal amount of overdose deaths." As I look back
over the Coroner's report, even now, it is painful. It brings back the
entire early morning hours of August 2nd, 2014, and the death that
was preventable, albeit not without great and constant effort. I take
anxious breaths as I read:

In consideration of the known circumstances surrounding this
death, the available medical history, and the examination of the
remains, the cause of death is ascribed to acute heroin toxicity. The
manner of death is accident. Briefly, this 25-year-old male was found
unresponsive in his room with a belt around his right upper arm
and hypodermic syringe in his hand. He was pronounced dead at
the scene. Items indicating injection drug use, including a spoon
with residue and a second syringe, and 870 mg of BT Heroin in two
baggies were found within the room. The decedent has a reported
history of previous illicit drug use and had recently completed drug
rehabilitation therapy.

Included in the Coroner's Report are the results of all the blood sample tests, which offered us no real surprises. Even though there had not been any public information about it at that time, we had heard about additives like fentanyl via the substance abuse recovery community. We had asked if they would be sure to test for them, but they found none.

What did come to light, however, were two significant facts. The first was that JL had very high levels of alcohol in his system, even when the blood was drawn 8 hours after his death. This would greatly increase the potential for respiratory, brain, and central nervous system depression and shut down. The other was the strength of the heroin, which is metabolized to morphine. A usual dose of morphine for pain relief after surgery is 2 to 15 mg. Sixty mg of morphine can precipitate death if someone is sensitive to it and a lethal dose is considered 200 mg. From what John and the doctors calculated, JL had approximately eight to ten times the maximum therapeutic concentration of morphine in his blood when it was drawn.

Given the fact that he had recently relapsed and had signs of having used several times in the previous week, he would have known how much to use. This was not a case of just getting out of treatment and his first use. This was extremely potent BT heroin, an unregulated drug "produced" in Mexico, where there are no standards in production in contrast to the heroin that comes from Afghanistan. Asian heroin accounted for approximately 93 percent of all heroin imported into the United States until recent decades, when Mexican drug dealers got into the business. Now, added into the equation are illicitly manufactured synthetic opioids in China shipped to Mexico and, because they are so much cheaper, mixed in with heroin or formulated into look-alike prescription opioids and tranquilizers. As if this wasn't bad enough for harmful drug use around the world, China genetically engineered the opium poppy seed to enable growth and production of three crops per year instead of one, dramatically increasing the supply of opium worldwide. Taken together, all of this has upped the ante in the dangerous game of drug-roulette in which it is impossible to win.

Dreamland, The True Tale of America's Opiate Epidemic by Sam Quinones is an exposé of the rise in the 1990's of the black tar heroin industry and the convergence with the explosion of prescribing of oxycodone by physicians, its illicit distribution from "Pill Mills," and the ensuing use of Oxy as a street drug. Briefly, the author explains that two young men in a close-knit Mexican family created a way to process opium that was less refined and cheaper to produce than the traditional white powder. It was easy to push because it was easily smoked. BT heroin was born. At the same time, a felon and his twin brother in Florida decided they could become millionaires—along with the manufacturers—by marketing OxyContin as a street drug. By scraping off the outer coating to reveal the pure oxycodone, heating it until liquefied, it could then be smoked or injected. OxyContin was introduced by Purdue Pharma in 1995 as a slow-release narcotic. *Since 1999, two hundred thousand Americans have died from overdoses related to OxyContin and other prescription opioids.* According to the American Society of Addiction Medicine, *four out of five people who try heroin today started with prescription painkillers.* Our son is one of those statistics, and fatalities. The rest is the opiate epidemic we are living with today. According to the Centers for Disease Control (CDC) life expectancy in the US has now dropped for the first time since 1918 due to drug overdoses and suicides. It is little comfort to know that we are not alone.

On October 30, 2017, *The New Yorker* published an exposé on Purdue Pharma and the Sackler family: "The Family That Built an Empire of Pain." The article links the Sackler's business acumen with direct pharmaceutical marketing to the rise of drug addiction during the sixties, as they got rich marketing the tranquilizers Librium and Valium. By 1973, American doctors were writing more than *100 million prescriptions a year* for tranquilizers with countless patients hooked. With the release of OxyContin, using techniques that were sometimes *blatantly deceptive,* Purdue launched a multi-faceted campaign, causing a shift in the culture of prescribing. Until the aggressive Purdue Pharma promotion of OxyContin began in the late '90s, doctors had been reluctant to prescribe strong opioids because of a long-standing, and well-founded, fear about the addictive properties of these drugs. Physicians were intentionally misinformed about the risks, Purdue claiming that some patients may experience "pseudo-addiction", but they were not actually addicted. Their scheme and misinformation was so persuasive that I still have intelligent professional friends who believe if you are truly in pain, opioids are not addictive. This is absolutely false. More significantly, how could the FDA let this go on? My frustration index skyrockets just thinking about it. The mounting evidence says that the Sackler's bear moral responsibility for the Opioid epidemic. As of this writing over a dozen state attorneys general have filed lawsuits against them and Purdue Pharma reinforcing this evidence.

Yes, we can be thankful that new ways to deliver pain relief were developed for patients with extreme pain from cancer and terminal illnesses. I have seen the need for it when my brother was in ICU dying from AIDS and when I cared for my sister who was dying of brain cancer: both had morphine drips. But the wholesale promoting and pushing of these drugs for every ache and pain, while knowing how absolutely addictive they are, is unconscionable. Had we understood the domination of opioids in a life when we first learned our son was addicted, we would have taken a more proactive approach to his initial recovery program. Much more.

I don't think it's in very many of us to deliberately choose destruction, but we play with it and it licks us and burns us, and can ruin lives.
–Dr. Sherwin Nuland in *Einstein's God* by Krista Tippett

6

REMEMBERING JOHN LEIF

A sorrow's crown of sorrow is remembering happier times.

—Alfred Lord Tennyson

August 8, 2014

JL,

Mom here. *You were so loved by so many friends and family. Did you know that? We have received dozens of emails, texts, cards, calls from your friends and ours who saw the post on Facebook that we put up the night you died. We go to sleep at night thinking of you, longing for you to be alive. We would not be sleeping a wink without medication; we wake up not wanting to be awake—or alive—and don't want to get out of bed and face the day because we know the reality will hit us that you are gone. I just can't write much, it is too painful, and I am in so much pain already. Unspeakable describes it best. If the words come out of my mouth or the ends of my fingers, it will make them real, permanent.*

Our home was full of flowers and cards and food, expressions of love for our son and tenderness for us. Johanna arrived from Australia, JL's cousins and friends and our friend Linda (another "mother" who loved JL since teaching him in fourth grade) all flew in from around the country. Everyone who knew and loved him had come for his memorial. Johanna and cousin Justine sorted through volumes of photos, scanning everything to digital files, as

Carman and Gabe worked on choosing songs to put all together for the tribute video montage.

August 8, 2014, continued

Dad here. *I have decided to try to share the "Message of Hope" part of your service. Mark and Marcy said it is usually the final presentation at a Christian memorial, words that share our eternal hope. The words are beginning to take shape, often around 3 am. It is full of contrasts: the "real" you vs. the "addicted" you. One so full of life and love vs. one so discouraged and sad. Deep down, way down in your heart of hearts, your spirit was true, pure, clean, and innocent. On the surface, however, you were suffering, scarred, and stained. Not at all unlike me—or unlike everyone else.*

By this time in the week, six days after his death, John and I were both emotionally spent. We felt like taffy stretched to its breaking point, but we knew we had to keep moving forward. Neither John nor I were unfamiliar with grieving and mourning. Most of us use those two words, "grieve and mourn" interchangeably, but they are actually very different. Grief is about what is going on inside us after a loss—how we feel. We have no more control over it than we have control over other feelings. In this sense, we are not asked if we want to grieve any more than we are asked if we want to experience loss. It happens to us, and our choice involves how we deal with it: do we treat our grief like something we manage and attempt to be over it as soon as possible? Or do we allow the natural process to move forward, not denying but attending to all of the messy and difficult feelings?

Mourning is the action of dealing with our loss—what we do, the common rituals, the external part of the tragedy. We must make many decisions that just cannot be put off, the ones in the first days and weeks after a death; decisions about our loved one's body, a funeral, notifying friends and family, government and legal details. But after those essential acts, we do have choices, and we can either face them or put them off. Some people put acts of mourning off indefinitely.

The decision to have our son cremated resulted in an unforeseen quandary: where would we "go" to mourn our son? John and I have visited cemeteries here and abroad where ancestors are buried, mostly out of curiosity to see what was inscribed on their headstones. John's parents were cremated, and their ashes are in a mausoleum and my brother J.D. had a traditional burial in a plot. We have never visited either—while there are people who visit their loved one's graves regularly. Perhaps the mourning ritual of going to a grave consolidates grief into a time and place where we can then walk away from it until the next year? My sister Susan and brother Joseph were both cremated and their ashes were shared with the family to scatter in places of our choosing. I think this may be why our photo and memorial areas hold significance for us: they are monuments to our loved ones, where we can pause and remember them anytime we want.

John and I have the important books that have guided us through waters similar to these before. Similar—losing two younger brothers, losing a sister, losing parents—but none of these were the same as losing a child. Nowhere near the same. We know "The Five Stages of Grief & Loss" that Elisabeth Kübler-Ross defined so well: denial, anger, bargaining, depression, and acceptance. But with each fresh experience of a death, each "stage" is unique.

How did we end up here? We did this together, we raised our children together. We were at alternate times too encouraging and believing, or too harsh and unsympathetic. Why didn't our parenting manuals prepare us for the real perils of the twenty-first century? And now, in the midst of what felt like mutual catastrophic failure, we had to interact with all the people who loved us and who loved JL and were there to help. When we felt overwhelmed, where did the pressure escape? Mostly toward each other; we two are safe. We know we can vent, and will both survive the hurt and still be a unit afterward. At least we hope so. We had never had to navigate a tragedy this deeply personal to both of us. *Our* son. Bone of *our* bone, flesh of *our* flesh. Severed, cut off, detached. We are both feeling the excruciating pain and the immense loss of blood.

Saturday, August 9, 2014—End of Week 1
JL,

    Dad here. *Looking through photos, it is good to see your smiling face as a young child. One birthday photo stands out to me, from when we lived in Birmingham—you must have been turning five— the table was festive and there were friends helping celebrate. Mom made yours' and Garfield's favorite meal, lasagna, and you had asked mom very specifically for an orange-flavored cake. You blew out your candles with your fat little boy cheeks all puffed up and then reached up to give mom a kiss. Happy, active childhood.*

    It is painful to see the sadness in your eyes—or was it trepidation?— as a young teen, and later after your accident and relapse as a 19-yr. old. Painful, sad, many regrets. John Leif. Who was he? Who are you? Where are you? How can we present you at the memorial, your life, your loves, your passions, your thoughts? We cannot. Only you truly knew the real you; you and God. I pray that you are at peace—that you know real peace, and real joy.

JL,

    Mom here. *We go to view your body today with Johanna…our legs are weak…*

John spent time in his office alone, looking at pictures and listening to JL's music from his iPod. He likes most of it and was thrilled to learn just how much John Leif loved music. But John was sad that he did not know this, that he did not share this with our son. We listened to all genre of music in our home, but rap and hip-hop became popular when our kids were no longer living with us, and we had little exposure to their playlists. A few months before his death, JL gave John a CD with some songs JL thought he would like.

Johanna and the cousins included some of those songs and others in his iPod playlist in the video montage including "Crossroads" by Bone Thugs N Harmony. "Under Your Spell" from a band called Desire sums up how John and I feel at this time: *"I don't eat, I don't sleep, I do nothing but think of you."*

John and I tried to think of how our son would respond to us if he were here. We were now living in the ethereal world of unanswered questions and could hardly stand it. Questions we never really thought about asking JL or discussing with him because there was all the time in the world, or so we presumed. Now everything he might have wanted to tell us, every opinion even about the most trivial of subjects, mattered to us, matters so desperately to us still, but the grave is final, and silent.

Sunday, August 10, 2014
JL,

Mom here. *Johanna and dad and I met the family at the church after their service was dismissed—we didn't want to have conversations about your death with people we are not close to—too much energy loss when we have so little energy left. Dad went over service details with Mark and the sound engineer and cousin Gabe, and I went over the set-up with Marcy and our friends. Then we went to see your body again—your empty shell—mortality put on immortality.*

Some of the family were still there along with a friend, chatting away in the room where you lay, as if it was a normal family gathering. I closed the divider between us and them but could still hear them talking. It was very distracting, drawing our attention away from you, so dad asked them to please be quiet. Sadly, we later heard through the grapevine, that some family members were very offended by this and didn't know why I had closed the divider, which was baffling. It seemed obvious to me, knowing what it means when someone closes a door, especially in that sort of situation. It seems you can't shut the door on dysfunctional family dynamics.

When it comes to remorse or deep sorrow, I want to be alone—or with the very few people I have invited into my inner world and with whom I feel comfortable because of mutual trust. Some people are comfortable with allowing others to observe and be included in their feelings of sadness. John is able to do this, however, and he is totally honest with any expression of his emotions. Growing up, our family was very expressive in most areas of emotions: joy, anger, happiness, pleasure, triumph, disdain, worry, etc. But in those areas of inner struggles, where one is emotionally vulnerable, where the shield walls are down, there was no encouragement to do so nor a model for expressing melancholy feelings—especially from my mother. Her way to deal with difficulty was to "put on a happy face," which seemed to have worked as a survival tool for her. I have made an effort over the decades to unlearn this strategy, realizing that it is not emotionally honest. Both JL and I had great poker faces; great for when we wanted to win at cards but could offer challenges when it came to close relationships.

Monday, August 11, 2014
JL,

Dad here. *Today was your memorial service. A time to remember you, and to celebrate your life. Everyone worked very hard on the tribute video, music, and multimedia presentation of your life. Your sister, and cousins, and all the people who shared, poured their lives into this day.*

It's late now and I'm tired, but I want to say I am so glad that we decided to set aside the afternoon from 2-4 pm for your friends to come and view your body if they wanted to. Many of our older friends said they would not want a viewing—they have unpleasant memories of being forced as young children to view grandparents after they died. Even though you didn't really look like yourself, there is something about being able to say goodbye physically that our humanity needs, at least for some of us. Most of your friends, especially those from out of town or who hadn't seen you lately, definitely wanted to see you. Dozens came and spent the afternoon, with each other, with you. Arm in arm in front of your casket—crying in disbelief—leaving for a break—then back to your casket, crying.

The foyer was beautiful with tables of your childhood mementos, photos, a guest book, and some seashells for your friends to write their goodbye notes to you on. They will be cremated along with you. Several hundred people came, many of them your friends, to honor you. You were loved so much because you loved so well. The sharing by family, friends, counselors, was awesome. Johanna did such a great job, sharing how she had been so excited as a five-year-old when mom was pregnant with you and how at first, she wanted a baby sister. Then she decided a brother would be best so she wouldn't have to share her dolls. Well, she got her wish—a beautiful "little" (almost 10 lb.) baby brother. She also shared how she had a hand in naming you: she insisted that you should not be just another John. So, Johnathan Leif Trang you became. She loves you so much.

I hope you were able to hear how you were loved. It was a powerful day. And the time of sharing a meal afterwards at our dear friends Chris and Ann's home gave some time for us to hear a little from friends how sorry they were that you had died and how much they will miss you.

August is monsoon season in our Sonoran Desert, and the afternoon storms were building as we were preparing for the memorial. It was hot, sticky, and oppressive, the sky filled with dark, boiling clouds. Later, rain finally fell, bringing a sense of release to the city as we all released our sorrows together. The day reflected our hearts so well, giving way to an evening that was beautiful in so many ways.

John and I had planned to leave the service quickly since we knew it would be over two hours long, in order to get everyone moving to Ann and Chris' home for the meal. What we hadn't thought about was that many of the people at the ceremony were not going to the meal, and they wanted to at least give us a hug and express their sorrow. As we rushed to our car and saw several sets of friends who wanted to do just that, John wanted to wait and interact. I wanted to leave. Anger flared up between us as we drove away; not the first time, and certainly not the last. Fortunately, Johanna sensed the need of those friends and stayed to receive their condolences.

Ann was a hostess extraordinaire, creating a beautiful setting for the memorial meal. Neither John nor I had anything left to give (emotionally or physically) to these concerned and loving friends who were grieving and in shock too, especially JL's friends. As I gave hugs to them, I smelled the alcohol that many had used to help them get through this very difficult day. I understood. We purposefully had no alcohol at this meal in support of those we knew were struggling with addiction or working their recovery.

There were several difficult interactions with some people who felt they needed to give us their insights and advice on our situation, despite them having no personal experience with either addiction or the death of a child. Some monopolized John by extracting details about our son's life that they did not know. Death brings many unwelcome visitors. Mostly, however, there was much sincere and empathetic love expressed by friends, in their quiet hugs and unassuming gazes into our clearly pained faces.

Friendship improves happiness and abates misery,
by the doubling of our joy and the dividing of our grief.
—Cicero

7

THE REAL JL

The great advantage about telling the truth is that nobody ever believes it.

–Dorothy L. Sayers

To Tell The Truth was a game show in the 1960's where a person of some notoriety and two impostors try to dupe a panel of four celebrities, through a series of questions and answers, into voting for the two impostors. At the conclusion of the questioning, the host would ask: "Will The Real Mr./Mrs. X please stand up?" I was reminded of this as we continued to receive letters and have visits from friends. We were able to see more of the beauty of our son's life, after so many years of dealing with the consequences of his non-sober life that made it hard to see "The Real JL." But the addicted are people too, human beings who feel hurt and shame, who need love and encouragement, who are interesting and intelligent. They are people who are complex and imperfect, just like everyone else.

This has been one of the most unexpected benefits of being open about our son's death, and how it continues to affect us. John and I have been able to hear perspectives on JL that there would have been no occasion to hear before his death. If it is for this reason alone, we will continue to be vulnerable and open. We found that if we force ourselves to squeeze through the narrow passageway of emotional honesty by taking the first courageous step into what appears to be an intimidating solid rock wall of public opinion, we find that it gradually widens and opens to a peaceful green meadow that brings with it surprise encounters. Openness not only helps us, the bereaved ones, heal. We now realize, from so many cards and conversations, that it is a gift, an invitation, to our friends and relatives to be able to share their feelings as well. We had never heard from any other parents who had lost a child to addiction, until we began sharing JL's story. We wish we had, perhaps it would have helped.

Our commitment "to tell the truth" permeated every decision we faced after our son died. The closing "Message of Hope," as a traditional part of Christian memorials, would be the time to share our hope. Death naturally brings thoughts and questions about what happens after we die into sharp focus. John worked on what he would say for days, through tears and exhaustion, because of the great love he had for our son and his desire to honor him, regardless of how he died. And there is an exaggerated elation, a euphoria, that can set in after a tragedy. We unconsciously respond to shock with random bursts of energy from somewhere deep within.

Even so, how could the father of a 25-yr old son who had just died from a heroin overdose give a "Message of Hope" at the memorial service? How could he have any hope to offer to his sons' peers and to his own friends and family? How could he find the resolve to dig into his soul and allow his ruptured emotions to become visible, not only to the light of day but to an audience of people who can't possibly imagine what this loss is like for him? John has always demonstrated sacrificial love, the way God loves, to me, our kids, and others. When things have been painful, dirty, or inconvenient, he has always stepped forward to do it, regardless of personal cost. Here is an excerpt of what he said to several hundred people who were gathered to remember John Leif:

"We are all here today because of one life—one individual life. One beautiful little baby boy; one curly headed toddler; one completely captivating young boy; one not too awkward adolescent; one bright-eyed, mischievous teenager; one accomplished, articulate, intelligent, handsome young man. Johnathan Leif Trang. Who was this John Leif? John Leif— sober and clean—was engaged with family and friends, and optimistic about life and the future. Kind, thoughtful, gentle. Bold, adventurous, daring. John Leif—addicted and using—was somnolent, absent, disconnected, confused, and disillusioned about life. Callous, unfeeling, unconcerned. Frightened, anxious, scared. But wait—how can one individual present such different faces? How can we reconcile the enigma of this individual—of any individual—of ourselves?

"The Real JL is not the shell that you may have come and grieved over this afternoon. The Real JL, the real me, the real you is something much deeper, much bigger, much more wonderful. At our core, there is something real in us that reflects the image of God, in every one of us. Life is very hard and presents challenges that can lead to us into slavery in so many ways: but 'taking the easy way isn't the easy way.' The Good News is that there is a way that leads to real life—that we can 'know the Truth and the Truth will set us free.' John Leif is free indeed and we can be too. I ask you not to let this horrible, tragic, holy, event pass without affecting you. JL's life has connected us for eternity. Please allow his life and death and the presence of God in this place today change you from the inside out—the healing, growth, and changes that you and I know we really need. I love you and really, really appreciate your coming here today to show your love for our son, John Leif."

If that shell in the casket was not really our son, then who was JL, The Real John Leif? In *The Four Loves*, C.S. Lewis beautifully describes the different faces and facets of love. There is *eros*, physical, carnal love; *phileo*, brotherly love; *agape*, which is called *divine love* because it is the unmerited love of a greater to a lesser. *Storge*, affection, is fondness that is derived from familiarity and is present without coercion. Lewis describes affection as "a humble and shy love. A love that is modest. Affection, by nature, is not loudly and frequently expressed, but seeps into our lives … Affection is responsible for nine-tenths of whatever solid and durable happiness there is in our natural lives."

JL "seeped into our lives" the day he was born and was an affectionate child and more sensitive than we realized or really understood. After having a daughter, we seemed to presume, at least subconsciously, that our son would be less sensitive. And in some ways, he was. I think that the onset of puberty, and the accompanying hormonal changes, affects mainly the external part of our nature, while *the essence* of who we really are remains the same while we mature into our personality. JL could emit bravado and liked to be in the middle of the action. If there wasn't any, he would find a way to make some, but as an introvert, this is where some of the pull for substances came in; as a way to be "more than" what he felt he was, especially around his peers. Even though most people who knew JL would probably not describe him as shy or perhaps private, for those who knew him well, he was, unless he was debating an issue or trying to prove a point. Then he could be lethal, which is why he was pursuing a career in law.

From the time JL was a small child, he had a loud and deep voice that sliced through the ongoing conversation in a group; not because he was shouting, but because of the timbre of his voice. He loved music from the time he was young and would listen intently to the broad variety of music we had playing constantly around our house and in our car.

JL, like John, was an "early bloomer," as opposed to many guys, who often tend to be late bloomers. By the time he was twelve he had to start shaving because he was being teased about his mustache. He had a lean but muscular build and grew so fast starting around eleven that he had constant pain for several years as the bones in his feet and legs grew so quickly. Even though JL was not tall by American standards at 5'10", he was that height by fourteen, and therefore seemed older, and he was the tallest of anyone in our families.

While reading about adolescent development, we learned that when a boy is among the first in his peer group to begin the process of maturation, they are at risk for emotional and mental turbulence in their teen years. Because they are developing normally cognitively, socially, and emotionally, but physically they look older, it creates a mismatch that can initiate difficulties with internalized symptoms (such as anxiety) and externalized symptoms (such as tobacco use and risk-taking).

After JL died, I came across some notes JL had written to me. One was while we were trying to choose an out-of-town sober living house for him in 2013. He had just separated from his girlfriend and his extreme anxiety was clear when he wrote:

> *"Mom, please, please can we wait until tomorrow to make the final decision on where I will go? This has been a very stressful few weeks, as you know, and this particular decision is the most overwhelming of them all—the moving, sorting, packing of my stuff, paperwork, etc. I want to be sure of this decision, so I can go truly wanting it for myself. Love, me."*

September 21, 2014
JL,

Mom here. *We watched an action/thriller movie last night. It was one of the first times I was ready to do so since you died because we first watched them at your suggestion and then with you over the years. It is so odd—you were so much a part of us that even something as insignificant as this is, deep in our subconscious, has* *to be faced after your death. And it brings to mind when you were 12 and wanted to watch Men in Black. I didn't want to because I didn't like American movies or TV. But you persuaded me, and we watched it and I laughed my guts out. So began many years of us knowing that you knew what we would like, be interested in, and able to tolerate when you recommended movies or shows— even the HBO series, Breaking Bad. We wanted to watch what you liked because we knew it gave us a glimpse into your psyche and soul. I will miss watching movies with you because I will miss you being with us and the awareness that you knew us in many ways better than we knew ourselves. Children are rapt students of their parents.*

September 5, 2014
JL,

Dad here. *I sent an email to Kyle, along with photos of him on the afternoon before your memorial service started—standing in front of your open casket, arm in arm with a few other friends. I just read the transcript of what he shared at your memorial. It is wonderful—I laughed and cried and smiled and felt God's presence in the love he expressed for you. I thanked him for loving you and for being a true friend. This was one of our daily prayers for you—to know and experience the kind of relationships and love that most people in this world only hope to experience. I thanked him again for spending the time and money to come and be a part of your memorial, and for being with us before and after, sharing words of encouragement. And especially for telling us more about your friendship with him.*

The past five weeks have been very hard—especially Saturdays. It just doesn't seem like it can possibly be true—you can't truly be gone. I don't think it is denial—mom and I are not wired that way—but maybe it is desire, just wishing, hoping it isn't true. Feelings of all sorts come in like floods overtaking a dam. It looks like we will be in the "stages of grief" for quite a while.

Kyle and JL had been friends since middle school. They were like brothers. They laughed, they fought, they argued, and they got drunk together. At the memorial, Kyle said,

"JL was the best friend a guy like me could ask for. As my partner in crime, JL and I definitely conducted more than our fair share of idiotic shenanigans. But our friendship was much deeper than that. I could tell JL anything. He was the only person on this earth that I could spill my heart to. And we shared some mutual struggles. No matter what point in our lives we were in, whenever we hung out nothing mattered but our friendship—almost as if time would stop for us to enjoy each other's company where we would just talk or argue about complete nothingness. But as my friend, JL was always there for me. In many ways, he was my therapist. A lot of where I am today and the major choices that I made are a direct result of JL's guidance and advice. JL was the most selfless guy I ever knew. Whenever I had a problem, he would stop everything to help. He always made time for me."

On a day in October, I was thinking about JL's baby dedication and the pastor's word for him, "Amazing." It has continued to surface in descriptions about him from random sources. With his miraculous, *amazing* birth he brought a second, deep joy to our lives that we could never have imagined, and to Johanna's too, especially as a young girl. She was thrilled to have someone to play with, to be a part of creating imaginary worlds with Playmobil, Legos, toy animals. They made up stories with JL's curiosity and inventiveness complementing her affection and "mommy-love" for their play families. We felt so much more like a family when he entered our lives. Johanna now lives half-a-world away and was an only child for 5 1/2 years until JL was born; now she is an only child again, which was yet another new reality we had to face. We thought we would move into the future together, expecting to watch JL find a love and life partner, marry, have a career he enjoyed, have children for us to know and love.

The future. What we all hallucinate being like putty that we can, by sheer force of will and determination, shape into what we want it to be. John Leggio, director of The Mark, shared his thoughts at JL's memorial service about this common view of life and our illusions about what we have control over and what we don't.

> "There's this thing called *powerlessness* in our life that we in recovery programs talk about a lot. Powerlessness isn't just for those who are addicted to chemicals. The chemicals are just a visible thing. We're all powerless, spiritually powerless. We all wrestle a lot with what we have control over in our life. Yet we teach our kids from the time they are very young, 'You can do whatever you want to do!' But I think a lot of times we're remiss in not telling them that there's so many things you can't do... and that's probably almost everything. You can't control life. You have to accept life on life's terms. And the smarter you are, the harder it is to accept this. JL was smart—what a challenge, let me tell you! But I think the older you get in life, you realize that you can't pull yourself up by your bootstraps. You have to turn it over to a Power much greater than yourself."

Also, in October, John called the director, Mike, at Joshua House—the first residential sober living program JL went to in January 2014—to let him know that JL had died. What Mike said confirms what I felt last spring: that JL's time there, although short, was significant for him spiritually. He said JL was a sincere, gentle spirit, very thoughtful, asking lots of questions, and trying *so* hard. He described JL as "Amazing"—that word again.

I continue to feel an imperative need to hear good things about our son, to affirm him as a valuable person, regardless of his weaknesses and flaws that may be different than mine or someone else's, but similar in that we are all fallible and fallen human beings. This is why a random conversation with our brother-in-law, Mike, has found a permanent place in my memory: he said, "When I look back, I can say I never heard a harsh word from John Leif." Yes, that was true to his character, and it was what made him so much like his grandfather Leif; he had a non-judgmental nature and an unexalted opinion of himself. That primal need is why even the slightest disparaging comment, however innocently spoken, and especially after JL's death, causes a wound and a subsequent re-action.

October 25, 2015
JL,

Mom here. *William Sky's mom called yesterday. She shared how she thinks of you and us every day, remembering all the times with you over at their house during your teen years and how much your friendship with William Sky meant. He and Kyle were your closest and oldest friends, since junior high. She said he is really, really sad with you being gone and is glad he has his new job to distract him. All she could say was how sorry she is for us. The empathy seeped through the phone lines and touched my heart.*

The call illuminated again the stark contrast between our "non-religious" friends and their ability to empathize and put themselves in our shoes, to express their love and sorrow with total acceptance of our son and us, and some of our more "spiritual" friends, who were quite silent and non-expressive, often at a loss for words. John and I felt it may have been due to a sense of judgment on their part towards us, but who knows. Maybe they were too far removed from any experiences with this element of life, as if they couldn't picture themselves in our shoes, where our other friends could very easily. Maybe they kept silent rather than saying something they felt would hurt us, but couldn't they think of anything comforting to say? Silence can be so easily misunderstood, and to us it was profoundly damning, and deafeningly loud.

One of JL's close friends wrote to us expressing how JL recklessly loved his friends: "JL was a great guy, a wonderful person, and even more importantly, a fiercely loyal friend. Your son holds a special place in my heart, and has helped me become the person I am today.

JL will truly be missed by all, but never forgotten." As many of JL's friends shared with us what they admired about him, it helped us remember *the big picture* of his life, and that he was not, and should not, be defined by his addiction. Through these conversations, we are reminded that The Real JL had the qualities and relational skills as an adult we valued most as parents. We are grateful he had so many extraordinary friendships.

January 18, 2016
JL,

 Mom here. *Dad, Johanna, Gerard and I went to see the third Hobbit movie—just as we would always go to the latest Tolkien movie together as a family each Christmas. Sadly, we remember last year with you being totally out of it because you were using heavily while at Restart Sober Living, even though we didn't know, and we were frustrated. You slept through most of it, and although you were high, you still wanted to be with us. These are the memories we have that it seems we have to deal with as they come. But I know that gradually over time we will have fewer of the painful ones and more of the ones of who you really were without the drugs.*

 Something we really didn't understand until after JL's death was how much our relationship with him meant to *him*. We knew how much it meant to *us* as his parents, but it is so hard to see the true essence of the person inside the exterior of the addict, the one you are resisting at every turn and whom you have anxious days and wakeful nights over. Like the marrow inside a bone that our dogs will single-mindedly chew on until they get to it; this is what the parents and friends of an addict are summoned to do if they want to remember who the *essential* being is hidden inside the shell that was once their loved one.

 We have heard that young people with addiction issues have noticeable problems with impulse control from the time they were young. John Leif didn't have a problem with this as a child, but after becoming an addict as a teenager, opiates *necessarily* stunted his normal development and the regulator in his brain that would normally kick in to help resist an urge or reflect before a temptation was short-circuited by the chemical changes from opiate use. He always had a very curious personality, he was mischievous, and exuberant. He loved life, but he was not an extrovert. Perhaps that led to some of the issues. I think being an introvert when you are in middle school and you don't know anyone is difficult. He found that alcohol caused him to loosen up—a benefit for people who are drawn to drink. It can take away tensions that introverts seem to feel when they are in groups of people.

Another area of research that is giving us more food for thought are new findings about traumatic brain injuries and addiction. JL had his first concussion when he was hit in the head at six years old playing soccer. The next one was when he was twelve and the youth director was horsing around and dropped JL on his head on the concrete. The third was a serious fall his freshman year of college. We never connected his concussions to his addictions and now wonder if offering his brain for research before we had him cremated would have answered some questions related to why JL had an addict's brain, other than the genetic tendencies in our families. How did those first two concussions play in to his being drawn to drugs? How did the third one after his fall affect his relapse?

Chronic Traumatic Encephalopathy (CTE) is caused by accumulated blows to the head by causes such as serious falls, athletics, or bombs. CTE triggers degeneration of the frontal lobe. Physical changes to the brain can appear months or even decades later. Impaired judgement and loss of impulse control are the resultant unmistakable symptoms no matter how long it has been since the initial injury. Someone not normally drawn to drugs or other high-risk behavior, will be likely to start.

Ultimately, does all of this insight and scientific knowledge that we have acquired by the twenty-first century help on a practical level? Will it be useful for parents as they raise their young children? As they take pains to observe the little ones they love so much, will they be more proactive in what they guide them into and, conversely, away from? We think it would have been helpful for our family had we known these facts.

While we are dealing with our loss of JL, I regularly think about the losses he experienced, as well as the losses all those dealing with addictions experience, and it brings more pangs of sadness. There are so many, many losses in their lives. I think in JL's experience, it started with losing his ability to be honest with himself as he told himself stories that bolstered the denial about just how addicted he was. In a sense, this is where dignity is really lost early on, even though externally nothing will seem to have changed yet.

There were the things he no longer enjoyed because all he could think about was getting high. There were the things he could no longer do well because he was not fully functioning, such as sports, study, or keeping his work up to par. All along the way, he gradually lost connection with friends because of trying to hide his impairment, or because of repeated excuses for not showing up or following through. Using opioids leaves you somnolent and usually alone. And especially important to him, he lost a consistent life of close, intimate relationships. Some friends and family got to the point of not wanting to be with him, because even when he was around, he was not present.

As JL fully succumbed to his addiction, he eventually dropped out of university, lost good jobs and dependable income. He needed predictability, and that is what an addict just can't have. It is stolen from them by their own choices. Addiction is so self-defeating. Some individuals lose their body as their own property when they sell themselves in exchange for substances. Many lose their job, their car, their place to live, and some eventually lose all freedom due to an arrest and jail for DUI or possession or dealing.

Any dignity that seemed to exist in some corner of JL's soul was diminishing year by year. Many times, after JL had pawned some treasured item like his guns, he would tell us about them before they were sold, embarrassed and weeping. It was so hard loving this son of ours and seeing him in this state. Our hearts were always torn, feeling like they were being pulled from our chests by warring emotional forces, wanting to pull him close and shelter him by force, yet knowing he had to learn to live with his choices. What we didn't realize or understand is how much his heart was being torn too.

March 18, 2015
JL,

Mom here. *Dad got your snowboard bag from the storage locker so he could use your equipment when he goes skiing. As he brought that big, long bag into the family room, I remembered the times we went shopping for ski pants, boots, a jacket. I remembered seeing you wearing them in photos from your trips, seeing your face smiling out from under your helmet and goggles as you sat on the ski lift in the mountains, surrounded by tall pine trees and white snow. Seeing your goggles and gloves as dad sorted through the different pairs—him trying them on for size—brought you right into the room—a video clip from years past when you would decide what to take as you would be preparing for a trip to snowboard with dad and William Sky. It was another pit of sadness for both dad and me to see your things and remember how, when you were clean, you loved to snowboard. Another reminder of what was lost in your life, eaten away, bit by bit, by an ever-ravenous foe.*

As our first year slowly and steadily passed after JL's death, each date or month or season brought back exactly what he and we were doing the year before. In March 2014, while Johanna and our two granddaughters, Anaëlle and Zaria, were here with us visiting from Melbourne, JL was at In Balance Sober Living house. He was doing so well, and some of our best memories of him clean, sober, and The Real JL are from that time. Videos of him reading stories to the girls, patiently listening and responding to their sweet childish comments, having meals together, are visuals we can now go back to and receive comfort from. Our favorite video clip—the last one before his death—is of John Leif sitting on the living room floor, the box of Duplo's spread around while they work on building a circus train, Anaëlle and Zaria playing and chattering away. These were Duplo's JL had played with for hours as a young child. They were familiar, saved for twenty years, for him to pass on and to play with his children someday. JL picked up an elephant to put on the circus train, and said, "Uh-oh, the elephant's foot is broken." Zaria, at three and with an extremely cute Australian accent that was pretty hard to understand at the time, responded: "That's OK, Bella and Brutus chewed on the elephant." JL, not understanding a word of what she said, patiently asks, "What?" Zaria repeats her sentence. JL understands and together they decide the elephant's other leg "is even better." Anaëlle chimes in and says, "The elephant can ride on the train sideways, with just his front feet attached." At that moment, all was well.

Addiction is a tough illness,
and recovery from it is a hard but noble path.
Men and women who walk that path deserve
our support, encouragement, and admiration.
–Sheldon Whitehouse

8

GRIEF PART 1: Denial, Anger, Bargains

What is hard for "microwave, quick fix" America
is that grief takes time...
Christian grief peers into the hideous face of death
with brutal honesty and tells the truth
by deeply experiencing the loss...

–Roger Edwards

Grief necessarily takes time because feelings can't be rushed. Being an impatient person makes this difficult for me, so I have to be intentionally patient, and slow myself down. I know from my own experience, as well as from observing others, that we may think we can take a shortcut to acceptance and peace, but grief will not magically disappear. Along with the passing of time, grief needs to be tended to. John and I both felt that the open wound in our souls that was causing us such pain would never close up, even though it slowly started healing over, creating scar tissue out of the edges of this jagged wound. John and I just weren't perceiving it yet.

One aspect of grief that creates an internal conflict for me is that on the one hand, while I want it to be over and done with due to the pain it consistently causes, I also desperately cling to it, afraid to let go of even the tiniest aspect of my feelings for fear that I will be releasing my lifeline to my son, as if I have hold on the string of a balloon and if I let go, it—my son—will float away into the sky and out of sight forever.

Saturday, August 23, 2014—End of 3rd week
JL,

Dad here. *Saturdays are the worst day of the week. Every Saturday seems exactly like August 2nd. The day the world changed forever. The day that the officer came to the door. The day that we sat in stunned disbelief. The Day—every motion and emotion we went through that day is vividly present and intensely painful.*

August 26, 2014
JL,

Mom here. *I am starting back into work—I need to for many reasons, mostly to have something my mind can be distracted by for a few hours. Dad and I still don't want to wake up in the morning. As soon as our eyes open—or even before—we think of you. It is a good thing we have each other. What a horror it would be to face you being gone alone—either physically alone, or like many couples, emotionally alone. And dad and I share many of the same emotions—vacillating hourly, disturbing thoughts, guilt—albeit over different things and in the ways we deal with them. We love you so much and feel we let you down in so many ways...*

My friend Ann L. shared an article with me that she read in the *New York Times* about "complicated grief" from *The Year of Magical Thinking* by Joan Didion. It results from losing a life love, is worse with losing a child, and is most common when someone experiences that loss of a loved one through a sudden or violent death. Psychologists report that the more awful the circumstances surrounding the death, the greater the risk of complicated grief. It can result in life disruption and neuropsychological problems. Yes, John and I now know complicated grief.

Elisabeth Kübler-Ross, M.D., was instrumental in research and writing about the process experienced when an individual faces loss from death and developed the "Five Stages of Loss" after learning more about the final stages of life and its common anxieties, fears, and hopes. We have been reading her books on dying and grief since my brother J.D. died in 2001 from HIV/AIDS. I wish I had known about them when I had the first of two miscarriages. I was only 26, and it had been drawn out over weeks as we waited while the doctors wanted to be sure there was not a heartbeat. I had never known anyone who had a miscarriage. I remember being on the verge of tears as I told some older women friends about it a few weeks afterwards. Their unified and cheerful response was "Oh, don't worry. You'll get pregnant again soon!" Those thoughtless words were probably meant to be encouraging, but they had the opposite effect. I walked away more depressed than ever. Having just experienced my first major loss of life, I was struggling with lots of conflicting and confusing emotions and thoughts. But I learned a lot through that encounter and discouraging time, and as I shared my grief, I began to hear others' stories that had been kept quietly tucked away, waiting for an understanding and empathetic ear.

Both John and I know all the stages by heart: denial, anger, bargaining, depression, and acceptance. Knowing them has helped us tremendously as we have had to process so many deaths in my family. Knowing them has helped us see where we are as we progress through our grief. Knowing them does not change the fact that we will go through each and every stage with each and every new death.

Neither one of us are given much to denial, which would actually have been good for us during those first few weeks and months. Kübler-Ross says that denial helps in an unconscious way to manage the shock and survive the loss. It helps pace feelings of grief. I've come to see how there is a grace in denial, and how important it is because it is the psyche's protective mechanism, giving us moments away from the pain. John and I both wish we were more inclined to denial. We needed some moments away from the pain. I seem to manage shock by withdrawing when I am around others, and perhaps that type of retreat is a form of denial, or self-preservation. I have always been afraid that if I crack open the door to my heart, everything inside, all that I am, will bleed out until there is nothing left; denying that I have any emotions gives me the time I need to let the shock roll through me, until I am able to feel, and face those feelings again. John is much more open and willing to live with his full range of emotions, regardless of how others might be affected by them, and regardless of the cost to him personally.

The five stages are tools to help us frame and identify what we may be feeling, and the stages are not necessarily linear. We move in and out and back again as we individually "peer into the hideous face of death" as Edwards said. Some of us more honestly from the start than others, reaping the benefits of wholeness and acceptance. Some imitative and self-deceiving, prolonging the pain through years or even decades.

As I have said, we are not given to denial in how we live life, but it is clear from our journal entries that we experienced it when faced with JL's death. Denial can be disbelief, and the feeling of being numb or paralyzed by shock is common—words we used in our journal those early weeks; a mental rejection, an inability and unwillingness to accept what happened.

August 27, 2014
JL,

Dad here. *Mom and I still feel deadened—paralyzed emotionally, as if our hearts have a neurological syndrome that prohibits response. You cannot possibly be gone. We cannot possibly have to face another day without you. The recurrent theme during all my waking hours is Why? How? What? Why has this happened? How could we have been so unwise—so ill-equipped to walk with you through the difficult times of your life? How could I have had the best intentions of being the best dad, and end up being the worst possible dad for you? Why are we left with only memories and broken hearts? What could we have done to change this outcome?*

Both of us were angry at random times in the first months, at ourselves mostly. Kübler-Ross tells us that this anger is guilt turned inward instead of outward toward others, even though neither one of us are blame-shifters anyway. This guilt was due to our intense love for John Leif and "is a natural and healthy reaction to the unfairness of loss," the unfairness of *us* losing *our* son. "We often assume that if we are good people we will not suffer the ills of the world...underneath anger is *pain*...anger affirms that you can feel, that you did love, and that you have lost." It is healthy, necessary, and hopefully progressive. Yes, even though being angry is not comfortable, especially for John, we knew it was important for our emotional health to feel it, not deny it, and thankfully it *was* progressive. We don't have the same anger, or the same pain now, that we had in the first year or two after JL's death.

August 14, 2014
JL,

Mom here. *I went to your banks yesterday with Linda to get your accounts closed, but I need to wait for your death certificate. I wondered aloud where we are in the grief process, as it seems we are not in too much denial. But the anger and the pain from feeling that a loss is unfair—I know I will have to deal with that because of my sense of justice, and I feel it now. How unfair that a 15-year-old thought trying a smoke of something that would be "fun" at a party would find it turned into an uncontrollable monster. It makes me angry and I want to know who first seduced you with that lie, but maybe it goes farther back than that—back to the person who introduced you to Oxy's—or back to your first tooth extraction and pain meds that we allowed.*

I am also feeling how unfair it is that I have now lost three immediate family members: my brother JD, my sister Susan, and now you. Of course, I can only, and ultimately, be angry at God who allows these things—yet that is futile and robs me of life. Trusting that God loves you more than dad and I do is what we had to learn to do while you were alive—we now have to re-learn it in your death. How long will this take? Corrie Ten Boom said "When a train goes through a tunnel and it gets dark, you don't throw away the ticket and jump off. You sit still and trust the engineer."

There is another side of anger after a loss that comes from looking at the other players involved: circumstances beyond our control, external influences from friends and society in general. We had to face these external enemies as well as the enemy within. After the first several weeks, some of our anger began to turn outwards: toward the drug dealers and cartels, opioids in general, and the secret-keepers.

September 26, 2014
JL,

Mom here. *I was driving your car today and had this strong feeling of anger at the damn drug dealers and Mexican cartels who have profited from the deadly heroin that led to at least fifty unintentional overdoses in Tucson since May 1st—you included. These are just the ones Dr. Cai knows of from his work at one facility. Being in your car brings memories of how happy you were to get it and working so hard that you could pay for it—achieving all that you had in 6 months. Then, your brain fooled you into thinking you could "tame the dragon" instead of "chasing the dragon." The dragon took over and you never thought you wouldn't live to see another day.*

John and I deal with our feelings of frustration with ourselves over JL's death differently, an experience we had no control over and cannot change. My husband wants to share his thoughts with people, process verbally, and needs more social interactions even though it eventually drains his energy. He is an extrovert, and because he works alone, he has the time for his emotions to regenerate. When my heart is heavy or I am processing intense emotions, I don't want to share those things with strangers over and over again. It takes more emotional energy than I have, so if I stay focused on work I don't have to go there. For me, sharing repeatedly when I'm in pain is like poking and prodding into a deep wound, causing it to continue to bleed. If I want it to heal, I need to leave it alone for a while. Of course, that is after I have gotten all the debris out. I don't want to carry that pain around inside me my entire life where it can fester, causing even more hurt down the road.

September 28, 2014
JL,

Dad here. *We received feedback from your friends regarding what an incredible guy you were while you walked here on the earth. I am so thankful and happy that you were able to experience the joy of great friendships. But I'm in a pretty deep "funk." It is a deep, profound, sadness. And anger—Why you? Why not me, or another one of your addicted friends? Anybody else but you? It is just a very dark time for me. I love you and I hope you can hear my words.*

Anger usually surfaces in the grieving process once we realize (somehow, deep inside) that we will probably survive, or that we have already survived what we thought we wouldn't. I think most people know that anger is a necessary stage of the healing process, although many aren't comfortable feeling it. They "manage" anger by avoiding it. Attempts to manage unwelcome and inconvenient emotion such as anger is like yeast dough in a pan too small for it: the emotions expand and spill over the edges creating a mess. No one should ever ask or expect a grieving person to deny or bury their anger.

I know from decades of experience in communities of faith, that having and expressing anger towards God is largely considered taboo, especially from those who consider themselves highly spiritual. Many people may feel it and be unable to understand it or even admit it, but I have always felt comfortable expressing my frustration and anger to God because He has the biggest shoulders, and I know from experience that He understands.

One specific source of anger for John and me after JL died was when the director of Joshua House sober living, Mike, said to John that "It was just his (JL's) time." Deep inside we believed he was speaking the truth, but it brought up strong feelings of anger and disappointment. Not at Mike, but towards God. Why did it have to be *our* son's time to die? John and I know several young adults who have overdosed at different times, and thankfully were saved, and while we are *so* thankful for them, I still ask the question: Why do some people get second chances, and others don't? So many people face times in life where something, an accident or an illness, may end their life entirely, but somehow, they survive it and keep going. Why couldn't JL have that second chance, was that too much to ask for? I've wondered if perhaps he had squandered his chances or lost his ability to change due to the hold heroin had on him. They are questions I won't ever know the answer to, at least not on this side of eternity.

November 24, 2014
JL,

Mom here. *Your cousin Gabe is coming down to spend Thanksgiving weekend with us. He has felt very compassionate towards us since your death and wants to be a support. We talked about grief and I asked him if he has any guilt since Susan (his mom) died—and he said "of course" and also with you. He wished he had taken the time to know you better as an adult. Since you and Carman (his brother) are 11 years younger than him, you two were always the "annoying little brothers." Then Gabe was a young adult and living in LA while you were both teenagers living at home. I really appreciate Gabe—I know I can count on him to be honest—it creates a comfort zone between us.*

Several months after JL's death, we were still struggling, going from the extremes of acquiescence to anger, faith to futility. Our feelings were changeable, wholly unpredictable; they reminded me of the waves as they come to shore at Mission Beach during a rip tide, coming in at random angles and heading out at different ones. We made it a practice when the kids were young to go to the lifeguards and ask them where the current was before we headed into the surf, hoping to steer clear of the danger if at all possible. When we were in our 20's, John and Susan were caught in a rip current at Newport Beach, as Susan's husband Mike and I watched helplessly from the shore. A lifeguard boat got there in time to save them. That was before we learned not to fight those currents, and how to walk or swim out of one if we happened to get caught being sucked out to sea. We taught our kids this as children, and just like we learned to understand the force of the waves, together John and I slowly learned how to walk out of the changeable, unpredictable currents of sorrow when they threatened to overwhelm us.

February 27, 2015
JL,

Mom here. *I got in touch with your friend Zach last night. We talked a few weeks ago while he was in a treatment facility. He just moved into a sober living community that has classes, groups, and grief counseling. He said he is working through his grief and guilt surrounding your death. He realized how much he had buried and how much it was affecting him. He felt unjustified guilt over not having been here to help you move when you left In Balance Sober Living because he was out of town. He is such a sweet guy and was a good friend, even though you only met him last spring when you were living together at In Balance.*

What Zach was experiencing is referred to as "survivors' guilt." When a person dies and we survive, we cannot understand why. So, we blame ourselves—there must have been something we could have done, right? The truth is that we will all die of something someday. Even though we will eventually come to realize that we have no control over almost any death, self-blame must be explored in order to be resolved and for us to find peace. It took time for John and me as parents, and JL's friends, to work through the distraction of our surviving while he died, to deal with the unanswerable question "Why?" and then sit with the reality that he was truly gone forever.

Something seismic happened inside both John and I the day our son died. Somewhere deep inside our beings, a fissure opened, and all our energy was expelled. All that remained was a lethargy so total that we had no will to do anything, or even just "be." By nine months, we still felt the gaping crevice would never close up, thinking that maybe it would only fill in with silt over time and not be so deep, and perhaps it was filling in already unbeknownst to us.

Deep inside we both craved escape from the intense pain. With John's background in pharmaceutics and our spiritual beliefs about not using mind-altering substances, taking drugs to alleviate our emotional pain was never considered. Not that we didn't have access to them; we took prescription meds for sleep, but also have used them judiciously for international travel to help get over jet lag. John and I have always had a healthy fear of using drugs other than for short term problems, and he would have been more inclined to drink to excess but didn't succumb. Perhaps we were even more sensitive to any substance use because of what had happened with our son. I do think that we could have both benefited from antidepressants—it would have made the first year less brutal.

A resource we could have tapped into would have been a grief group, especially since none of our close friends had experienced the death of a child. We didn't know about groups like Grief Share, Grief Anonymous, and The Compassionate Friends (TCF) which are nationwide with groups in many cities, ours included. A friend who lost her daughter said "The single most useful thing I did was attend the TCF meetings. It was very cathartic to hear other stories. We groaned, we laughed, and we also understood that a child's death is so horrendous that people really don't know what to say, so they say things that are sadly cringe-worthy." Perhaps by writing our journal and talking so openly with friends and strangers, we unintentionally gained the catharsis that we needed while it also left a record of our grief that we can now share.

But during that year, we longed for relief. To run somewhere we didn't feel the pain of thinking about all that happened and wonder what it meant and how we made so many mistakes. But where could we run? No place on earth would be far enough to get away from our own minds. It would only be by leaving this life too, and that was not a choice we would make. The lethargy and pain continued.

Even ten months after JL's death, we were both still facing bouts of anger. John described it as seething under the surface, making it hard for him to want to express it. He had feelings of futility brought on by trying to clear away debris in his office, sorting through files from years of accumulation. I was sorting, too, and read some of my journal entries from the 1970s; I marveled at how zealous and misled we both seemed to be back then. We were both experiencing frustration, wanting so much to get it right, to make a difference in the world and seeming to do neither. Our son's death caused us to hold a light up to all we did. The anger we both have is directed at ourselves still, at our inability to have been the perfect parents, to have made it safe for our kids to live in this world. We have countless parenting books on our shelves, but what good were they? This is what a death like JL's, or a suicide, or any random accident causes most parents to feel. Most parents want to shield their kids from serious harm and want to raise them to be functioning, self-reliant, contributing members of society. When things go awry, John and I have a tendency to look long and hard in the mirror, full of regret. Pointless, perhaps, but we are and always have been prone to self-examination. We don't make excuses and we hold ourselves to a higher standard than anyone else expects of us. It seems that in reality, we are only punishing ourselves.

Bargaining is the third stage of loss. Trying to negotiate and somehow change the past. John dabbled with bargaining, albeit in a purely theoretical sense, when he wished he would have died instead of JL. Our mutual bargaining stage was about regrets— wanting to wind back the clock. Our journal entries are full of "if only's," evidence that we were living in the past, in a land that is hard to escape, and that can feel like an endless maze with no way out.

October 3, 2014
JL,

    Mom here. *It's one of those days when it feels like the world should stop—everyone should know and understand that an important soul has left this world—but it doesn't. It's dad and me and our world that has screeched to a halt like one of those test cars they put dummies in and send flying towards a brick wall. Our heads snapped back, and we are concussed. Yet, in reality, our outer world goes on taking care of the business of life—work, bills, doctors, calls, and other relationships. Our inner world wants to stop spinning relentlessly forward around the sun, hour after hour, day after day—we can feel it spinning. We long to back up to August 1st to somehow change the outcome, to rewind for that second chance.*

    When I was young and home sick from school, we were allowed to watch daytime TV—a special treat because the TV was never on in the daytime—my mom was not the soap opera type. I can still hear the announcer's voice from *Let's Make a Deal*, one of the shows I liked to watch, picturing myself as one of the contestants who was offered something of value, and then given a choice to keep it or exchange it for a different item that was hidden from view. If you chose the different item, you could get a really great prize or a "zonk," something of little or no value. Bargaining after our loss—after getting our zonk—felt like we were trying to "Make a Deal" with God for a second chance.

November 1, 2014
JL,

    Mom here. *Dad and I are in Fresno with Rafael and Elizabets, receiving comfort and love from them as we share about your life leading up to your death, and especially being all alone that August morning. Your dying alone is one of the hardest aspects of your death* *for us and one I often picture in my mind's eye and weep over. I wish we could change what happened.*

Rafael and Elizabets are our oldest friends—we have known each other since John and I were first married. We lived next door to one another, played music and traveled together as a band. Elizabets was not a musician in the band but was my closest friend and confidant. She has a gift for empathy and has blessed our lives with wisdom and unfailing love. Rafael is one of John's soul-mates that he depends on for honest input and support. If we ever needed them, it was then.

November 15, 2014
JL,

Dad here. *Another Saturday. How can time continue to mark the minutes, hours, days, weeks and months? How can I be so self-absorbed with my loss, my pain, my grief, over losing you, over missing you? I am so sad that you are not here. Selfishly of course, so that I could hug and kiss you and watch you grow in wisdom and understanding. Yet, mom and I continue to be encouraged by so many little things God has done to sustain us since the moment of this huge event. A death, a passing, a rebirth. Your life, your passing, your rebirth.*

Our bargaining during this time also focused on the future, asking God to stop these tragic and untimely deaths in my family, and to protect our daughter, her husband, and our grandchildren from anything other than a normal, healthy life. Our countless "Please, Lord" prayers looked more like begging: on our knees, John and I totally defeated, with only a thread of hope and faith that kept us pleading.

The will to save a life is not the power to stop a death.
–Elisabeth Kübler-Ross

GRIEF PART 2: The Blues

Does justice never find you? Do the wicked never lose?
Is there any honest song to sing besides these blues?

—Switchfoot, *"The Blues"*

Honesty. That is one of the main themes that ripple under the surface of "The Blues." Expressions of honest feelings, whatever they may be at the moment, which for most of this genre are themes of lost love, painful relationships, and dashed hopes; I have heard that it was developed out of the songs of the slaves as they struggled in captivity in an unknown land, away from all they knew and those they loved. Even as black musicians and singers became part of the music scene in the 1920's, their lives were still filled with difficulty, exclusion, and heartbreak, and yet privileged white Americans and Europeans were drawn to their music. They were drawn to the common emotions expressed; drawn because the majority of humans have or will experience heartache in their lives. Although it seems counterintuitive, most of us feel consoled by songs that express what we are feeling deep inside but may have a hard time putting into words. In order for me to be honest, I have to acknowledge the blues. By bringing it up to the surface and facing it in a beautiful way, our souls can begin to process and perhaps even find a way to deal with life's hardships. Tolstoy said: "Music is the shorthand of emotion." How true this has been for John and myself throughout our lives.

The fourth stage of loss and grief is depression. When we had mucked about in the past for quite some time and ended up in the present and the place in our world that JL had occupied was now empty, we couldn't escape. Even though we had so much to live for, life felt totally pointless at times. We moved in and out of this stage throughout the first year following our son's death, and at times still experience depression. It is not a comfortable place, but appropriate sadness is normal. We can "invite depression to sit with us without looking for a way to escape ... when we allow ourselves to experience depression, it will leave as soon as it has served its purpose in our loss."

Depression is where we tended to sit and park, waiting, during the journey of grieving our son. We vacillated between our confidence in being together with JL again for eternity, and the painful and raw feelings of present loss. Neither of us were willing to rush the process—we had only one time to grieve this loss and we wanted to allow ourselves the grace to experience it to its fullest extent. By six months after John Leif's death, we were not in *constant* emotional pain; it began to ebb and flow, like sitting in our car, parked on a beach front cliff in California, overlooking the ocean at sunset and watching the waves as they come in and go out, predictably, rhythmically, incessantly...

October 7, 2014
JL,

Mom here. *Dad and I learned yesterday that a dear older neighbor's son shot and killed himself Sunday night after a life of struggling with addiction and alcohol. He was fifty-nine and left a wife and daughter. At eighty-one, our friend is heartbroken beyond description and asked me through tears "Will it ever get better and be bearable?" I told her it does, but very slowly. I can say that now, two months later, your death seems bearable, even though we don't want to bear it, even though we wish it was not real.*

It hit me again that many times this world is just too much for some people, myself included. There were times in my life that I did not want to go on living, even though I had been given so much: a great love in John, two beautiful children, a blessed life. What more did I need? Why do some of us feel the emptiness of this world so profoundly? I don't know, but I do know that if it wasn't for my relationship with God and support from John, I would not have kept on.

One of JL's friend's mom, who knew him well because of all the time he spent at their house, recently shared through tears as she remembered him, "He was such a gentle soul and I think the world was too much for him."

November 19, 2014
JL,
    Mom here. *Dad is still waking up and going to sleep thinking of you and feeling sad. I think this is because he thinks that if he could do it all over again, he would be the perfect father. Maybe it's fatalism on my part, but I would probably not get it right even if I was given the chance to change this tragedy. Depression for both of us.*

It is interesting to me to learn how similar the effects of opiate addiction on the brain are to the effects of depression on the brain. The grief after loss is the worst depression we have experienced. John and I were both sad those first months after JL's death, but we were also depressed, as we responded to such an extreme stress. From what we understand from research on depression, it brings about physical changes in the brain, and in particular, the amygdala, "the pleasure center." This area is deep in our brains and is the same area that is affected by opioids. It is responsible for emotions such as anger, pleasure, sorrow, fear, and sexual arousal. The amygdala is activated and depleted when a person simply *recalls* an emotionally charged or frightening memory, and when a person is sad or depressed. Since August 2nd our pleasure centers had been activated and depleted. We experienced the loss of all normal pleasures and desires including continual indigestion and loss of appetite, decreased energy and sexual desire, and a general inability to feel joy.

As the holidays approached, although we didn't realize it, we entered a new room in our House of Grief: the empty place left by JL's death at the family gatherings. Even when JL was not sober, he was still part of the plans and had a place at the holiday dinner tables. We felt his absence profoundly. We understand now why, when thinking about grief, the advice is to allow oneself a full year in order to experience the loss through all of the seasons, anniversaries, birthdays, and holidays. It is in passing through these special events without the ones we love, that we are able to experience the loss of their presence in this *particular* situation, and therefore able to fully experience the grief. For us, the memories are not all good—there are many sad or troubling ones. We must grieve those too, it seems.

November 26, 2014
JL,

Mom here. *A friend asked me how I was feeling about you and this upcoming holiday. I told her that yes, holidays will be hard for dad and me. We have so many conflicting memories from recent years of you not "showing up:" not being present emotionally because you were using, or not showing up on time. We want to try to re-create new memories based off years before, when you were your real self, perhaps by going through older photos. Can we do this?*

It was sweet and bitter getting Thanksgiving greetings from JL's friends via text or Facebook. They were so kind, demonstrating concern about how John and I were because of families being together, and our son no longer with us. We had a great day serving at a Thanksgiving Day benefit brunch, where again, much love and sympathy was expressed by our friends; yet through the conversations, as the words came out of our mouths and back in to our ears, it brought up the regrets about how we did not understand the deep struggles with which JL lived.

Acute grief normally begins to lessen within a few months after a loss. Looking back, I would say that was true for John and me, although there were times when a specific date or memory would trigger fresh intense depression well beyond the first year. The professional psychologists and lay counselors we met with, and from extensive reading on grief from loss, say to not criticize ourselves, or others, if our grief does not behave normally. Depression that follows loss is based on specific identifiable sorrows. The concern comes when depression is prolonged and excessive and less specific. It is then classified as "clinical" and worthy of seeing a specialist to get treatment. Our grief was definitely specific and identifiable. Although it wasn't clinical, we wished there was a treatment for the pain we were enduring.

November 12, 2014
JL,

Mom here. *I was seeking comfort today in Gold by Moonlight, by Amy Carmichael: "In hours of oppression we were not left to grope in the wilderness. There may be darkness about our ways and yet we are never left without moonlight with which we can gather gold." There were so many times during your life we were definitely groping by moonlight, not sure if we would find gold—then—or especially now.*

November 21, 2014
JL,

Dad here. *I am OK with this sadness when I have lots of work to do, and a lot to think about. But at night, at bedtime, in the morning, all I think about is you. And then I am sad, yes, very, very sad. But I am also thankful for all of the wonderful—full of wonder—years that you were alive living with mom and me. What a precious gift you were, are, straight from the hand of God.*

Throughout the year following our son's death, there was not only the grieving process, but acts of mourning our loss through the intentional decisions we made, the steps we took. They didn't just surface in the first days or weeks. Some were unavoidable, but some, like this one, were our choice, and unintentionally brought more agony:

December 2, 2014
JL,

   Dad here. *I drove down to the sheriff's' office today to pick up the photo CD from when they found you at Garage Mahal. As I drove, I was listening to "Sights" by London Grammar: "What are you afraid of, I know that you are." Years ago, our friend, singer-songwriter Annie, spoke of the "altars," or markers in our life, that we can look back to and remember and worship the Lord. I began to cry on the way down First Avenue. Thinking about your last night here with us. Thinking about the last night of your life. Thinking about Thanksgiving morning 2007. I stopped and cried in front of the Tyndall parking deck where you fell—an altar. Thinking about all that you went through.*

We are told that nothing can separate us from the love of God. And just as that is true, so it is true that nothing can separate us from grief and sorrow over our only son's death. Even with our conviction that we are only separated temporarily, and that we grieve with a strong sense of hope, we still have deep, painful, grief. Death may be the natural occurrence for mankind while on this earth, but it is referred to by Paul as "the last enemy that will be abolished." Isaiah the prophet and John in Revelation assure us that in heaven, "God will wipe away every tear from our eyes, and there will no longer be any death, or mourning, or crying, or pain."

   In the meantime, however, John and I are still living on planet earth. We were still experiencing the shock of our son's sudden death after five months, and the lack of emotional energy as the consequence of the "stress response" to that shock in our bodies and brains. This is defined as an automatic response to a real or perceived physical and/or emotional threat that triggers the release of stress hormones. They cause our hearts to pound, muscles to tense, and breath to quicken, preparing us for "fight or flight." Normally, the built-in feedback-loop allows our brains to turn this response off when the threat passes. If it doesn't, the high levels of stress hormones can lead to many problems, such as immune system deficiencies and depression. Our complicated and intense grief kept our stress hormones high.

December 19, 2014
JL,

   Mom here. *When I think of you any time, but especially when I see your face in a photo, I feel a weight of sadness and a physical pain in my chest. I take a deep breath because I can't believe that I will never see your face again—in person—on this earth. Your being dead is unacceptable. I don't want it to be true.*

John and I travel to Melbourne, Australia (Oz as we call it) twice a year, usually for December and January and then in the summer. John is able to continue working since his research is all done on his laptop. We have been so blessed to be able to be with our granddaughters since their births, watching them grow up, enjoying them as we see the world through the eyes of children again. We were especially looking forward to this time of being with Johanna, Gerard, Anaëlle, Zaria—and being away from the physical reminders of our loss.

December 25, 2014
JL,

   Dad here. *Mom's and my first Christmas morning without you. To say that we missed you, your presence, your smile, is so inadequate to describe the deep sadness. Of course, it is great being with Johanna, Gerard, and the girls. Christmas morning with children. Lots of gifts and hugs and kisses. And memories of our lives years ago when you and Johanna were kids. I am thankful for those years—for those memories.*

One day, we took the girls to a park with a miniature train and pony rides. They absolutely adored the ponies, and loved petting their soft muzzles and manes even more than riding. Yet, even with these loving interactions with our granddaughters, I realized that my lack of emotional energy and wanting to be alone were because I carried my grief over with me, halfway around the globe. It underlay everything else and took so much energy to process. When John and I were quiet and thought about JL, visualizing his face, we both felt a deep, deep ache in our hearts, and we still couldn't believe he was really permanently gone from this life, our life: this world, our world. Were we moving backwards in our grief, back to denial and disbelief?

January 17, 2015
JL,

Mom here. *Even when I am swimming laps here in Oz, I am remembering you and I tell you I love you and I miss you. I am a broken record; really broken.*

People die by the thousands every day—in America, around the globe. This thought struck me tonight as I watched the evening news with tornadoes in the Midwest, war in the middle-east, famines, and many families torn apart as the death tolls continue to rise around the globe year after year. We know families are grieving and we feel compassion and empathy for them. But it is impersonal—we are removed from them physically and relationally. But when it is a person, an individual, who matters to you, who is entwined in and around your life like a vine, it is so very different. Of course. What Augustine wrote in his *Confessions* about the loss of his dearest friend touched me the first time I read it years ago. It is particularly poignant to me now:

"My friend died. My heart was utterly darkened by this sorrow and everywhere I looked I saw death. My native place was a torture room to me ... all the things I had done with him—now that he was gone—became a frightful torment. My eyes sought him everywhere, but they did not see him; and I hated all places because he was not in them, because they could not say to me 'Look, he is coming,' as they did when he was alive and absent. I marveled that other mortals went on living since he whom I had loved as if he would never die was now dead. For where could my heart fly from my heart? Where could I fly from my own self?"

Many times over the years when I would fret over JL, I had taken courage from Augustine and his life. He lived a licentious life, full of the excess of a wealthy young adult—not unlike many young Americans today. His mother, Monica, prayed for him for years. He had a spiritual epiphany as a thirty-year-old, leading to a life change, and became an inspiration to his generation, as well as generations down through the millennia. I knew "miracles" like that could and did happen, and I think this is what makes it hard for John and me now. We wonder *Why did we not get our miracle, the thing we wanted more than anything?* Maybe instead of hoping for a miracle and being overly optimistic, we should have been a little more realistic and accepting of JL's very real struggles. Then, together we might have made different choices.

April 20, 2015
JL,
    Dad here. *Beautiful as the spring morning was, it met me with a wall of despair and sadness. Anger at myself for failing you so, at God for allowing it to happen, at you for being gone. The thought of never knowing the joy of holding your son, my grandson. The last in the Johan, Leif, John, John Leif Trang line. Selfish thoughts and great sadness. Solomon said "Better is the day of one's death than the days of one's birth. Vanity of vanities." I am finding no consolation.*

April 22, 2015
JL,

Mom here. *Some dear friends shared in a letter about their son who committed suicide nine years ago, at about your age, and how they are finally making a new will. They have not faced some details surrounding his death until a year ago, especially his mom, who said she dealt with it by making denial her "friend." The dad wrote: "We wrote a will 30 years ago. It was simple—give the kid everything. Now we haven't had an heir for almost a decade. This loss is a recurring source of grief for me."*

It seems that fathers have a particular sense of loss when they think of their heirs—especially sons—passing the baton. The sense of leaving a posterity is now gone. And we have both felt the loss of having to change who we leave things to. Instead of dividing it between JL and Johanna, now it all goes to her. Yet there are things like the guns that have no interest to her or Gerard. It leaves us in a place of sadness. There is a deep hole, a bottomless well that we can't seem to fill up—not even with all the tears we are shedding. One more area of our lives we have to grieve.

We continued to post monthly on JL's Facebook Memorial page. There were many likes and comments on the posts, most saying how courageous John and I were to have not curled up in a ball in self-protection, to keep facing and sharing our grief and pain, and the process of grief we were going through. It helped many of our friends to not hide their grief after loss, as people tend to do because of discomfort. Others don't want to hear anything after the tragic news. They want you to "move on." But we don't care what others think we should or should not do. "To our own selves be true."

May 23, 2015

JL,

Dad again. *It is a good thing mom has continued to write. I have lots of pages with sticky notes. They all say about the same thing: I love you. I think about you every day, sometimes all day. I miss you—your smile, your eyes, your voice, your hugs—I still can't accept that this has actually happened. That you are actually gone—that this is truly our new reality. Painful—profoundly sad—inconsolable. I cry thinking of you.*

> *After great pain, a formal feeling comes.*
> *The Nerves sit ceremonious, like tombs.*
> —Emily Dickinson

10

THE MAZE

To walk safely through the maze of human life,
one needs the light of wisdom and the guidance of virtue.

−Buddha

No one has the capacity to break your heart like your child, because no one else is literally a part of your heart, as a child is. The first time I saw my son was when his almost ten-pound body was pulled from the incision in my belly and laid on my chest after hours of non-productive labor. The gasp in the delivery room from the team of doctors and nurses on the other side of the drape just below my chin caused me to panic, picturing something wrong—a deformed or dead baby. But it was only the enormous size, compared to our daughter at five pounds, that brought the astonishment. Clearly, at 5'4", I was no match for his girth.

The last time I saw his grown-man body alive was thirty-six hours before his death as a 150-pound, 5'10", beautiful twenty-five-year old man. When this son who was our flesh and bone died—a unique and singular human being made from the combination of two very different gene pools—something inside of us died, too. Even with a physical separation as final as our son's death, the intangible connection between us as a father and mother and their child can never be broken. Yet, this event shattered what was once our lives together. It took the unique puzzle that had been built over the years and not only disassembled it, but forcefully scattered the pieces. We found ourselves on hands and knees, trying to scrape the pieces of our lives into a pile, gather them up, put them back together again.

How did we end up here? We were radical "Jesus People" in the 1970's, (part of the "Jesus Movement" concurrent with the "Hippie Movement" of the late 60's and early 70's) and played in a band at coffee houses and outdoor festivals while we worked and went to college before having children. We were married eleven years, then our daughter was born, and six years later, our son. While John taught at Samford University School of Pharmacy in Birmingham, Alabama, I home-schooled our two children, a sometimes difficult task due to their age differences. We wanted to build close relationships with our children by spending lots of time with them. And I remembered being increasingly bored in school, and I didn't want our children to experience that. Real learning should be engaging and bring joy. When we moved back to Tucson in the mid-nineties to be closer to our families, John began his pharmaceutical consulting firm and we continued schooling at home. As part of a homeschooling network, we enjoyed some field trips and group events, but it was just we three at home much of the time. Johanna entered regular school in eighth grade, which left John Leif and me rattling around at home alone for his third grade. We made the decision to put him in a small private school beginning in fourth grade, and he flourished.

Tuesday, September 2, 2014—One month since John Leif died
JL,

 Mom here. *Dad and I find that we still really don't want to get out of bed in the morning. We know it will make your death real, and unspeakably painful. When we wake up, we hold hands and sometimes look at each other. At other times, we stare off into space. It has been one month since you died, and it seems like ages ago. So many sensations have been circulating around and then spilling out of our hearts. It feels like nothing is left. Sleep escapes us, like a caged* *animal who, at the slightest opportunity, charges out of the door. We still take medication to sleep and probably will for quite some time—we make no apologies for it. Awake, we drag ourselves through the day. We both need to get back to work projects, which momentarily occupy our thoughts, and force us to move forward. We continue to swim. Slowly re-reading On Grief and Grieving, we find we are normal with these feelings—though dad cries a lot more than I do.*

When Johanna and JL were young, we took them and my parents to England to meet some of my mother's relatives. We visited Hampton Court Palace, just outside of London. It was spectacular in every way. One of the parts that we thought would be fun to see was the Maze: the most famous maze in the world. It is referred to as a "multicursal" or "puzzle maze" and is known for confusing and intriguing visitors with its many twists, turns, and dead ends. A maze is a left-brain puzzle, logical and analytical, often with false passages and many choices—you can easily get lost and confused. We did, and we were glad we were in a public place where we knew someone would eventually help us out. While I was thinking about the years of living with JL and his addiction, it seemed like we were *living* in a maze. We were definitely lost and confused much of the time. No amount of analyzing or logic seemed to change things. As we were trying to put the puzzle pieces together and figure out what led up to his death, the memory of the maze surfaced. With it came the same feelings of confusion, disorientation and panic—for no discernible reason other than our world had been upended. For me, figuring out and understanding the details of how and why it happened seemed urgently important, as if that understanding would bring peace to the chaos I felt.

September 10, 2014
JL,

Mom here. *"What holds us so very close together? Anxious vigils, the chill of fear, the rain of tears: of such strange things Gold Cords are made, the hope that refuses to despair." The words are from Amy*

Carmichael, who worked in India her entire life trying to save babies and little children from temple prostitution, with many successes along with failures. We empathize fully. I have a note in the margin there from July 2009 with your name. You had told dad and me in May 2009 on our way back from Australia that you had relapsed and were using Oxy, which rapidly progressed to BT. The following months and years were full of poor choices and decisions by us as you struggled with recovery and relapses. If we had only known then what we know now. Yet, as Amy Carmichael said above, those struggles held us closely together. And now, those "gold chords" are what God is using to hold dad and me together as we live without you being here.

Throughout the years since we found out that JL was using BT in the summer of 2005, we attempted to learn how to *not* be "codependent." Sadly, JL died while we were still in the process, albeit we had come a long way. My family of origin was *very* codependent and although I would not have been able to define it as such when I was a young adult, I knew the relationships were not healthy and I did not want to duplicate them in my own life. Even with that strong desire, I did not realize that the patterns of behavior I had learned growing up, that had been passed down to me unawares, were entrenched so deeply in my psyche that it would take years, decades, of intentional counseling and study to "unlearn" them. Many times during our group therapy at The Mark I was baffled and felt thick-headed while trying to "get" the points about codependency. Fortunately, our relationship was not as much of a struggle because John's family was much healthier, and our codependency was considered "simple" (from one family background) as opposed to "complex" (from both families). With complex codependence, it is estimated there is a 60 percent chance for a person to become addicted. But it was with others, in groups at church and my family where codependency was deeply ingrained, that the battle was fought to have healthy, balanced relationships instead of ones that were emotionally destructive and one-sided. I hadn't yet learned detachment.

Our journey together with JL as he attempted to find lasting recovery, was full of ups and downs. But it was not like a roller coaster ride. There was never anything fun or exciting about the highs and lows, but rather, it was an arduous trek through steep mountains and deep valleys. Sometimes pulling him from in front, sometimes pushing him from behind. In rare and precious moments, walking calmly beside him.

In the beginning, we were definitely pulling him against his will because he had found peace from the turbulence of adolescence that some of us experience more deeply than others. And bliss. He found bliss in opiates, the magic potion that seductively draws a person in and never lets go without a life and death struggle. Fortunately, when we found out, he was a 16-yr-old with enough normal frontal cortex left to know he was in trouble and want help and, more significantly, we had enough leverage over him as a minor to enforce conditions we hoped would insure his recovery.

In looking back through my journal from the summer of 2005, I found information I had totally forgotten—the passing of time had selectively deleted from memory. Three weeks after JL had gone cold turkey off of BT, we were already regularly doing urine tests for opiates. He was taking trazodone, as suggested by his doctor to help with sleep and general mood enhancement. Trazodone is an antidepressant of the selective serotonin reuptake inhibitor (SSRI) class. Gradually, his attitude had become uncharacteristically demanding, and at times aggressive. Of course, his body and mind were craving opiates, which we did not fully understand or appreciate, so he was not the real JL. I decided to urine test for a few other drugs. I both wanted and needed to get to the bottom of it. I was right. He tested positive for marijuana and Ecstasy (MDMA), a methamphetamine that alters mood and perception. We were shocked. John and I were told it is common for addicts to switch drugs, and that we shouldn't bother testing any longer but instead get JL into a residential rehab program. Again, we thought we could manage it at home.

We also didn't realize how much he was drinking. Because our focus was on drugs, that is what we tested for. We didn't understand at the time that alcohol is just another drug and a companion to drug addiction. We knew that JL didn't drink and drive—he was frequently the "designated driver"—and so we *assumed* that when he was going to friends' houses or parties, he wouldn't drink. We, of course, were wrong. There were many creative ways around this problem, as we found out much later.

What is insightful about turning around and looking back is that, as John reminds me, "hindsight is 20/20." I see how many times we were given advice by people who knew addiction and those who are trapped in its grip and how many times we did not fully take it. We were woefully myopic, too close to the problem to see it clearly or objectively. In our misguided compassion and listening to our son's pleas, we always did a *modified* version of the action steps that were advised. We just didn't seem to understand how deadly the monster of heroin addiction was, and that aggressive and long-term solutions were *absolutely* necessary to save our son's life. So, instead of a residential rehabilitation program, or the next best option of the intensive outpatient program—where we would have been attending meetings and learning alongside our son four times a week—we chose a once a week outpatient meeting. Because of this decision, the three of us had to repeat the program several times over the course of his attempts at recovery, when it was really too late for us to implement this critical information.

October 18, 2014
JL,

Mom here. *We found an IT guy to retrieve the data from your phone without having your super security passcode. The call log only went back a few days, but as I searched through the names to see who you called, I saw what I was after: Alex—from Restart Sober Living, where you had been here in town December of 2013—a name you would never have been calling except to get drugs. We looked at all the text messages with him, starting the very week you went there after* *your detox at Compass Health last Thanksgiving—messages about "sharing a dab for $25" and meeting him and "needing a place to shoot some shots."*

Then there are some texts the first week in January while you were here detoxing after being caught, and you and Alex were kicked out of Restart. He was texting you and you stopped responding. You were serious about staying clean. The next text is July 31, the Thursday afternoon before you died, asking if you could head over, and there was an address. I decided to pursue the owners and find out about Alex, why he was a house leader, and what they knew, before we contacted the sheriff and the Drug Enforcement Agency (DEA).

When I called the owners of Restart to ask about Alex and told them what had happened, they confirmed what I thought. They had made him house manager, but after New Year's Eve and finding out that JL and Alex had been using, they removed him and told him he would never be allowed back. They gave me his mother's phone number, but I could never get through to her, and I have never gotten any response from Alex. I don't know if he is still alive or not. Since JL's death we have heard that Restart is referred to as "Relapse in a Box" by the recovery community. Like many so-called "Sober Living" homes that are poorly managed and supervised—maybe started with good intentions or maybe not.

We put off contacting the DEA for some time. It was just too difficult emotionally to head back down into "the basement" of our lives and open up this particular box and rummage around in it; why bother inflicting more pain on ourselves voluntarily? When we finally did, the officer took down the information, but said that they only have time to follow up on leads for the big dealers as opposed to the guys who sell to friends. I had hoped that if they found Alex, it would lead to his dealers. I never heard back.

John and I also put off watching some documentaries that friends had suggested to us about the Heroin Epidemic, sources, and government failure. We still haven't watched some of them and now I'm not sure why. Perhaps it's an attempt at self-protection from more pain. We know if we immerse ourselves into what is actually continuing to happen day in and day out—not only in America, but all over the world—not only are we vividly reminded of JL, but we will feel we should do something. We don't know what we could do to actually offer real, lasting help.

November 9, 2014
JL,

Mom here. *I feel like the period of searching surrounding the details of your death is almost at its end. I am feeling that there was not just one reason, but many. As in all aspects of life, it is complicated, and I have to accept that there are reasons beyond my finite human ability to understand. But some of them I do get. Now that time has passed and I am able to see more of the tapestry of your life—not woven by mistake, but the result of living in an imperfect world where God grants humans the double-edged sword called choice.*

I believe some of the reasons for your death at this time were to end the deep suffering and guilt that you endured every day with the tension between wanting to be clean and sober and the constant struggle to satisfy the dopamine cravings in your addicted brain, that place where the receptors had changed and the only thing that spelled pleasure for you was heroin. There had been too many cycles of relapse and recovery for you to want to go through it all again and again. You had not had any significant period of sobriety since before your fall in November 2007. After your experience last New Year's Eve (2013) and the intense desire you had to be clean, your spirit was willing, but the cravings grew. Without the medical help you needed—and that we didn't support—you were wandering away from your spiritual foundation and your commitment to never use again.

We made continuous attempts as a couple to get through "the maze" and piece together the puzzle; John's answer to the "Why?" piece continued to be that he was at fault because he was an imperfect dad. I should be content with that answer too, since I was an imperfect mom who made many mistakes, but that doesn't satisfy me. I know too many other parents who are equally imperfect, albeit in different ways, and they still have their children alive and well on this earth.

> *Heartsick, Heartbroken. To know love is to know pain.*
> *What could be more common?*
> *Even so, each broken heart is so singular that*
> *with it we probe the Divine.*
> —Rumi

11

NO PAIN

I will love the light for it shows me the way,
yet I will endure the darkness because it shows me the stars.

−Og Mandino

In the early 1980's, one of the urban catch-all phrases we used was, "No pain, no gain." Jane Fonda made it popular in her aerobics videos to motivate us to exercise through pain in order to gain the most from our fitness workouts. I remember John having discussions with my sister Susan about this motto. In applying this principle to life, she had taken it a step further and would say, "No gain without pain." That is, if it doesn't hurt, it isn't worthwhile. She proposed, in her pursuit of vibrant spirituality, that if it hurts it must *necessarily* be good. John, ever the logician, reasoned with her that most *mottos* are not absolute truth, but they can be applied to certain situations at certain times, and their converse can also be true. Something can be worthwhile and beneficial without pain, such as enjoying natural pleasures of eating, exercise, sleep, and esoteric enjoyment from sharing love, receiving a gift, a smile from a friend, enjoying music and art: "gain without pain." If something hurts, it may not be good. It may actually be hurtful, dangerous, or even deadly: "pain without gain." Our natural, built-in response to pain causes us to pull our hand away from a flame or to back away from a snake in our path because there will be no gain from being burned or bitten. As adults, we can learn to avoid *unnecessary* pain through experience, education, and gaining wisdom.

John and I were both raised with strong work ethics and, because of the general culture of the 50's and 60's, we were taught delayed gratification from our earliest days. When we raised our kids, we strived to train them in the same way. However, there were only two of them as opposed to the larger families we grew up in where we were all part of making the family run smoothly—parents and kids. In contrast, our kids were freely given our time and attention. Our parents had no extra money with which to indulge us. Even though we were not wealthy, our children had more than they needed and abundantly more than we had growing up. We know we overprotected our kids in so many ways just like the parents of their peers. When I asked some of JL's friends about their family dynamics and why they think they got involved with drugs, several of them said their parents were preoccupied with their careers and *under involved* with them, while they were *overindulged* with money their parents gave them in lieu of being with them.

It seems there is not a "formula" for getting it right or getting it wrong. I think one reason we want "the formula" for raising healthy, happy kids (and why there are so many books and lectures promising it) is because we love them so much, we don't want them, or ourselves to experience pain. We forget that pain is part of life and work, effort, and normal, healthy challenges help us mature. It is natural to seek pleasure and to avoid suffering, especially for those we love. It's easy to see how addiction to drugs, other substances, and activities that affect the "pleasure center" of our brains, are very hard to dislodge.

At times I wish we could have protected JL more from the *real* perils in this increasingly dangerous world. Spun a cocoon around him that he could have stayed inside until he was older, more mature, wiser. Of course, he would have shriveled and died. Larvae cannot remain in a cocoon past their time. And larvae are not butterflies. So, we would have felt the need to help him out, being the ever-enabling parents that we were, reducing the struggle by opening his cocoon. Yet, *without the struggle,* the necessary enzymes wouldn't be forced into his wings, and he would have emerged crippled—a butterfly who couldn't fly.

From my earliest memories, my knees and legs ached at random times with varying intensity. Sometimes I thought it was from running or playing too hard. At other times, it seemed like it happened when it rained in Tucson—which wasn't very often—and there were many times they ached when it wasn't raining. But being in a large family growing up in the 1960's, there were not many options for relieving that pain. My parents would sometimes rub my legs with witch hazel, which made my legs feel good temporarily. Sometimes they would wrap my knees in an Ace bandage to help while I was at school. There was one thing that never happened: I was *never* given any medicine to relieve my pain.

My leg aches continued into adulthood, and I tried my best to figure out what was causing the pain. It wasn't until we moved to Arkansas where changes in weather were so frequent that my hunch was proven correct: a dramatic change in barometric pressure, usually accompanied by rain, caused my bones to ache. In Arizona, the pressure could change without ever seeing rain, and so it had been hard to put the pieces together. Yet even as a young adult, I was still hesitant to take even aspirin. My how things have changed.

Most likely, even if my parents had known of a drug that would relieve my pain, they were not worried about me having to suffer a little pain. They knew that pain was an inevitable and bearable part of life, important in forging resilience. I developed an empathy for pain from my experience which, sadly, most likely played into why John and I did everything we could to help our kids *avoid* pain. Now we are experiencing the result of those mistaken applications with the loss of our son. We found these same thoughts expressed by Sam Quinones, as he discusses this at length in *Dreamland*. He believes that pain avoidance is largely responsible for the opioid epidemic in America because it is intertwined with our culture of supremely valuing comfort and prosperity. How we wish we would have had these insights decades ago.

November 27, 2014 – Thanksgiving Day
JL,

 Mom here. *When I went to bed, preparing to get up in the morning to work the annual benefit brunch at the Raging Sage, I remembered Thanksgiving 2007. We received a call at 5:30 am from University Medical Center emergency room telling us you had fallen 15 feet from the parking garage wall—but you were fine. We thought we'd come later but decided we should go then. By doing so and talking with your friend Oliver (who they would not let in to see you because they thought he had pushed you) we found out you had actually fallen five stories—65 feet. On hearing this, the ER docs went into action. Not pleasant memories to go to sleep to.*

Thanksgiving weekend 2007. The dorms were empty as most of the students traveled home to be with their families. JL was staying in town to be with us for the holiday. Along with his friend, Oliver, they spent the evening playing video games and drinking. Underage, but drinking. We were unaware of how much he and his friends were drinking at the dorms. We presumed there were sufficient barriers in place to keep alcohol out. Wrong again.

There was an unusual thunderstorm rolling in that night, and like all desert dwellers, the guys wanted to see it. At about 3:00 a.m. they bought burgers and drove up the ramp to the top level of the five-story parking deck on campus to get a good view of the lightning. There is a decorative fascia structure which is separated from the deck by about two feet, and the boys, being rock climbers, climbed out onto it to sit and watch. Sometime around 4:00 a.m. they heard a car driving up the ramps and saw that it was campus police.

We know they had normal underage responses to seeing police, being out in the middle of the night, and having had alcohol, even though they weren't drunk. Instantly, JL had a plan. He thought they could quietly climb one level down and then casually walk back up, as though returning to their car. As JL quickly crab-walked backward to get out of sight he made one move too far. Over he went, backwards, between the fascia and the parking deck. After the first fifteen feet, he landed on his head on a small platform and became unconscious. He continued to fall off the landing and the rest was between the buildings in a narrow space—which saved his life. He hit several pipes on the way down, breaking ribs and vertebrae, and then was in open space for the last fifteen feet—where he landed legs first, causing a compression fracture in his back.

Meanwhile, Oliver turned around and JL was gone. When he realized he had fallen, he jumped back up on to the parking deck and ran toward the police cars frantically telling them his friend had fallen. They drove down to the bottom level and found JL still unconscious and bleeding. In the confusion and rush, they didn't seem to hear from Oliver that he had fallen from the top floor. The ambulance arrived and whisked JL away. The police were suspicious that Oliver had pushed JL, so they wouldn't let him into JL's room in the ER. Meanwhile, JL regained consciousness and told them he had fallen 15 feet—that was all he remembered before passing out—so he was just under observation when we received the call. It was only after we arrived and talked with Oliver and heard the story and relayed it to the doctors, that scans and tests began.

Thus began five days in the hospital with stitches, morphine, then oral opioids, and fitting for a body cast. So also began his relapse. JL had been clean from opioid addiction since June 22, 2005, almost two and a half years. It was the last sober period of any length for him until his death. He returned to the University of Arizona (U of A) for the spring semester of 2008, living in the dorm, back brace and all. He had to quit his job after he fell because he could no longer lift heavy things.

During the following months with him on opioid pain meds, he couldn't wean himself off of the drugs. The orthopedic surgeon wanted him to do physical therapy for the pain in his back from the compressed vertebrae and broken bones, which he did for a while, but it seems it was too much effort. Drugs were an easier solution, and the receptors in his brain had been reawakened. The dragon was out of its lair.

After JL had pimped the doctor for as long as possible, in the spring of 2008 he began buying Oxy's on the street. That is how he met two new friends that were dealers in prescription opiates. Like JL and so many of his generation of addicted young people, they were intelligent and from solid families. They were at the university and had addictions but did not want to use BT—it was more dangerous because of the random potency and the probability of it being laced with something else. So, they sold Oxy's to support their own habits of using opioids.

Since JL died, we have heard from both of these young men. One we knew and knew he was an IV opioid addict but didn't know the backstory or about him and JL and the Oxy connection. After surviving an overdose, he left Tucson in the spring of 2014 to try to get and stay clean, since for him, living in the city where you have all your connections was like being a five-year-old in a candy store with open bins. He stayed clean, although he does regularly use cannabis. And since he is very intelligent, like JL, his head tells him all the reasons that he doesn't need AA or spirituality or community to stay clean and sober. We continue to worry about him. John and I are convinced that without community—without the presence and pressure that many close relationships afford—the quality and viability of a sober life is not tenable in the long term.

The other young man is thriving. He contacted us via phone months after JL died and introduced himself. He is very involved with AA in his community, has been clean and truly sober for over seven years, and is an inspiration to all those around him. In his weakness he has become strong. Another great paradox, counterintuitive to our culture that values power and control. Although he is highly intelligent, he started his re-entry into "normal" life by being a laborer. He is wise enough to know he cannot ever think he has it made in regard to his sobriety.

A young friend who is a recovering heroin addict shared her thoughts with me regarding her continuing to be a part of AA/12-step meetings: "The ritual of getting drugs and using provides structure for addicts in an otherwise totally unstructured and chaotic life. That's why AA meetings are so important. It's having a structure, a positive ritual, to replace the destructive one."

In the summer of 2008 JL finally got another job, but by this time it was not enough to support his normal spending and his Oxy habit. JL had to eventually switch from Oxy to BT because of the expense: Oxy is multiple times more expensive. When JL died, each 20 mg Oxy on the street sold for $40 or more. During this relapse period, JL began to pawn things like his guns and his video game equipment and took out auto title loans, all without our knowledge. At some point in the ensuing years, he had dipped into his refund of his student loans from an unfinished semester at the university. Due to another relapse and recovery program, he was unable to finish that semester and the loan refund had gone into his bank account, again without our knowledge. He was responsible for his student loans. When that money ran out and we finally heard about the pawning and the drugs, JL began one more re-start down the road to recovery—which included working and paying us back for getting items out of pawn before they were gone. These items were then put into our storage locker where they were out of his reach.

Along with *Dreamland*, John Temple's book from 2015, *American Pain*, gives details about the Oxy epidemic and how the American Pain "Clinics" started in Florida, and preyed upon people struggling in Appalachia and the Rust Belt. The book documents not only the rise, but the fall of those involved in these pill mills including one doctor who made $1.2 million in the 16 months she worked there and the main owner, a young felon, who made $40 million. Some are still serving prison time while others were acquitted; and the toll in human lives? Too costly to count as the statistics we hear on the news just continue to rise, in a nation where a culture of avoiding pain at all costs is a subliminal message many Americans continue to buy into.

November 29, 2014
JL,

   Mom here. *I remember having prayed over the past few years that if you needed to be arrested and go to prison in order to bring a life-change, then so be it. But today I thought I would not have wanted you to experience what life in prison would have meant—it would have been 24 hour a day pain and anxiety for us. Maybe your instant death was the most merciful way to get off the merry-go-round. For all of us.*

   Reflecting back over this journal entry, I am struck by how intensely I was trying to make some sense of JL's sudden death, and the empathy I felt, both for him and for us. I was groping for comfort and the thought of any more pain was unthinkable. Years after his death, my thoughts revert back to being more objective about prison possibly being a positive experience for JL as I have heard more from those in the judiciary system and stories from those who are addicted.

   We have a friend who is a federal judge here in Tucson and has a daughter who is a recovering heroin addict. He has told us it is disappointing that our society handles drug and alcohol problems, along with co-occurring mental health issues, in the judicial system because there are long term consequences that create extra hurdles for their futures, such as criminal convictions and exposure to career criminals in prison. He can, however, send people to residential treatment programs multiple times, which is usually what it takes. It can be a help for weary families, because there are other sets of eyes on their loved one and services they wouldn't be able to afford on their own. If we could get rid of the felony convictions and have "drug court" for federal offences as we do for state, it would be far better. Drug courts have been initiated across the country and they are very successful.

Two of JL's recovering friends and one young friend I've recently met, all did stints in jail or prison because they were caught with enough drugs to be incarcerated. They are alive and well and functioning in society now and that experience was a wakeup call for them. It was the same for Tracey Helton Mitchell, who wrote *The Big Fix: Hope After Heroin*, the story of her life as a heroin addict and her recovery. There are many others. Of course, it is not a reliable "solution," but it seems for young addicts, a lengthy time of being truly clean and sober gives their brain and body enough time to heal so they are able to envision, and then want, a different life. A life without opiates.

> *The aim of the wise is not to secure pleasure,*
> *but to avoid (unnecessary) pain.*
> —Aristotle

12

SECRET LIVES

The face is the mirror of the mind, and eyes,
without speaking, confess the secrets of the heart.

–St. Jerome

With JL's iPhone unlocked, I tentatively sorted through some of the photos, unsure of what I would find, unsure if I really wanted to see what was there, but very sure that I would continue to wonder if I didn't. He kept his phone secure and very private. There are reasons people keep secrets. With a sudden death, that privacy is lost, and many well-guarded secrets are exposed. One photo was taken in the last few weeks of his life. A self-portrait, standing in front of what appears to be a public bathroom mirror, dressed in black slacks, shirt, tie. Dressed for work, perhaps. He was staring directly into the mirror, reflected directly back into the lens. What was happening in his life at that moment that caused him to want to document it for himself? My guess is that he was attempting one more time to remind himself of what he was doing (using again) in the hopes that it would urge him to make a change, but we will never know.

August 17, 2014
JL,

Mom here. *I wonder if you were going to tell us you had relapsed several weeks before your death—after your oral surgery, while being* *on Percocet—and that you were using again? Were you going to ask us for help Thursday night before your death when you were here for dinner? Did my saying we knew about your getting drunk in June while we were out of town change that by putting you on the defensive? Or were you waiting to see what we knew and then just not tell us? You had taken that tack before and over a month had already passed. I still remember the frustration in your voice that night when you said you had been planning on telling us about what happened in June...*

It was June 2014 when John and I left for a trip to the Midwest and East Coast. I am prodding myself now—like trying to get a stubborn cow out of a barn—to go back to that time and bring up these memories, which are both painful and frustrating. There were so many things we didn't know JL would struggle with while we were away. Especially this time, while we thought he was doing so well. Of course, we were not mind readers or responsible for his feelings or choices, but we knew that it was never wise to presume that just because things were going well for an addict that meant they would continue.

JL went four-wheeling with some of his old friends up the back road of the Catalina Mountains on the northern perimeter of Tucson. He, John, and friends had done it many times. It is a rough and steep road, but a challenge they loved. While we were away on our trip, we talked with JL several times, and he told us about it and how fun it was. What we didn't know, until the week before he died, was that JL did not go back to the sober living house that Sunday night, specifically because he was drunk. When he got back to town, at some point when he began to sober up, he called the house to say he wouldn't be home until the next morning because he was staying overnight with friends. When he got back, the house leaders knew (the addicted and the alcoholic can't fool each other) and they worked through it with JL. His addiction counselor told us that if a child loves his parents, they have a strong desire to not disappoint them, so they wait until the parents are not around to relapse. He was supposed to tell us but waited until after we got back, and even then, put it off for several weeks until *we asked him* about it a few nights before he died. He was, of course, embarrassed and ashamed. It shows us how much guilt and self-condemnation he felt for his addiction. What a self-defeating cycle.

He explained: "While we were in the mountains and sitting around eating, all my friends were drinking. I said 'No' repeatedly, but finally caved in and had a drink." As an alcoholic, he could not just have one—or even a few. What is hard about this for us is feeling frustrated that his friends didn't get that they were not helping JL by drinking around him and offering him alcohol. JL would never have said that it would help if they didn't drink around him. It was impossible for him to say he was an alcoholic. It is the same wherever we go.

But should we be surprised? John and I were the same at their age when we also had to learn this lesson in a painful way. It was in the mid 1970's and we had become friends with a young woman, Valerie, who moved into our townhouse complex and who went to our church. We had her over for an Italian dinner for her birthday and splurged by having a bottle of wine. (This was before inexpensive good wines—we were on a student budget and rarely drank anything.) We had a great time, and then we didn't see our friend for months. I ran into a mutual friend in the store one day about six months later and asked where Valerie was. She said that Valerie was an alcoholic who had been sober for quite a long time until she had that wine at our house. Then she had "fallen off the wagon" and had been drinking ever since— and was so ashamed that she didn't want us to know. We were heartsick and grieved.

We had no idea she was an alcoholic and wondered why she didn't just tell us she couldn't drink. But because of the stigma associated with being called "an alcoholic"—especially with the faith community—she didn't want to say she was an alcoholic or refuse our hospitality. From that day onward we did not drink alcohol, even when we moved to the Southeast for John's professorships for thirteen years. We realized that there were people whose very life depended on being sober and who needed the solidarity of people around them. When we moved back to Tucson in 1994, we felt at liberty to begin drinking again but were very selective as to when and with whom.

Recent statistics indicate that in the past two decades, Americans who drink are drinking more, and dying because of it. Yet 30 percent of Americans don't drink at all and another 30 percent average less than one drink per week. If we choose not to drink, there should be no apologizing or embarrassment. We are not alone—unless we are keeping company with the top 20 percent who average 15 to 74 drinks per week.

We have never found out who the friends were on that weekend in the mountains. JL would never tell us, and I think they are embarrassed. We can only hope they learned something from this experience. That episode of drinking in June began his final relapse. And even though it would be a few weeks until he was taking Percocet before his oral surgery, it triggered his pursuit to numb himself and seek the drugs that would cause his death.

Saturday, August 16, 2014—End of Week 2
JL,

Mom here. *It seems you needed to keep your friends and relationships separate from dad and me because you felt we might be critical of them—a logical conclusion. But we now know that you knew quality people and knew how to have good relationships. We also know you could use people to cover or enable your addiction.*

Why were John and I surprised that we didn't know everything about our young adult son's life? We didn't need to, desiring to respect his autonomy as an individual, separate from us as his parents. There was still this aspect of secretiveness that we knew was there and, of course, we were never sure if the secrets pertained to him just protecting the privacy of his friends—which he felt strongly about—or covering his trail by keeping us disconnected from any potential source of damning information.

We had so much personal and private information already about John Leif because of the interactions surrounding his addiction and cycles of sobriety and relapse. Since he was trying to go through the university and get his degree, and because we wanted to support him as much as possible, invasive interactions became part of our relationship. Drug testing at home—watching him pee into the cup so we would not be fooled by any of the latest schemes—caused a total lack of privacy for him. There is so much that whittles down and erodes dignity for alcoholics and those who are addicted.

JL's friend James, who was his companion in using opioids from the beginning, visited us some weeks after the memorial. It was good for him, and us, to talk about our son. We asked him for any information on his drug use history and how JL actually started using, but he gave us very few details. We are sad that JL never wanted to tell us those things, even when he was clean. I imagine that it would have been embarrassing for him. I know he felt we were judgmental toward the friends he really loved, unable to separate their addiction issues from them as people; but even more, was our concern for him hanging out with friends who wouldn't lift him up or influence him in a sober direction. He thought he could be with other addicts and not let it negatively influence him, but he was wrong.

September 14, 2014
JL,

Mom here. *William Sky came over today for lunch. Dad and I enjoyed hearing him talk about his favorite memories from when you two were young—many things we didn't know, such as times when you were probably 12 or 13 and he stayed overnight. You two would go out after we were asleep and smoke pot in a glass pipe in the carport. He confirmed what we thought—that you really didn't like pot and preferred alcohol. He said it was you who advised him to take the job in Utah this summer and the possibility of you getting a job* *with him, too. That was two days before you died. He also said how incredibly brilliant you were and joked with you about being your personal assistant when you were a billionaire. You had the potential for so much and were robbed of it so young.*

John and I had some of JL's good friends over for dinner in the fall after his death. They were concerned about us and we were concerned about them, especially Cory, since he was the one who found JL dead that morning. He said he will never forget the sight he met as he broke into the room, or the shock he had. I can't imagine how horrible that must have been for him. We will never forget that morning either.

But the conversation moved on to some fun stories about them all in monkey and banana costumes running around Speedway at night, while they were freshmen at the U of A—just having good, clean fun. We discovered that they had all been with JL on July 4th as we looked through the photos on his phone, something we didn't know at the time. My mind started clicking as I heard this. *Was JL reminiscing because he knew his time was short? Did he have a sense that he would relapse fully after being on Percocet?*

And so, it went, again. Me wondering what was in our son's heart and mind, trying to understand what he was feeling, projecting how I might have felt if I were in his shoes. Fear is what I think would have been foremost in his mind, even dread, perhaps, seeing himself do something he knew was not going to end well, but also knowing he couldn't stop or tell anyone—least of all his parents because they have such high hopes that he was on a recovery trajectory that seemed certain. How I wish I could have known how to allow JL to share when he was not doing well without him fearing that we would get mad or *do* something. That's what parents' roles are, right? To *do* something to help or change our addicts? Instead, we needed to be supportive while not enabling, letting him work through his own choices while giving whatever wisdom we could have to help guide him. It was a tightrope we had been forced to walk, suspended high in midair between two skyscrapers. None of us wanted to be testing our balance as we made our way forward, teetering from side to side.

One of my younger brothers, JD, was a winsome, fun, brilliant young man with tons of friends, including me. He was extremely knowledgeable about plants and a well-respected landscape designer here in Tucson. But he was also a risk taker, and ultimately those risks cost him his life. As the first son of my Italian father, after three daughters, he was the "Golden Boy." Lots of dysfunctional family dynamics were woven into the fabric of his life—a life cut off in its prime. Overprotected and indulged by both of my parents, this only served to allow him to take risks, and then expect someone would be there to remove or minimize the consequences. There was always a way out with few consequences, or none at all.

His friends and colleagues were in shock when they learned of his death and its cause. Even though he had been in ICU for two months, my mom, who managed the office for his business, told everyone, including his closest friends, that JD had pneumonia and was improving every day. None of them knew he was dying of AIDS, and we, his siblings, had no clue what my mother had been saying, wondering instead why none of his friends had come to see him when visitors were finally allowed. When we knew he would only have one more day, I called his two closest friends and asked. My mom had told them he couldn't have visitors. When they came to the hospital, they wept in sorrow. John and I were so frustrated with my mom and what she had done. We understood that the actions she took were because she wouldn't allow herself to believe JD was dying. Denial was her friend, and secrets were how she kept others from the truth that would cause her shame and pain.

December 4, 2014
JL,

    Mom here. *It is raining today and wonderful for the desert. Kyle came over yesterday to sort through the photos from your phone and computer for us. Dad and I know there are things you would not want us to see—we want to respect that. We don't want to see them anyway,* *but Kyle does, and will delete all the "X-rated" ones, only keeping the ones that he and we want. He said he has never seen himself drunk or blacked out, and you had photos and videos of him and others in those states. He said it was hard but OK. John is worried it might cause him to relapse. I think it will do the opposite. He is a young man of integrity and wants to be of help to this world. These are places he will never want to go again.*

In speaking with Kyle recently, I asked if there were any photos or videos of JL drunk or blacked out from when he sorted through them. There weren't. It seems that no one else was regularly taking photos of their group drinking bashes, and I'm pretty sure when JL was using opiates, it was not in a group. He kept that part of his life as secret as possible.

As we sort through 25 years of our photos of JL, there is a memory attached to each one. With each memory we are taken back to a specific moment in time and to a particular place. Many times, we are able to remember the details: Nunu and he sitting and playing the piano when JL was about 3; Grandpa Leif holding JL on his lap at our kitchen table in Birmingham; JL and Johanna cooking with Nonna while she cared for them when John and I took our first trip to Italy. Or when he was an adolescent, before drugs—target practice or camping with John, boogie boarding at Mission Beach, riding the go-kart behind our house or swimming in the pool with friends— real joy evident on his face. Later on, during periods of sobriety, his clear eyes and genuine smile were often seen as we traveled together as a family, visiting friends and family in the West and East coasts, or Norway and Italy. Although there are missing photos—missing because JL was not in a state where we would have been having fun and taking photos together—there are also more painful photos when he would show up but not be *present,* revealing to those of us who knew JL well the inner conflict and turmoil that he lived with, the loss of hope, dissipated dreams.

While in the midst of living and dealing with the addicted JL, many times we did lose sight of The Real JL, of who our son really was, and any understanding of how much *he* wanted to be free of his addiction. Recently, a picture unexpectedly came to mind, a photo I took in the fall of 2011. It was JL standing in the bed of our black Tacoma pick-up truck, baggy shorts and t-shirt, talking animatedly on the phone with a friend, wide smile on his face and bright eyes. John and I were in Phoenix for a meeting with JL and his counselor on his return stay at a detox/recovery center. This was his first clinical detox and inpatient experience and we paid for the 30 day program. He left after two weeks, against counsel from all the staff because they felt he was "compliant but not willing to do the work." We could not force him to stay since he was over 18. He felt he was fine and wanted to get back to Tucson, a girlfriend, and possibly the university. He was a different person, he was the son we knew, but he relapsed almost immediately. Within three weeks we were driving him back. When we dropped him off I said, "I don't want to see your face again until you return as my son, not some shell that looks like him." After a week of being back, he called us and said "I am really enjoying being here!" telling us that all he knew was that this time "God must have performed a miracle because I have heard other addicts talk about their desires changing inside but I have never felt them myself—and I didn't want to fake it." That change occurred during the first week and he just *knew* he was different. We were thrilled.

He came home after two weeks. Really, he should have gone directly into a sober living program for at least a year, but all of us were *again* overly optimistic about what being free from opiate addiction required. Remember, there was no public information, no news exposé on a heroin epidemic, no numbers on how many young people were dying—it was all still hidden behind a curtain, out of sight. (It wasn't until 2015 when *NBC Nightly News* began their series on the opioid epidemic and the public conversations began in earnest.) JL returned with renewed hopes and plans to finish school and get right into AA again…but. He spent Thanksgiving on a trip with a friend, and there was lots of drinking. When he came back, although we were testing for drugs, we were unaware of the excessive drinking. We left mid-December for Australia. John and I still did not understand that being alone is one of *the* major triggers for addicts, nor how our leaving affected him. How odd it seems now. We enabled him in so many ways, yet when it came to taking trips, we didn't let his addiction issues keep us from them. While we were in Oz, he let us know he had relapsed to BT, and we immediately called the recovery program counselors to ask what he should do. They reiterated that he needed a minimum of 6-to-12 months of sober living program and suggested a few. Looking back through our notes and seeing that we did not insist JL do this, I am again filled with regret and incredulity at our decisions. We were still partially supporting him as he was attempting to regain his life and continue with college. It would be a full year before JL entered his first sober living program and a full year of continual relapses.

The sad truth about addicts and alcoholics is that their entire lives orbit around their addiction, like planets circling the sun. This thought struck me the other day as I was in the grocery store and walked past a shelf with gourmet pancake mixes. I remember buying a can of it for JL at least a year before and then finding it in his apartment after he died, unopened. It was a sad reminder that, when he was not clean and sober, he never got around to things he would normally enjoy—like cooking good food, rock climbing, camping, snowboarding, four-wheeling, shooting. Heroin became the center of not just his solar system, but his entire universe. That's the nature of opiates.

Life becomes narrow and lonely and miserable, and yet an opioid addict can't get out of the cycle because they have no will power left. Many of JL's good friends had not had much interaction with him since his serious relapse in 2009—except during a few sober periods when the real JL would surface, and he would contact them and get together. That is what happened over July 4th weekend, the month before he died, when he was together with his friends when they were all in town, and they looked at old photos and had such a great time. It is why they were all so shocked when they heard he had died—he seemed to be doing so well. He was able to hide his struggles, even from his good friends. He so longed to be considered "normal."

Wanting to be normal is why JL could never really allow himself to become an integral part of the AA community. He would not *incarnate* himself into it, because he didn't want to be identified and known as an addict/alcoholic—present tense. JL struggled with it because he thought once he had gotten clean and sober, he should no longer be considered an addict. Several of his friends are still struggling with this. They do have a point, as the *Associated Press* states in their new policy book for 2017 that "addict" should no longer be used as a noun. "Instead," it says, "choose phrasing like *he was addicted*, or *he used drugs*." In short, separate the person from the disease, reports Maia Szalavitz for *National Public Radio (NPR)*.

We have learned there is a distinction between "addiction" and "dependence." *Addiction* is a chronic, primary disease of the brain that is manifested by compulsive substance use despite harmful consequence. *Physical dependence* refers to adaptations the body makes to ongoing use of a drug with the result of withdrawal symptoms if the drug is stopped suddenly. In order to avoid withdrawal symptoms, some drugs need to be tapered off slowly when no longer needed, as with some medicines for diabetes, depression, heart disease and opioids like buprenorphine for treating addiction. Drugs like opioids and alcohol commonly result in *psychological addiction and physical dependence.* Understanding these two conditions can help to remove the stigma while acknowledging the need for recovery programs.

May 25, 2015
JL,

Mom here. *Dad and I called your friend Peter also. He had contacted us through Facebook and asked if we would be willing to talk with him—of course—even though we had never heard of him. It was an amazing and encouraging conversation. He shared how you were such a loyal and encouraging friend and supportive of him and* *your other friends. And how you did it because you genuinely cared. You encouraged him to stop selling and using opiates because you knew he was better than that. He said you called him mid-July, as you did other friends, and so he was shocked to learn about your death shortly thereafter.*

This is hard, excruciatingly hard, for me to think about and write, even now. In early July 2014, JL had had his wisdom teeth pulled. He had been on Percocet for several weeks and, as we now know, he had started shooting heroin again. We did hear from one friend who is a recovering heroin addict that when he saw JL over the July 4th weekend he could tell he was not clean—and he wished he had given him grief over it. This was three weeks before his death. In making contact with all of his friends in July, was he reaching out for help? Was he hoping someone would sense he was calling for something more than to chat? Did anyone have any premonitions that they didn't act on? Was he calling to say his goodbyes knowing he was going to not survive this relapse? Questions. No answers. And no specific warning. Just one life on a train roaring down a track that we, his parents and family and friends, for some reason and given his history, couldn't see heading over a cliff.

When JL graduated from high school in May 2007, we thought his life was moving forward on a fairly normal course with a predictable outcome. He decided to go to the University of Arizona, as many of his friends were also going there. For JL's first year at the U of A in 2007-08 we allowed him to live in a dorm, which we now view as a mistake. We were under the impression that the students were closely supervised, given that there were thousands of eighteen- and nineteen-year-olds all living together, but they weren't. In 2008, we decided that rather than continue to pay dorm fees that we would never see again, we would buy a house with rooms JL could rent to friends. We had done the same thing with Johanna five years before. However, there were increasing issues with the rental house by 2009: mostly 19-to-20-year-old renters without much regard for cleanliness, some we didn't know, and lack of commitment to the lease.

After being in Melbourne for six weeks in the spring of 2009 for the birth of our first granddaughter, we flew up to Seattle instead of returning directly to Tucson. My sister Susan had been battling breast cancer, and it had metastasized to her brain. The doctors had operated, she had gone through chemo and now there was nothing more they could do. She was going on to hospice.

JL was just completing his second year at the U of A. He called us while we were in Seattle to say that he had been using Oxy and that he was going to wean himself off. He wanted to let us know before we got back home. We accepted this, not realizing at that time how potently addictive Oxy was. Our thinking was that at least it wasn't heroin, right? We can hardly believe this now, but this is a clear example of the lack of truth surrounding prescription opioids at that time. After we got back to Tucson, I turned around and flew back to Seattle to take care of my sister for her last five weeks. John held down the fort in Tucson and had interactions with JL who was living at the rental house and working, but all seemed fine. After my sister's death on July 17, then her memorial, John and I returned to Tucson, and started packing for another trip to Melbourne where John had a two-month commitment as a visiting lecturer.

Before we left Tucson, in early August, we found out JL was using BT again: Out of the blue one day, two of his close friends, who were not addicts, called us and asked "Will you give us your permission to break down JL's door to his bedroom? We haven't been able to get him to answer his phone or open the door and we're afraid he's overdosed." They had been with him recently and could tell he and James were using again. We said "Yes" and anxiously awaited their call back. When they broke in, and JL finally woke up, he asked what all the commotion was about and why were they there. They confronted him about his using, which he denied, but then foils, a scale, and a blowtorch were found, and it was clear that JL was, indeed, using again. His friends called us and asked if they could come right over and talk, sharing how they had noticed JL distancing himself from his friends and spending all his time in his room with James. They were very worried for him, and we couldn't thank them enough for letting us know. We confronted JL, and at first, he was defensive, then contrite, and then he asked for help. He started back at The Mark outpatient program, and they would do urine drug tests until we returned late September. This was a very difficult autumn for all of us—handling grief over my sister's death, and grief over a second time around with JL's heroin addiction. Naïvely, we had thought it was something in the past that we would never face again.

After we returned from Oz in early October, we heard from one of JL's roommates that while there were friends at the house, JL came out with his 9mm Beretta, unloaded, and was waving it around. He had been drinking (almost a handle of rum we later found out). JL was cross-addicted: moving from one addiction to another, from one substance to another, each one he thought he could handle, but he couldn't. No one addicted to opioids or alcohol can; it took huge amounts of alcohol to give JL the numb feeling he was used to with opiates. His friends were freaked out and afraid. His ex-girlfriend was there with another guy, and JL was jealous and very hurt, so he covered it up with alcohol-fueled bravado. A totally human thing to do, even though it continues to hurt just to think about. It was so out of character for the real, sober JL.

During the eighteen months he lived at the rental, they had a break-in while they were all gone, and a lot of valuables were stolen. Even though JL denied any knowledge of it, we always suspected that it was someone who was involved with JL and the drugs, since being involved with drug dealers *necessarily* involves criminal activity. He had parties where all sorts of people came and went and had opportunity to see what was in the house.

We made the decision to move JL home and move his other roommates out of the rental house and rent it to someone else. Now he had lost the house that was a step in his independence and supposed to be an investment that he would work towards owning for his future. What became clear was that JL would be vulnerable to relapsing to opiates when—not if—alcohol no longer did the trick. So, we were advised that he should start on a new drug treatment for opioid addiction: Suboxone.

What is striking to me as I remember these events is that we still didn't see JL's alcoholism in the same light as his opiate addiction. Why didn't we realize that they were one and the same monster with just two slightly different heads? Why didn't we get that he needed treatment and the recovery tools—which he so resisted—for his drinking as well? We knew that the programs taught that they were not to be using alcohol, but we just didn't understand the interplay with drugs nor the severity of how alcohol affected his addicted brain. Yet, when I look back at our overall attitude toward underage drinking, it is not surprising. Although we did not condone party drinking or drinking to excess, we still thought having minimal alcohol with meals was fine, but JL could not just have the minimum. He clearly had Alcohol Use Disorder (AUD) along with 20% of college students, which is defined as "a chronic relapsing brain disease characterized by an impaired ability to stop or control alcohol use despite adverse social, occupational, or health consequences."

Many parents of teenagers feel party or binge drinking is "just a phase" that young people go through and, after experiencing it, they will emerge with a more balanced and level-headed approach in their twenties and beyond. Sadly, this is often not the case. It is estimated that half of underage and college age persons binge drink at least once a month. This typically occurs after 4 drinks for women and 5 drinks for men within about 2 hours. I'm sure JL and his friends stood firmly in this group.

Some months after John Leif died, we went by the mobile phone store where he had worked to get help figuring out how to use his smartphone. We just couldn't face that chapter of his life any sooner. We spoke with his co-worker, whom he was close with and who shared her thoughts at his memorial service. She told us how, when JL came back to work after his oral surgery, he was acting very strange. This was the last week of work before JL died. She said he came in one day sweating and shaking with some vomiting and clearly very fearful and struggling. He had told her previously about his past drug abuse, and she was concerned and wondering what he was using at that time. But she had not met us and did not know how to contact us—another area of secrecy in JL's life.

After JL's death, when we heard from David at In Balance that JL had cocaine in his urine test, which was really shocking to us, this all started to make sense. It seems that he had progressed from the Percocet before and after his surgery, to BT. But he also had to finally get back to work and needed the cocaine to get him "up," using a toxic mix called *speedballing*. It may have been even more toxic than normal, because it seems that the BT he was using was intermittently laced with something else and/or was super potent. Hearing this information about JL's last week alive left John and me weighed down, once again, as we walked out of the store, climbed into our car, and drove away. One more step on JL's path in the last week of his life where, if there were less secrets and more interactions between the people who loved him, his life might have been spared. But there's the rub: addicts are good at keeping their circles of people separate from each other. It is purposeful, not just an oversight, but it is so detrimental to their well-being and hopes for recovery. The whole point of AA is that it is a community. We all—and especially addicts/alcoholics—need community to be whole, healthy humans.

Nothing makes us so lonely as our secrets.
–Paul Tournier

13

COMMUNITY

Why then do we wonder that heroin is everywhere?
In our isolation heroin thrives...
and our very search for painlessness led us to it...
Heroin is the final expression
of values we have fostered for thirty-five years.

–Sam Quinones, *Dreamland*

Once again, this is hard for me to write. I drag up memories from several years ago, remembering the events, remembering the expressions on JL's face, remembering the strained conversations, the frustration, the anxiety in all three of us. Wishing we would have had some other option, wishing we would have known something else he and we could have done to change the course of events...

By January 2013, we knew JL had relapsed badly. He drank constantly. We had been paying for his rent because he had been enrolled at the university, but we said we would not renew his rent for the coming spring. We were not going to keep the commitment we made since we found he hadn't completed the fall semester. JL moved back home February 1st and we began seeing his addiction doctor together and this time followed his advice to look for a sober living home for JL outside of Tucson, away from his network of users and dealers. We finally found one in Prescott, Arizona. Even though they preferred JL to be done with withdrawal, they accepted him. He really did not want to leave Tucson, not because of drug availability (he knew he could get drugs anywhere) but because of his relationships. He had several close friends and a girlfriend, and they were important to him. So, after much procrastinating and waiting while we thought he was starting to detox, we drove him up in mid-March. We later found out that he used Oxy even that morning.

We had such high hopes for this son of ours. "The Cave" is a song by Mumford & Sons that I had hoped would become true for JL in Prescott—becoming part of a community, a band of brothers. *"It's empty in the valley of your heart... I know the shame in your defeat. But I will hold on hope, And I won't let you choke, on the noose around your neck..."* The two young men who ran the program were intense and hardcore purists when it came to sobriety: No Medication Assisted Treatment (MAT) to help through the transition or recovery. No Harm Reduction included in their philosophy whatsoever—abstinence only. JL was able to have his prescription for clonidine, but they even fought that. Clonidine combats the sympathetic nervous system response to heroin withdrawal thus making things slightly easier for the individual. It also helps to prevent restless leg syndrome—a common, lingering, symptom in withdrawal that make you unable to get comfortable, due to involuntary tingling and twitching of the limbs. A pounding heart is common along with sleeplessness, which clonidine helps, so the addict is more likely to see their detox all the way through. Of course, detox is the first and easiest step on the road to sobriety.

A few days after he arrived, the fifteen guys at the house loaded into a van and drove all night to the National Youth AA Conference in Fresno, California. JL was so excited about the conference—it was the boost he needed. This was true of JL every time he started back into recovery. He wanted *so* badly to be free of this death-trap and knew he couldn't do it on his own. They didn't sleep much on the trip and when they drove back, he came down with the flu and had a high fever. The program did not allow cars or phones, and the guys were expected to have work within two weeks, or they were out. They could not be at the house from 8:00 to 5:00 daily, so even with a fever, JL was out walking around Prescott in the cold trying to find a job. He got one, but on day two had to go to the ER because he was so ill. He had cracked his ribs from coughing.

We got a call telling us that they could not keep JL in the program because they had no one to stay at the house with him— no exceptions. It was very discouraging to us and JL; it just felt so legalistic and unaccommodating. Here was a desperate addict who actually wanted to be there, to be part of this small tight knit community, something he *really* needed, and he was being turned out. Hopes dashed to pieces due to legalism once again, for all three of us. I still feel angry about it. We later learned that it is not uncommon for sober living programs to kick residents out after a few days for some supposed minor violation in order to bring in another paying resident, while they keep the payment from the one they remove, thus boosting their income. We have no idea if this was, or was not, the motive in JL's case.

JL found another sober living house in Prescott with more gracious leaders, but less community. He moved in and recovered. He found a job selling vacuums door to door, commission only. We were proud of JL doing work that was not of any interest to him or intellectually challenging. He needed his car to get to work twenty-five minutes away, since there were no buses to his work. So mid-April we drove his car up to him. He seemed to be doing well and was developing a network of friends in Prescott, which has a huge recovery community, along with a huge alcohol/drug abuse population. In late September, he called to tell us he was moving back to Tucson. His work was not supporting him, and he needed to move out of the sober living house because his six months were up, and they needed the room. He asked if he could stay with us until he found a job and a place to live. We said yes.

When he arrived back in Tucson in early October, he seemed fine, but he began the addict routine of sleeping all day and staying up all night. After giving him a week to rest up, we insisted he go out and find a job. There are two important steps we should have taken *before we ever agreed* to allow him to return home: call the director of the sober living house where he had been, to confirm what JL was telling us; and drug-test him the minute he arrived. In retrospect, once again, we were overly optimistic. Our hopes outweighed justified caution. We later found out, after our suspicions were aroused and we finally made that call, that he had started using again, and had been kicked out of the sober living house. It is so hard to think your child is lying to you when you know him to be a truthful person. Sadly, the survival instinct in an addict, the fear of the physical tsunami that will come without the drug, overrides all positive traits and qualities of the same sober individual.

Early November 2013 when we realized he was using, when all along we thought he had been clean since March, we began the search again for a place for him to detox. Our insurance did not have any mental health benefits (which is how any substance use is covered) so he had to get into the public system, which took time. Finally, he was able to detox at Compass, a bare bones public system detox center, where you sit in recliners and get fluids while your bowels let loose, you can't sleep, and you shake. One more time. Thanksgiving weekend he moved in to Restart Sober Living in Tucson when his three days of detox were done.

About two weeks later in mid-December, when JL still did not have a job, I called the Restart house manager, Alex. I asked him if JL was actually getting up and out and looking for work. He assured me that JL was out of the house by 8:30 a.m. every day, trying really hard, working his recovery and going to meetings. What we didn't know until a month later in January, was that the house manager was actually dealing BT to JL and they were shooting up together. None of what he had told me was true.

During December, my mother, JL's Nonna, was in the hospital for open-heart surgery. Even in his compromised state, JL's love for his grandmother drew him to visit her. JL didn't show up for Christmas Eve and we only heard from him later that night. I remember so clearly the conversation I had with him, angry and frustrated: "Don't bother coming for the family Christmas Day dinner, showing up late as usual and not being *present* and involved." The next day he showed up at the last minute, looking straight at me; was it in defiance or wondering if I would say something? Somehow, he had pulled himself together. Sadly, I vividly remember all of us having wine with our Italian Christmas meal—in total disregard for his supposed sobriety, but by this time I felt that if he wasn't going to take his sobriety seriously, then why should we? We were all demoralized.

Our family went to the latest *Hobbit* movie with JL on New Year's Eve 2013. We were told he was clean and working his recovery, but we knew something was up because JL slept through the movie. Unknown to us, he had used BT. This was during a time when my instincts were telling me that my child was using, but I was trusting others at a program to be testing my son, so I felt he was safe. I *wanted* to feel he was safe. JL then went to someone's house and spent the night there and woke up with Radial Nerve Palsy in his right arm. It was paralyzed from his shoulder to his fingertips. (Radial Nerve Palsy/wrist drop is sometimes referred to as "Saturday Night Palsy" because when a person is inebriated and falls asleep with pressure on their arm, it can result in the nerve being pinched, causing the wrist to drop and hang limply. It takes 1-2 months for it to return to normal.) He said he had slept on it wrong. He called us from urgent care the next morning, trying to figure out how to keep from going back to Restart sober living house for the (very infrequent) drug test they had to take. He said he was too sick, and he was trying to get us to pay for him to go to the ER, which had a high co-pay. We smelled a rat and said "No."

He did go back to Restart in the daytime, and they did a test and kicked him and Alex out. So, he came to us and began to tell us the story. He had been using ever since he came back from Prescott and was afraid to tell us. Of course. Other than the days he detoxed at Compass, as soon as he went to this sober house, he began using again with the house manager and other guys who were there dealing and using. After all the pain of detox, he had not stayed clean at all. I'm sighing again, even now.

John and I had been struggling with the decision we had finally made to remove JL from our private health insurance policy. There were several reasons, but the overriding one was that we felt he needed to figure out that he was responsible for his own health care, whatever that would mean. Our insurance had no mental health coverage anyway. At this point in his life, he would have to go on to public assistance, since he could not hold down a job with benefits. It was a very difficult decision, as my journal entry describes:

July 22, 2015
JL,
 Mom here. *I was sorting my desk and found notes I made from a conversation with Linda in January 2014—the day after we took you off our health insurance and you went on public health services. It was a step in letting you take care of yourself and be responsible and not continuing to be your safety net. I was feeling guilty about it and having much anxiety. Linda was so affirming of how enormous a step it was for us. She fully empathized with how scary it was because every week it was a new issue with your pattern of addiction and it had been a very long ride for us all.*

JL tried to get back in to Compass on January 2, 2014 and spent twenty-four hours in the waiting room. There were no beds available, as holidays are some of the busiest times, so he came back home in the midst of withdrawal. He went back again the next night and it was the same story. We had some Suboxone leftover, and since that is what they use at Compass for detox, we agreed to let him do his detox at home and to make an appointment to see his addiction doctor to get enough for a few more days.

Meanwhile, we didn't realize that JL had been taking his few extra dollars from here and there and drinking. He was totally alcohol-dependent again. I first realized it when we went for an appointment with his counselor John Leggio on January 10th. JL reeked of alcohol. That Sunday, the 12th, he was dead drunk in the daytime when we tried to wake him up. I took his keys and began searching his car and found piles of empty small bottles of vodka and rum, but buried among them all I also found another bone-chilling surprise: a dozen used syringes with BT in them, a spoon, cotton balls, and the other paraphernalia of an IV drug addict. I was horrified. John was hoping they were not his. Until this time, we had always assumed JL's BT use was limited to smoking. I also checked the liquor cabinet and found that he had cleaned it out. I was livid. We brought this to him as he lay on the living room sofa and attempted to get the truth from him. He did not remember drinking all the liquor due to having blacked out, and his explanation about the needles was that they were from friends, but of course he would not mention *who* the "friends" were.

The next words out of John's mouth were: "JL, you can't stay at home anymore, you need to be out of the house tomorrow morning." He looked at us through despondent eyes and asked, "Where am I supposed to go?" John and I wanted him to start by going to Compass to detox from alcohol but when he called they couldn't promise that he would have a bed. So once again we allowed him to detox at home, after talking to his doctor to find out that he needed to use benzodiazepines to keep from having seizures. The conditions for allowing him to do this was he was not allowed to drive his car or go out. Meanwhile, JL called many sober living houses, finding very few openings. Salvation Army has a six-month program, intense and with a great success rate, but JL wanted to go to a house that we both heard great things about. But he needed to be sober for thirty days first, which is so difficult because after withdrawal, intense cravings start from this parasitic drug that demands to be fed and sucks the life out of its victims. He was just treading water since he detoxed, and the likelihood was high that he would relapse if he was not part of a sober living community and beginning to work the 12-steps.

And, like most people with life-threatening addictions, JL had no healthy community of friends. For a child who had grown up in a family where relationships and community were a priority, it is disheartening to look back at the way we inadvertently disconnected our son from that invaluable lifeline during his adolescence, just when he needed it the most. Just when having a peer group became the most important dynamic in his life.

For seventh and eighth grades, JL and his class of twelve sixth-graders from the private elementary school were going to be merged with the private high school. We had been told previously that there would be a separate middle school, where it would have been easier for JL to make the transition to public high school. We had seen the negative effects that a private Christian high school had on my younger brothers, JD and Joseph, decades ago. That is where JD's drug habits started. In his experience, it was an intellectually boring atmosphere and such a legalistic and constricting social world that he needed to do something for a challenge and fun. So, he dealt drugs to the school and church leaders' kids. Because of this, and because of observing other families' similar issues, we had already decided that we wanted JL in public high school, but he wanted to go where his classmates from the past three years were. So he started two days at the private junior/senior high and then we changed our minds after we had second thoughts and some negative interactions. We yanked him out and away from all his friends, and put him into public middle school where he knew no one. His life changed forever that day.

Initially, JL still wanted to be involved with youth group at church because his friends from his elementary years all went there and he enjoyed it, but by the beginning of eighth grade, his friends had changed, and he really did not want to go any longer. We were fine with that because we had become disappointed with church as a place where we had hoped to find real fellowship, union with kindred spirits where you would most expect it, but community was non-existent. So JL's tie to a group, a *community*, was cut, and he needed to find a new one. We failed to realize how important this was for him, especially as a teenager. The eight hundred public middle schoolers had been together since they were three-year-old's in preschool, so they knew each other, and their parents were connected to each other. Our son was an outsider, just when he really needed to feel he belonged to a group. So, naturally, he had to find a new peer group, which he did, but in this very cliquey school, it was the other kids who were also strangers and outsiders that he ended up with as friends. JL started his first day with a broken foot in a giant moon boot. To a shy twelve-year-old who absolutely feared and hated change, this was anathema.

We look back on this decision as the first decision we made that had far reaching negative consequences for JL's life. He wept after two months and said he didn't think he could be good there. What we ignored was his exposing his heart and doubts to us, along with his deep desire "to be good." He was suddenly exposed to a whole new set of temptations, unhealthy behaviors, and earlier exposure to alcohol and drugs that neither John and I, nor JL, were prepared for. JL knew himself and his weaknesses, and we didn't honor that because of *our* issues with the systemic hypocrisy we continued to observe in the Christian school, as with so much of organized Christianity. Hypocrisy and pretense have rankled deep within me since I was young: "Showing brass for gold," as they say in India. But hate, even hate of hypocrisy and partiality, can blind us to what the truly important issues are.

June 2, 2015
JL,

Mom here. *Dad and I drove up to Oak Creek Canyon for a few days away for our anniversary. It is peaceful and green, and we have many wonderful memories of spending anniversaries here. We remember August of 2001 when we brought you and Johanna up here for a few days before you started junior high and before September 11. Momentous times. Funny how physically being in a place brings* *memories up—seemingly out of nowhere. You had a broken ankle and were hobbling around on crutches as we walked to Slide Rock. We spent time in the cabin playing games like Risk—you took over the world as usual—your ability for strategic planning had been fully functioning for years.*

We also drove to Lost Canyon Young Life Camp at Williams. The Tucson leaders invited us up to see what they do and how it blesses the high school kids, most of whom are from non-Christian homes. We both wish you and Johanna could have been a part of Young Life—it is so fun. But you had grown up with so much Christianity that you needed a time away from the organized aspect of it to find your own faith.

At his new school, JL just happened to find a friend who was a risk-taker, who loved all the sports he did and who become one of his closest friends—and later, fellow opiate and heroin addict. JL had been transplanted which, even when done carefully is traumatic for plants, especially young ones. It is not hard to see how being introduced to substances would help dull the stress and anxiety of the abrupt transition he had experienced. John had been, and always would be, a totally involved father with his kids and spent most weekends with JL and his new friend James, either dirt bike riding, shooting, climbing, or having paintball competitions. They were risk-takers, like John and me and many of my family. Sometime during eighth grade they began using Oxy's but we do not know how or where they got them. During their freshman year of high school they were introduced to BT heroin at a party where some older kids were smoking it. We don't know the exact details because no one is talking – still.

February 7, 2017
JL,

Mom here. *I received a call from your friend Zach today and we caught up. He is in a rehab facility after an overdose of muscle* *relaxants. He is on an antidepressant as depression and loneliness are his underlying issues. I also think the wealthy life he comes from is a heavy burden. He has said he just wants to make money, but as I've said before, kids who grew up with so much have a huge struggle to consider an adjustment in lifestyle with the need to work and slowly accomplish goals. You may look for the easy and fast way and it is not there, and so depression can set in.*

Talking with many of JL's friends who are struggling with addiction brings up new regrets about how we raised our kids. John and I wholeheartedly agree with Sam Quinones conclusions in *Dreamland,* now that the floodgates of opiates have been released, regarding parenting and what we as Americans can do to change the dynamics that are destroying our families. Children grow up more isolated than ever before, not part of a close-knit community, and it is in that vulnerability that addiction thrives. We, as the parents of Millennials, have medicated behaviors that could have been treated with plain old exercise and outdoor activities. We have hovered and over-protected our children from experiencing any pain, and have created consumers of our children from the cradle.

And although we cannot change the past, we feel a surge of hope for the young children being raised today and a strong desire to add our voice to the message we hope other families hear, that things need to change. We cannot expect government drug agencies' attempts to stop illegal and increasingly potent drugs from entering our country, our communities, and our homes as *the* solution. We, the parents, are the door-keepers to a holistic future for our children and grandchildren. Our society, all of us, are responsible for this epidemic and together we must be willing to spend the time and money to reverse it.

How frustrating it is for John and me to be suffering these results when we home-educated our kids with goals of being a close-knit family that allowed them to be children longer and have a bit of the life we knew growing up in the 50's and 60's.

John rode his bike all around Los Angeles as a 12-14 yr. old, and our sports were not organized and regimented, but happened in our neighborhoods because our moms were home and watching. And, of course, drugs had not arrived in our neighborhoods or schools. Our children were not raised with neighborhood streets where kids were out playing after school. Regrettably, they were mostly alone due to modern demographics and lifestyle, and much of face to face community had disappeared. Our kids were not raised by a village, and it does take a village to raise a child. It takes community to stay healthy, even if we are not in recovery. Life lived in isolation is not life. We need each other to experience being truly human. All of the young adults with addiction issues whom we know of from our son's generation (and the very, very few still alive from our generation) resurfaced into life via AA/12-step groups, and many with medication. And if they are not still an active part of a group, then they are involved in some type of community and/or in a service or action group. They have learned that those tried and true good old 12-steps work—there is a reason for each and every one of them. I believe that the reason there are at least a small percentage of opiate addicts who are sober and alive is directly related to the degree to which they are involved in a community.

The need for connection and community is primal,
as fundamental as the need for air, water, and food.
–Dean Ornish, MD

14

PRIMUM NON NOCERE:
First, Do No Harm

*It may seem a strange principle to enunciate
as the very first requirement
in a hospital that it should do the sick no harm.*

–Florence Nightingale

Before August 2nd 2014 we hadn't heard of "Harm Reduction," but it is a phrase that has become commonplace since our son died. Harm reduction is a way to help those with addictions stay alive *while they also work* to become sober using medication, social services, and a strong 12-step recovery program with vibrant community. We wish we had heard of it before. We had an "all or nothing" mentality for gaining sobriety, one that was unrealistically idealistic, but our son's generation and subsequent generations face a threat that is unprecedented. It is the bane of living in a society where potent drugs are easily available to children before they have the wisdom to turn their backs on the flashy lure dangling in front of them baited with a deadly hidden hook.

In terms of drug abuse, harm reduction accepts that a continuing level of drug use in society is inevitable (a realistic view) and holds forth a set of strategies directed towards reducing negative consequences associated with illicit drug use. There are several organizations, such as Harm Reduction Coalition, working tirelessly in this area in order to address the adverse effects of drug use including addiction, overdose, HIV, hepatitis C, and incarceration. For opioid addiction, some of the main types of harm reduction social services are clean needle exchanges and safe injection sites.

Medication Assisted Treatment (MAT) is also finally gaining acceptance as a response to drug addiction in the US. It is a cultural shift from the view that addiction is a "moral failure." The Hazelden Betty Ford Foundation, a leader in drug treatment, used to subscribe almost exclusively to the abstinence-only model, based on an interpretation of the 12-steps of Alcoholics Anonymous and Narcotics Anonymous popularized in American addiction treatment in the past several decades. But in 2012, they announced they would begin providing MAT. As the latest research tells us, it takes five recovery attempts and eight years to keep just one year of sobriety, and on average *10-12 recovery attempts* before an opiate addict can *maintain sobriety*. Remission for Substance Use Disorder (SUD) occurs at five years, when relapse is no greater a risk than for the general population. It is easy to see why reducing harm while individuals make it through these recovery attempts could be life-saving, especially since a heroin addict averages only five years of use before dying from an overdose. Experiencing trial and error, and even relapse, *is to be expected*. It is a part of making changes in life, in all our lives. It is not failure. To expect otherwise is a set-up for failure. We look back and see that our expectation of the unattainable "perfect recovery" for our son was utterly unrealistic.

As I re-read our journal, I am struck by how many times we mention that we wish we had supported JL getting on Suboxone in January of 2014 after he had confessed to us that he had relapsed again while at Restart Sober Living. When we all went to see Dr. Cai, right after that confession, he felt that JL *must* be on a maintenance dose of Suboxone for at least a year, 4 to

6 mg daily, in order to be able to function and work, and not relapse. He felt sober living programs alone failed. JL was drawn to this medical solution because he knew deep inside that he was not able to muster up the "willpower" to stay clean. But he was concerned about being back on Suboxone because he remembers how horrible and long the withdrawal were several years ago—so much worse than going cold turkey off BT. Of course, it would have been. In 2009 the prescribed dosage that JL started on was 32 mg per day, which was *eight times as much* as is currently prescribed. JL also felt guilt about the expense, knowing we would have to pay for it until he was stable and found a job. Funny, I vividly remember the dejected look on his face that day as he sat in the chair across from us at the doctor's office. Why didn't I absorb it and act on it at the time? But John, JL, and I allowed our over-thinking and idealism to prevail. *We* felt certain that the programs actually did work. *We* rationalized that he just needed a less stressful job and needed to stay in the recovery community longer. In hindsight, we see our reasoning, once again, superseding someone who really did know more, not only about addiction, but about our son. He was detached from the emotional parent/child relationship. Dr. Cai wanted the choice to be John and mine and so, in the end, we decided that we would not move forward with Suboxone. We wanted JL to look for a sober living place. What we didn't really *hear* was what Dr. Cai said: **"This young man cannot relapse again. He will not survive."**

We obviously think that having JL on Suboxone would have changed the course of his life, that he would still be alive, and we would not be living every day with this sorrow, but we don't know how long JL would have stayed on it, or if he would have relapsed. Science has taught us that stress cues linked to the drug use (such as people, places, things, and moods), and contact with drugs are the most common triggers for relapse. Suboxone alone is not a magic bullet, unfortunately, and addicts can cheat while on it, but it *is* one step in harm reduction, and it *does* buy time for addicts to begin seeing the potential for their lives to return to normal.

What would we give to have more time with JL clean and sober, and the harm reduced in his case?

Below is a sampling of the journal entries that began shortly after our son died and continued on throughout the following year. They were consistent and repetitive, revealing how sorry we were for the choice we had made to not support our son in something he was highly motivated to do.

Sept 24, 2014
JL,

   Mom here. *We met with Dr. Cai today and asked if you had told him you were injecting heroin, after you detoxed, and we all went to see him last January. He said no, but you had told him you bought Suboxone on the street because you were so afraid of relapsing, which is why Dr. Cai told us then that he felt you must be on Suboxone for a long time in order to survive, stay alive, and be productive. A few weeks before, on New Year's Eve of 2013, your friend died of an overdose and you woke up with radial nerve palsy. You told us you had fallen asleep on your arm, but I wondered if it was from you damaging it with a needle while shooting heroin. So far, I haven't been able to find any research suggesting this as a cause.*

   *Dr. Cai told us, "**Opioid addiction is the terminal cancer of brain illness and addiction**. You have almost no way to fight it and win." He said to be assured that you tried your best, and he wanted to make sure we told others that your life was taken away by this illness and not by who you are. We left with heavy hearts knowing we both had not wanted you to do Suboxone because we were just tired of the cycles...*

JL hadn't told us that a friend had overdosed and died on New Year's Eve. He never told us about any of the other young people he knew who died. Perhaps out of fear that speaking it out loud would make it real. We only found out later when we were with John Leggio and he asked us if we had heard. This young man had been a client in and out of the program at The Mark and had a child with a girlfriend who is also an addict and who overdosed that night, but was revived. I believe that fear from this death and the wrist drop caused JL to stop using heroin that day, to try Suboxone again by getting it on the street, and ultimately have to rely on alcohol in another desperate effort to be clean.

September 25, 2014
JL,

    Mom here. *What is so sad to us is that dad and I let you down when you were trying to tell us that you were afraid you wouldn't make it and survive this disease without the Suboxone. And what we didn't get was the gravity of Dr. Cai's warning that you could not relapse again and live. We talked you out of the life-saving choice to be on Suboxone. Dad thought you just needed to "work harder" at your sobriety and really want to be clean and I was tired of being Mom "the enforcer." We refused to pay for the Suboxone. It was expensive, and our health insurance wouldn't pay for it. You didn't want to press us to spend more money on your addiction. We didn't know about harm reduction or understand…*

October 20, 2014
JL,

    Mom here. *I had a dream about you last night. It was a jumble of things and places, but you showed up and came to Dad and me wanting help. You had a big red area on your thigh where you prepared your drug, and you only had a bit of it left—some white powder. We were racking our brains together to think of what options you had: you couldn't stay with us, and we said that if you went to a sober living house, which you had done many times before, you would just relapse again as soon as you left. We just couldn't find any option. And then we remembered Suboxone and that Dr. Cai wanted you on it. So, we decided to do it. That was it. Wishful thinking, even in my subconscious, trying to figure a way out of the Maze together. And, my deep, desperate desire that we could rewind* *time and do it over again, a second chance to get it right. But there are rarely second chances, or maybe we'd had a lot of them and somehow got it wrong over and over again. Why didn't we "get it?" I heard someone once say, "If you're fortunate enough to get a second chance, don't waste it."*

October 27, 2014

JL,

Mom here. My heart breaks as I think again of you at our appointment with Dr. Cai last January saying, "I never want to use opiates again." It is a sadness I will always remember and feel strongly about because we didn't get that you needed more than Heroin or Alcoholics Anonymous to support that desire. You needed physical help, too. And I tell people this every time I tell your story, and someone says they know someone or a relative who is an opiate addict. Maybe it will give someone else a second chance for their loved one before it is too late.

March 2, 2015

JL,

Dad here. Mom and I keep going back to the bad decision we made to not have you on Suboxone. How foolish we were, to make a life or death decision like that based on optimism and practicalities. All I know is that I believe if you had been on it as Dr. Cai urged us, you would be alive and functioning today.

March 4, 2015

JL,

Mom here. What grieves me the most is the knowledge that you wanted so, so badly to be free of the addiction, to be normal—and you kept trying so hard. But the truth is that heroin will usually win, especially when it latched onto you before your brain was fully formed around age 21-25. I saw a very interesting panel of experts speaking on Charlie Rose and with new imaging data it clearly shows how the *frontal lobe is physically changed and impaired by various drugs, but particularly by opiates.*

All this knowledge did was bring up sadness and regret over not having JL on Suboxone. These regrets felt like a river I had been thrown into and no matter what I did, I was not strong enough to fight the strength of the current and swim to the bank, much like the emotions Eric Clapton expressed in one of his songs, "I feel like I'm drowning in a river of tears." As John and I entered the eighth month after JL died, ever so gradually I felt a change had begun, as if I was flowing *with* the swiftly flowing current, and felt confident that when the time was right, an accessible shore would appear, and I would be able to climb out on to safe, dry land.

March 10, 2015—John Leif's Birthday
JL,

Mom here. *Dad and I drove up Mt. Lemmon highway and found the place where you and William Sky did your first rock climbing camp in July of 2000. We buried some of your ashes at the foot of the rock face and spread some to the wind. It was not very emotional for either of us. The emotion I daily carry is sadness and regret that we didn't have you on Suboxone for the duration. Could we not accept anything but a "perfect" recovery? When I think of you daily it is remembering how many times you started over, went through horrible withdrawal, and tried so hard to be free and live a normal life. At dinner last night with Curt and Heather, she shared that a friend lost her 21-year-old son a month ago to a heroin overdose. What can we do to get this message out to people—to be a help?*

Our regrets remind me of being stuck in a multiple-lane roundabout while driving on the left-hand side of the road in Australia or England. When we can't figure out which exit to take in order to get on the right road, we just keep driving around in circles. The regrets we carry became even more vivid and painful when we read testimony from other young addicts who portrayed themselves as *exhausted and frightened* before they started on Suboxone, just like our son. They acknowledged having "loved" their chosen opiate but not what turned into a miserable existence dominated by drug-seeking to avoid "dope sickness." We have several of JL's key fobs from the many NA and HA meetings he attended, testimony to how many times he purposefully went through being dope sick in an effort to be free of his deceptive lover. I'm looking at one I have on a thumb drive from HA that says, "No More Suffering."

May 30, 2015
JL,

   Dad here. *It seems like each Saturday is more bizarre than the past. Forty-three weeks without you—it is unbelievable. Heroin overdose deaths of twenty-somethings are in the news every day. An NPR clip on a father whose daughter overdosed was interesting. There are parents who try to hide the facts by saying "He died suddenly," "She died accidentally." But he, like us, simply told the truth. Twenty-five-year-olds don't die "suddenly and accidentally of unknown causes." In 2014—in the past decade—they die from heroin or opioid overdoses. It is a national epidemic.*

   Every week this subject is brought right before our eyes—either in the news or from hearing about another friend who has lost someone from heroin or opioid overdose. A young friend who is a musician and worship leader lost his younger brother to a heroin overdose. A month before that we heard about friends who lost a daughter who had been on methadone for years and then in the hospital due to an accident and sent home with pain meds. Days later she was dead. We were in San Diego watching the news in early October 2016 as they did a segment on the illicit fentanyl being manufactured in China (and not pharmaceutical quality so no quality control), shipped to Mexico and either mixed in with a little Oxy or just left "pure" and sold as Oxy—causing thousands of overdoses, seizures, and deaths. The news showed photos of couples in cars passed out and dying as bystanders walked by and then called 911. Now, fentanyl is disguised as, or being mixed in with, other drugs unbeknownst to the users, and fatalities are mounting.

NBC Nightly News recently reported on "Heroin Safe Zones" in Vancouver, Canada. These are medically supervised legal injection sites, called InSite, that are part of a program of harm reduction. They have seen a 35 percent drop in deaths near the center. "Before InSite was opened, many body bags passed through the corridor, and it's terrible to see," said Dr. Ronald Joe of the Vancouver Coastal Health Research Institute. But isn't this just enabling and promoting heroin use? How would we have felt if JL was using at one of these sites? The foundational belief behind this experiment is since using heroin isolates the user, addicts need a place where they can use and not be in the shadows, alone, and more prone to overdose. In a safe place, they may begin to consider getting clean a real possibility and will actually be connected to people who can help.

Svante Myrick, the 29-year-old mayor of Ithaca, New York, is stirring up controversy with a proposal for a supervised heroin (and cocaine) injection facility in his city: "What we're proposing is an entirely new approach to 'the war on drugs,' one that's based in public health instead of criminal justice," Myrick said. **"Nobody recovers from a heroin addiction if they've died from an overdose."** A scientific review done in 2014 of 75 research articles found that supervised injection facilities, or safe rooms, has indeed reduced the rate of overdose.

I have no doubt that bringing heroin use out of the shadows in ways such as this, would likely have changed our son's trajectory. It was hiding his addiction from friends and family, due to shame, that perpetuated the private use of heroin. I think that if he, and other addicts, were using regularly while facing other addicts, not only would the shame begin to disappear, but the realization that their life was being wasted would surely be awakened. It may help those struggling to see hope as a real possibility at the end of a long, dark tunnel.

"Many body bags passed through the corridor, and it's terrible to see." Yes, John and I can confirm that seeing a body bag up close—and especially with someone you know inside—is terrible to see. You will never think the same about drug addiction again.

Perhaps it is impossible for a person who does no good to do no harm.
  —Harriet Beecher Stowe

15

AN OUNCE OF PREVENTION

If you know the enemy and know yourself,
you need not fear the result of a hundred battles.
If you know yourself but not the enemy,
for every victory gained you will also suffer a defeat.
If you know neither the enemy nor yourself,
you will succumb in every battle.

–Sun Tzu, *The Art of War* (Chinese military strategist,
5th century BC)

For Buddhists, craving is the source of human suffering and the misery of those ruled by cravings for drugs is just an extreme form of the attachment to material things that compromises any person's happiness. The Dalai Lama put these brain changes in terms of the "action cycle" of karma in Buddhist belief: Once you make a choice to use drugs, *consequences are unavoidable.* The powerful changes that occur in the brain and body with the abuse of drugs reinforces his belief that it is necessary to "put up the barrier before the floods come"—that is, to focus as much as possible on prevention.

I wholeheartedly agree with the Dalai Lama that education is central to preventing drug use and that education must create an environment which will instill a sense of purpose and connectedness, rather than materialistic values that cannot produce happiness. He acknowledged that once a person becomes addicted, Buddhism may have less to offer, and that medical science may be the best solution to treating their disease. As a Christian, my beliefs diverge in what I believe can be done once addiction has set in. Yes, medical science is very important, but there is also prayer and request for help from God—and even miracles. And we believe that there is a resting place, heaven, and that we will not be in an endless cycle of karma.

"Know your enemy" is a phrase that repeatedly returns to my mind when I am looking back on the years of our children's adolescence. Regrettably, what we have learned is too late for our son, but not for millions of other sons and daughters. I believe that we are at war with an enemy that, as it is taking the lives of our children, it is also taking the future of our nation and our world. The wisdom from Sun Tzu holds such significance for all of us at this point in the battle against opiates. Knowing ourselves includes knowing and understanding our children well, and knowing their friends and their families. Knowing our enemy is knowing what our culture currently believes and how our society is battling our mutual challenges—as all other parents through the ages had to know in order to survive.

March 12, 2015
JL,

Mom here. *Today I thought of our society and the cloud of ignorance that lies over it, like a blanket smothering the flame of wisdom, especially in how kids get sucked into harmful things like drugs. Dad and I should have been more informed as parents and known what was happening and been equipped to prevent your being introduced to opiates as a young teen. Since we were unaware before that happened, we could have at least been able to effectively intervene early, when it could have changed the course of your life—like it has for many of your friends who were put in serious long-term recovery programs right away. We were naive and optimistic.*

Our neighborhood does not seem like a war-zone. It is nothing like the inner-city neighborhoods where young people have to do so many things they really don't want to do in order to survive. But drugs are no respecter of person, social status, or socioeconomic demographics. JL was in his own "ghetto": a walled-up community, isolated in many ways from real risks, and so risks of another sort were a draw, especially for those drawn to challenge and risk, those of us who seem to need it to thrive in this life. I think that is why JL related to hip-hop and rap songs, because he was making his own edge, his own risk. It is well-known that during adolescence when the brain experiences dramatic developmental changes, it is more vulnerable and primed for risk. Add the normal lack of defense for dangerous experimentation to families who are drawn to risk and you have double jeopardy. This is the time when "An ounce of prevention is worth a pound of cure."

November 13, 2014
JL,

Mom here. *I was thinking today about how many times during recent years I wanted you to take a walk with me so we could have uninterrupted time to talk, especially this year around my birthday. But you would be defensive and on guard, thinking I had an agenda. You knew I could tell when things weren't going well, so you didn't want to talk. What hit me now is that if Dad and I had really been listening to you, you actually did express your deep feelings and fears, albeit subtlety. But as Elizabets has said to Dad and me, "You two are a formidable force." We made it hard for you to be honest. And we didn't accept or receive your feelings without trying to change them. I think of the recent times last January and the decision re: Suboxone and my body slumps...*

Our daughter Johanna gave us a book over a decade ago: *Tell Me No Lies* by Bader and Pearson. It was written to help couples learn about the complexity of honesty versus deception in marriage and how to recognize how lying can lead to serious trouble. She was reading it for insights regarding her relationship with a significant other. Why was she handing *us* a book about lies in marriage, when she was all too familiar with the total honesty we practiced in every area of our lives? The reason lay in Chapter Three, "The Lie Invitee."

As we talked with Johanna about what she wanted us to grasp from the book, we began to see that John and me, and especially me, were so focused on telling and hearing the naked truth that we failed to consider the feelings of our kids and how we went about actually eliciting the truth. Basically, the authors say that very few of us are aware of the person who acts as a censor, promoting deception while they demand the truth. We forget the emotional aspect of the equation, asking questions in a way that indicates we can *accept* the truth. Never really getting that both of our kids really wanted to please us, and therefore wanted to be honest with us, we "invited lies" because as teenagers and young adults they were at the stage in their lives where they needed to try things out for themselves and many of those things were not acceptable to us. So rather than risk our disapproval or a lecture, they learned to just avoid the truth by giving us only parts of the story.

Not giving them the freedom to be less than perfect in the area of moral judgment caused them to also not feel free to share their feelings and questionings, which would have led to more truly honest, emotionally intelligent interactions. If we could change one thing, knowing what we know now, it would have been to create an emotional environment that encouraged our teens to share openly about their urges, peer pressure, and fears—and for John and me to have listened as empathetic, informed, and loving parents. It may have changed all our lives.

March 14, 2015
JL,

Mom here. *Our friend Emily is in town for her nephew's private memorial service—her sister is destroyed. Who could have guessed* *six months ago when she was consoling us over your death that we would be consoling her over her nephew's death? I hate the drug lords in Mexico and the dealers here and the pharmaceutical companies' deception about prescription opioids. "The War on Drugs" has failed miserably. But what is the solution? Sure, if there was no market for them, they would go elsewhere. But drug "pushers" are aptly named. When you push an addictive substance on naive young people, you have your market—captive and perpetual. It is so angering.*

We recently watched a satirical documentary called *How to Make Money Selling Drugs.* It starts out telling how one can climb the ladder from small time drug-dealing to becoming the head of an international drug cartel, interviewing dealers and law enforcement agents along with experts from a variety of fields. Mid-way through, the film shifts to the facts surrounding our failed prescription and illegal drug policies while treating drug abuse as a criminal offense instead of a public health issue. And of course, there is all the money. It was released in 2012 with the implicit hopes to see our attitudes and policies towards drug abuse change significantly. I so appreciate these types of efforts to educate us and create public awareness that will help prevent increased addiction in the future. Yet I feel frustration at the snail's pace that change in society takes, especially for life and death issues, but it is like trying to rebuild a dam after a river has flooded and broken through. It takes many people with different skills working together on all the various complex aspects to eventually succeed.

Never wound a snake; kill it.
–Harriet Tubman

16

DESIGNER GENES

"You can choose your friends but
you sho' can't choose your family,
an' they're still kin to you no matter whether
you acknowledge 'em or not,
it makes you look right silly when you don't."

–Atticus in *To Kill a Mockingbird*, by Harper Lee

For those of us who grew up wearing Levi 501's, shrink-to-fit jeans, there was no better staple for our wardrobe. They never wore out, didn't show dirt, and the more you wore them between washings, the better they felt. We patched them, embroidered them, made cut-off's and skirts out of them. Anything and everything looked good with them, and still does. When 1979 rolled around, a new type of blue jeans hit the markets: designer label jeans. Sassoon, Vanderbilt, Calvin Klein. I don't remember when I personally bought my first pair of skintight designer-brand knock-offs (we were still poor grad students), but we did gradually succumb to the new fashion trend. Over the decades, although we've worn flares, bell bottoms, and now jeggings, I still prefer my Levi 501 original straight legs jeans.

Sometime in the early 1980's, I remember John explaining to me, in a way that I could understand, what our genetic makeup involved—from handing down our hair, eye and skin colors and other physical characteristics, to our health strengths and weaknesses. He would look at me and tell me how cute he thought I was, and say I had "designer genes." We have had a lot of laughs throughout the years when one of us displays a trait from one of our predecessors, a quirk or characteristic that we don't particularly care for perhaps, and we jokingly chalk it up to "those designer genes."

While John was in his doctorate program in Pharmaceutical Sciences in the late 1970's, a few of his friends were in programs for gene research. This was the beginning of the era of "genomics," which studies an organism's complete set of DNA, including all of its genes. And there was "genetics," which studies individual genes and their roles in inheritance, something that has become a booming business due to curiosity about our ancestors and how they have influenced every aspect of our lives.

While we knew that there were diseases with a genetic component, such as heart disease and diabetes, we did not understand the same could be true for addiction. When it came to engaging in behaviors that are unhealthy or self-destructive, such as smoking, using drugs, or excessive drinking, we felt it was an excuse to blame it on a genetic trait passed down through our forebears rather than a choice an individual makes. Whenever someone acted as if they had no control over their choices, we used to repeat Flip Wilson's line from his 1970's TV persona *Geraldine* when she would do something she didn't want to own up to: "The Devil made me do it!" We thought that placing the fault on the Devil was the ultimate blame-shifting. At a home Bible study we attended in the 1970's, the leader taught that when Christians sin, there is an actual demon inside, *and the cure was to cast it out,* whether it was lying, anger, lust or any "sin." We never went back, knowing we had control over our behavior choices. When it came to genetics, we sincerely thought each of us could "Just Say No" to our obvious, and not so obvious, habits regardless of the bad fruit hanging on the family tree. This was our mindset because we were attempting to rely on God to help us choose healthy behaviors instead of taking the path of least resistance. We did not understand that *addiction is more than having a bad habit or making poor choices.*

It was a simplistic belief for what we would gradually come to understand are complex and deeply rooted problems. And while we embraced the beauty of grace in our lives, we thought "genetic predisposition" seemed to cross the border into the territory of abusing that grace—what we referred to as "sloppy Agape." *Agape,* one of the four Greek words for love, describes the unmerited love of a greater to a lesser: God's love to mankind. Due to becoming better students of our society and culture, we began to grasp that God could use scientific knowledge alongside spiritual wisdom. In fact, we began to see the same wisdom shine from both sources.

Because of those early beliefs, as a couple, we naively thought we could teach our children by example that a person could drink minimally. With this belief, we embarked on a well-planned approach to allow our kids to try alcohol as early teens. This was the Italian half of my family experience. Drunkenness was not acceptable. At family gathering with all the relatives, there was wine for the adults, *pink ladies* for the kids: Seven-Up mixed with a dash of red wine. No big deal—at least that's what we thought. We reasoned that if our kids grew up seeing alcohol used moderately, never to excess, and not very often, they would learn by example how to imbibe, as I had. They would learn not to abuse alcohol because they wouldn't be drawn to it like a magnet due to never having tried it. Of course, we were only going by our own nuclear families' experiences; we had no input from experts, much less any reason to even think to ask for it. We had no clue about the genetic traits and tendencies of alcoholism and addiction, because the random alcoholics in our family trees seemed like that: random. What we failed to do was shake the family trees to discover what was being hidden secretly underneath the leaves. When our kids were teenagers on our first trip to Italy with them in 2002, they had wine with our meals. Not mixed with soda. I recently looked back through our photos and saw JL on that trip, thirteen years old, sitting at a table next to Johanna in a restaurant with a glass of wine. He is clearly buzzed. Why couldn't we see that? What was going on in our minds?

From my experience with my two sisters, there was never a draw to any excess with alcohol. I didn't know about my brothers because they were so much younger than us and I wasn't around during their teen and young adult years. History has proven there was a serious family addiction issue that surfaced when my younger brother JD was diagnosed with AIDS due to drug abuse as well as other high-risk behavior.

As we began attending the family groups with JL at The Mark, we were challenged by the current research and statistics to reconsider the genetic factor for our son's alcoholism and addiction. John's family was fairly easy to assess as they were more up-front and honest: his maternal grandfather, of German-Dutch descent, was a card-carrying alcoholic who was thrown out of the house when John's uncle was a teenager and big enough to physically remove his father from the house and warn him to never come back. We don't know anything about his maternal great-grandparents since the connection was severed. But we looked at John's parents and saw that they, as part of a church where drinking was frowned upon, never drank and we presumed that was the reason neither John nor his two sisters had any problem with alcohol: they had not been exposed to any regular or excessive drinking. John experienced some excessive party drinking in his senior year of high school and early college. After that, we met and had no time or money to party and no inclination to drink or communal influence to do so. Actually, the opposite was true: our community of friends when we were in our 20's were all trying to get sober and clean from drugs to pursue spiritual renewal.

My mother's family is more complex. Her family was English and Presbyterian, and although drinking wasn't prohibited, it wasn't part of their daily life. What we didn't know, until about fifteen years ago, was that alcoholism permeates her family. Because it is never openly discussed, is always covered up, or is written off as old news and minimized, it smells suspiciously like stigma and shame. After some prodding, however, I was able to find out from my mother that, aside from family members we knew of, several of her uncles were alcoholics. Had we had this knowledge, I think we would have changed our strategy.

Many of our son's friends and other young adults, (and in fact *every person* we have asked who uses or has used any drug), *always* had experiences with alcohol first. No exceptions. It is clear that **alcohol** is actually the gateway to mind- and mood-altering substances. In all of Australia's references and communications, "AOD" is used: Alcohol and Other Drugs. Alcohol is, of course, considered *a drug* and should be treated as such. When we first started group therapy at The Mark, I remember JL arguing with us about marijuana not being "the gateway drug." He was technically right—marijuana came *after alcohol,* but, as history has proved even in his life, marijuana was the gateway for illicit drug use.

According to the CDC, people who use marijuana are *three times* more likely to be addicted to heroin. We know many of our son's friends tried all the drugs beginning with marijuana, just as he did, and latched onto the uppers like cocaine and meth, or the downers like opiates, or just stayed with using pot and alcohol "recreationally." How did they manage to do that? We now understand that one reason some people can stay with using pot and not go on to other drugs is tied to their genetic propensity for addiction. The new highly potent pot multiplies the already unanswered questions, especially about long-term health and mental health effects on adolescents. Thankfully, decriminalization is opening up the opportunities for much needed research and regulation.

The truth is that those who are addicted to drugs are almost always co-addicted to alcohol. JL's friends didn't realize how hard it was for him to be around others who were drinking and stand alone as the only one who couldn't. Our relatives were unaware of this, too, during many family dinners and times eating out together. We had learned the hard way decades ago, as I related, that if we have love or concern for a friend or family member who is an addict or alcoholic, to take the path of self-sacrifice when we are with them and not drink. Regardless of their saying "It doesn't bother me" or "It won't affect me" or "It has to be my commitment not yours" (as our son would say) we realized that it does affect them. They are the "odd man out" and many times will later, when away from others, drink alone. How would anyone feel being the only sober person on a night out on the town or at a party or wedding or dinner? I realize this could be complicated given the alcohol saturation into our culture. We need to think of our abstinence like being a part of a walk against AIDS or Cancer in solidarity with them in their life and death battle against a disease that may take their life away. Protecting young people from exposure to *any* mind-altering substances, including alcohol, until as late as possible or until after twenty-one when the brain has almost fully developed, is imperative—*especially* if there is genetic predisposition. This is one reason there are more success stories for opiate addicts surviving from the previous generations because opiate use started at a much later age than the current trend, and the drugs had substantially less potency and additives.

October 4, 2014
JL,

Mom here. *I have been thinking about all of the things you were addicted to: smoking, chewing, alcohol, pornography, gambling, and wondering if that would have been different if you hadn't had early exposure? What if we had been more protective of you until you were older? Even so, it seems if you have those inherent traits and genes of an addict, you will be addicted to one or many things* *regardless. I have told John that he is addicted to "more." It seems whatever he does, he can do to the extreme and his brain still seems to need more. I believe it is a genetic thread, a chemical need, woven into his DNA since conception, just like all the other traits we inherit from our predecessors, and one that will continue down through successive generations, from his mom's and my mom's families.*

Of course, it is that same tendency to pursue more, in John and others, that also keeps them pursuing the best—the search for finding the perfect solution, the perfect home, in order to be their best and do their best for those they love. So even if it is eventually discovered that there aren't "addictive" genes per se, scientists already know that some people have more of, or lack of, certain chemicals in their brains than the majority of the population. Those deficiencies or excesses lie beneath the spectrum of addictions and mental illness or health. These are the attributes, personality traits, that we are all born with and that we all have to live with. Those who have reward sensitivity as a personality trait will tend to seek more rewards, but their brains have difficulty maintaining a balance. They release more dopamine than the average Joe, which is exciting, and so starts the cycle of seeking a repeat of that excitement. Research shows that much substance seeking, even interest in them, begins here. Jenny Valentish in her book *Woman of Substances* cites a specialist who "suggests *thirty percent* of the population of US has what he calls Reward Deficiency Syndrome, which increases the risk of obsessive-compulsive, impulsive and additive behaviors." Yes, JL likely would have been addicted to something and learning how to manage his life. But had he not had *early* exposure and use, he might still be here learning how to have that manageable life. Dr. Nora Volkow, the director of National Institute on Drug Abuse (NIDA) has written and spoken extensively on the physical attributes of addiction and tells us scientists know that *early exposure greatly compounds the genetic predisposition for addiction.*

The Millennials as a generation have early teen, even pre-teen, exposure to all manner of experiences that had previously been reserved for young adults. Maturity comes from having responsibilities, not from partaking in sophisticated behaviors and privileges. Both of our kids were hard workers, self-reliant, and very responsible at an early age, but we were blindsided by what JL was being exposed to because he remained so responsible as he was beginning to experiment and use substances. His habits of self-discipline and responsibility kept him at a higher level of functioning which may have contributed to his living longer as an addict while also causing him to be more conflicted internally.

A few months after JL died, two of his friends from the sober living home were in town for an appointment and came over one night for dinner. We heard about how much they missed JL and how close they felt to him. We found out about their past, their families and their addiction history. The younger one, who was 19, came from a family similar to ours. He started drinking young too, getting drunk in junior high, and it made me wonder why this happens so much earlier to millennials than it did to previous generations. I think it is because when most of us we were young, we did not go to other people's houses without our family or stay overnight, and we certainly did not have parties at that age. What are we as parents thinking and allowing now? I know we did not want our kids to do these things so young yet felt we didn't want to be overprotective. John remembers a lot of freedom as a teenager in the 1960's, but he didn't get drunk the first time until he was nearly 18. Society has changed significantly in the past 50 years.

My friend Emily grew up with a mother who was a functioning alcoholic, a single mom, who worked a good job her entire life to support herself and her children. Emily grew up with a repulsion to alcohol and a commitment to never drink. Six months after our son died, her nephew died while high in a car crash in Mexico. She said: "He was doing really well for 6 months, then a slip up, and he is no more." He was 30 and had been clean for many months but relapsed on heroin and meth. Another life extinguished. I'm sure he didn't want to be addicted, but he started using while young, his grandmother was an alcoholic, his mother was addicted to heroin, and so it was an easy role to fall into. That environment of addiction was waiting for him from day one.

John has often said to me, "There are reasons people do the things they do. They may not be excuses, but they are reasons." The reasons for those who become addicted out of all the kids who experiment with drugs, are validated by the statistics that are heavily tipped against those with familial and genetic traits towards addiction. The old belief was that 10 percent of our population are or will become addicted to alcohol or drugs, but I have heard that figure is now closer to 20 percent, as more accurate data is available and more substances are being pushed on our kids at an earlier age.

John Leggio from The Mark shared about this change at JL's memorial service: "It is no longer accurate to say, 'The apple doesn't fall far from the tree.'" What he meant is that we can't look at the families with poor parenting or absent parents to find the source of addicted young people. John and I were operating under an outdated philosophy: we still thought the apple didn't fall far from the tree and so were intentional in how we lived our lives and the example we set. But, the fractured society we live in has more influence than parents because of the time children spend away from us and with their peers: in person, via social networking, and the media. It is a dangerous world to grow up in. Children who might have experimented with substances during, or after, college are now exposed to them in middle school, giving genetics a preemptive strike.

I had a conversation with a friend whose brothers are "career" drug addicts and dealers. She said that when they finished high school, they decided that they didn't want to go to college or get a nine-to-five job. Their career choice was based on the easiest thing they could do to make money, be with fun people, and "chill." Dealing drugs fit the criterion. They could move to Hawaii, live cheaply, and just "chill" the rest of their lives. And that is just what they did.

Their quality of life is horrendous, however; their young children are living in campgrounds or their car, sometimes going to school, being physically molested by various people. It is heart wrenching. One of her brothers died while in his fifties a few years ago from complications due to the hepatitis and alcoholism he had lived with for years. Her other brother is still alive—this is the life he knows, and he continues to choose it.

As we talked about JL and his drug and alcohol history and the rehab/recovery programs he was in, she felt that recovery programs can be a scam with no long-term benefit. When I asked about her experience with them, her knowledge was limited to her brothers—who had only been in court-mandated programs and as soon as they were done, they returned to the life they knew, where they were comfortable. There was never even a fleeting thought of recovery for them. There was no will to do anything but continue "to chill."

I pointed out the huge difference between her brothers' generation of drug addicts, our generation from the 1970's, and John Leif's. They are at opposite ends of the spectrum of addiction. Millennials, kids who became teens in the era of 9/11, didn't make a "choice" to be a drug addict or to make it a career. They were enticed and ensnared at a very early age in the midst of their normal lives with trying something that just looked like it would be "fun," never knowing what the consequences would be. They found themselves in a trap which, once the door had snapped shut on them, they needed, and sooner or later *wanted* help to get out.

April 10, 2015
JL,
   Mom here. *I have been thinking about the phrase "severe mercy," and how your death was a mercy for you to end your constant*

struggling of trying to be free of an addiction that it seems you would truly never be free from. My question is still: When will it really feel like a mercy to us? Why does it still feel so severe? When will we be at peace with God—who allowed your death? Was there truly no other way for you?

It seems there wasn't, given the choices we all made at various points along the way. Perhaps it relates even more to the choice JL made in 2004 to try opiates with no knowledge that he would be one of the twenty-five percent who are genetically wired to become immediately addicted. As Mitchell said in *The Big Fix,* total abstinence was her only option: "I have two drinks, then four, then I lose count. Then I wander down the street and get some heroin…The night ends with me in the coroner's office. Because that is the way my using goes. It is simply how I am. There are people who can do 'just one more.' Then there are people like us (addicts)."

We live in a century where we have an advantage in trying to understand the complicated world of addiction through scientific research. The growing mountain of knowledge has made it clear that addiction is a disease of the brain and that according to what spells "pleasure" to an individual's reward loop will determine what they become addicted to. Once triggered, it will take a concerted effort to get and stay clean. I have seen and known of many people who have overcome active addictions. But almost all of them were not opioid addicts. Most of the memoirs written about addiction were by those addicted to uppers like cocaine or speed or methamphetamines. As the growing statistics reveal, opioids are another realm entirely. And the ways in which they not only alter brain chemistry and create a physical addiction, but bring about overdose and death, will keep them in a class of their own when it comes to treatment and recovery. Addiction is as complex as our genetic makeup and the human brain. We lived this truth for ten years with JL.

We act as if simple cause and effect is at work.
We push to find the one simple reason things have gone wrong.
We look for the one action, or the one person,
that created this mess.
As soon as we find someone to blame,
we act as if we've solved the problem.
–Margaret J. Wheatley

17

THE SECRET KEEPERS

*Forgiveness is important in families,
especially when there are so many secrets
that need to be healed –
for the most part, every family's got them.*

—Tyler Perry

In the first month after JL's death, one of our friends who lives out of state called to express his condolences, and to offer empathy for us as one parent to another. It was a vivid example of the fact that what we had just experienced was every parent's unspoken and worst fear, and ultimately, an unimaginable one. With compassion in his voice, he told us that the only words that came back to him again and again were "What a waste of a beautiful guy."

Those words were meant to be comforting, probably meaning that heroin stole the life of a beautiful guy, but they had just the opposite effect on both of us. Clearly, our raw and open emotions were a harsh filter, and all we received from those words was that our son's *entire life was a waste*: useless, purposeless, futile, squandered, having no value. Again, the image of the druggie as someone who *wants* to be an addict, who, given the choice, would remain one the rest of their days—they would make *the choice* to live in the margins, not contributing to society but taking from it.

In retrospect, we understand and appreciate the effort our friend made to take the risk of saying what he felt. It can be so hard to know what to say to people who are grieving that some friends say nothing. But as parents of someone whose life "was wasted," not just implied perhaps, by a friend, but clearly by society, we absorbed those words to confirm our own conviction that we had not parented well. If we had, our son would not have gotten into this mess, right? The steps to forgiveness toward our friend didn't take long. Toward ourselves has taken much longer.

As I've said, John and I are just wired to be absolutely honest, and that has not changed in our dealing with or sharing about, our son's life and death. While he was alive, we were discreet about his addiction because we felt it wasn't our story to share. It was his. It could affect his work and relationships. It was our place to encourage him to be open about it, especially with close friends and family, so there could be less enabling and more real support. JL understood that our close friends knew about his life because they loved him, and we relied on them for moral support and prayer. But once he died, all of his life's story became open territory.

I do understand why parents think they are doing what is best for their child by not disclosing the truth about their addiction, especially after a death, and covering it up like a blemish. But, as we remember from being teenagers with acne, the more goop you put on to try and cover it up, the more it stands out like a malignant growth. So, too, with addiction: the cover up adds more shame and perpetuates the diminishing of the person underneath. It invalidates *them* as a person and keeps them in the shadows. It says they deserve to be shamed; and, after a death, it doesn't celebrate them and who they really were, nor does it allow friends and family to process their grief openly, which is the only path to real healing.

National secrecy. Communal secrecy. Familial secrecy. Cloaked as "Discretion" it perpetuates the problem. What it did for us when we found out that our son was addicted to heroin was to create a puzzle that we were forced to try to put together in the dark with many missing pieces. No one would talk. When the drug bust happened at his high school in the spring of 2005, and the administration didn't call a meeting of all parents to alert us to what was going on, one wonders what motivation was behind that decision? Clearly, it wasn't what was best for the rest of the students, families, or our community.

Years ago, while working through our angst with the systemic problems in organized Christianity, and continuing to run into absolute resistance and denial, we came upon a quote that finally explained why we were not, and never would be, making headway: *"If you speak about the problem, you become the problem."* This wisdom came from an important and insightful book, *The Subtle Power of Spiritual Abuse.* But the subtle power of abuse is not limited to churches: governments, schools, communities, families—no one wants to be seen as part of the problem, especially with drug addiction. So, if we just keep troublesome or messy things secret, if we don't speak about them, we can all just get along.

The truth of this philosophy was something that might have helped me understand the reactions I would receive throughout my life, starting in my own family. I have many memories from when I was growing up, hearing my dad tell me, "Mind your own business." I don't remember specifics, but many times I was inserting an unsolicited opinion about some blatantly unhealthy or dishonest scene I was witnessing and felt the pressing need to say the true version of what had happened.

From information I have found out as an adult, embarrassment due to something considered shameful was a common motivation for our parents and grandparents to keep secrets and not be upfront and honest. John's paternal grandparents emigrated from Norway at the turn of the 20th century. They met in the Midwest and raised their family. While we were visiting family in Norway several years ago, we saw some unidentified babies in old photos and asked about them. At first no one seemed to know— but with a little persistence and lots of humor, we finally found out that both his single grandfather and single grandmother had left illegitimate babies in Norway and never spoke about them. Until a few years ago, none of John's family, including his father Leif, knew that his father had two half-brothers. One had actually visited Leif's family when he was young, and he was told it was "an uncle." We shake our heads now and wonder what possessed them to behave this way; that is until we put ourselves back in time 100 years and realize the shame and ostracization that they would endure when society was not as understanding and accepting of unplanned pregnancies and births.

In my mother's English family, secrets seem to have been a way of life. There would not have been any speaking openly about anything that would not support the image of a good and upright family. This was common and based on strong cultural mores such as: "Don't air your dirty laundry." Pride based on self-righteousness, for they really were good and generous people, seemed to be at the core of the cover-ups and "putting a good face" on everything. Victorian repressed attitudes towards anything related to bodies and sex were also standard. I have no doubt that underlying secrets are part of the reason there are so many surface problems with various addictions in my family. My father's Italian family was different in almost every way. His parents had emigrated from Southern Italy where the poverty was endemic after WWI. They lived in a world where you had to fight your way through many social obstacles. Being blunt and forceful was a way of life. They were generous with meals and hospitality, but they seemed to feel a strong need to hang on to anything they had. One of his sisters was the most selfish woman I ever knew. My mom remembers going shopping with her and my Nonna, in the early years of my parents' marriage, and the two women would take several pieces of undergarments into a fitting room and come out with them all hidden under their clothing—shoplifting. They justified it because the store owners and the government were all rich, and my relatives had to take what they could. They had pride too, although not the self-righteous kind. It was more akin to vanity.

Ultimately, my parents' family of origin dynamics affected their relationship and those of our entire family. They were from two different worlds and relational systems. Extremes abounded, with both joy and anger. When our friends, who know my parents and love them and have spent time with them as senior citizens, see and hear about the turmoil in my family, they have a hard time reconciling the two opposing views. Even their grandchildren, who love them dearly and experienced so much love and affection from them, have a hard time believing some of the stories from family life during my adolescent years in particular. My response to all this has been: "John and I dearly love my parents and have a wonderful relationship with them. They are people of great integrity, character qualities and strengths, and a simple but strong faith in God that has carried them through all the hardship, turmoil, and loss. But they had poor relational skills." They are not alone. The posterity of many of our grandparents is not in good shape today.

May 1, 2015
JL,

   Dad here. *I have been in a really deep blue funk—still. Dr. Cai would probably call it clinical depression. The best thing I can come up with is profound sadness. Then your cousin Gabe sent his new CD. He has written a dozen really great tunes. "Don't Be Lying" was based in part on conversations he had with you. I called him and he told me that when he was writing the song, he was thinking of all the ways we limit our own potential by lying to ourselves, doubting ourselves, or puffing ourselves up so we feel we don't need help from others. And he thought of you and your struggles with addiction and that wove its way into the song—honesty woven creatively into a great song. At the first listen, my spirit began to lift.*

Don't be lying if your heart is saying otherwise
You can lie to others but you're really lying to yourself
—Gabe Kubanda, "Don't Be Lying" ©2014 Kubanda Music Publishing

18

HOPES AND DREAMS

I know how men in exile feed on dreams of hope.

−Aeschylus, Agamemnon

After JL's death, John and I did feel like "men in exile," forced into separation from our son, banished from each other's' lives. We are not just on different continents, but in different worlds. And hope? Any hope would have been just that—a dream, a fantasy, vanity. To the people we interacted with as we went about our business, nothing appeared to be different about us. They couldn't see the empty space between us, the void JL left in our lives, the pain of this separation. Of course, this is common to us all when someone dies: our world stops, but the rest of the world is still turning, spinning perpetually around, untouched and unmoved by an event that paralyzed ours.

"Hope deferred makes the heart sick, but desire fulfilled is a tree of life." Hope was definitely deferred while John and I hung on for the last several years of JL's life, waiting for our desire fulfilled for him to be clean. I recently read an article entitled "Grieving the Living: Letting go of old versions of ourselves and others in order to make room for the realities of today promise of the future" by Dr. Susan Writer. I wish I had read it a decade ago. She shared on the Community Alliance for Healthy Minds (CAHM) website about relating to loved ones diagnosed with a mental illness or who have become addicts and how we can "lose the living." She says:

"Their behaviors are altered. They are not themselves—or at least not the version of the people that we have grown to know and love…our relationship with this loved one changes and we often feel a deep sense of loss. But we must grieve the relationship of the past if we are to create a new one in its place for the future…we must learn to accept that person's new identity as it emerges and develops. But we all must honor these changes in our loved ones and recognize that if we are to have any relationship with them, we need to learn to adjust and adapt on our end…we must 'grieve the living' to allow for life to move on."

In hindsight, I think we were grieving the loss of our son over the decade of his addiction, the son we had raised and known since birth, but we weren't able to fully adjust and adapt on our end soon enough to allow for the changes that needed to develop for his good.

His death took all hope of a sober and content son in this life away. Lost hope is what crushes parents when their child dies a needless death, an ignoble death to many. Had he fought in a war and been killed in action, to society it would have been a noble death. Most people who are separated from the life-and-death battle with addiction can't see the struggle that this generation of young people are fighting on a moment-by-moment basis against an enemy that is in their brain, in their body—not outside it— one they can't shoot and kill or put in prison. But we, as parents and friends, see it and wonder how much longer can they fight before they lose? Drug addicts and alcoholics are viewed as people who *want to be* addicted and drunk, and if they didn't want to, they would just stop. Simple, right? How easy it is to sit in the seat of judgment, looking down from high on the hill of moral superiority, especially when you have no real firsthand knowledge or experience with the issue. This is not to say that many, probably most, older alcoholics/addicts have lived with their demon for so long that they really do not want to change. I have relatives like this, I see men on street corners like this, where even the mere idea of the work it would take to become sober and maintain it is too much effort for their addicted bodies and minds to bear.

September 8, 2014
JL,

Mom here. *Every time I walk past the large photo of you in the Arizona room—a place I walk past many times each day—I take "an anxious breath." That's what I call the involuntary, short catch breath that happens to me when I am anxious or upset. It lives below my level of consciousness, and I can't control it. The pain of your death is so deep. You were so much a part of my life, both you and Johanna, since your births. God asks us, His children: "Can a nursing mother forget her own child? Even if she could, I can never forget you. You are inscribed on the palms of My hands." Any mother who has nursed knows that you cannot go long before you must have your baby at your breast, even if you must wake them, and I suppose even if you don't fully love them. It is self-preservation. And we can never forget the children we carried inside our bodies for 9 months, never. You are inscribed—engraved, carved, etched—in my heart.*

In Greek mythology, the river Lethe was one of the five rivers of the Underworld that flowed through a cave. Poppies and other hypnotic plants grew at the mouth of the cave and all who drank of the water experienced complete forgetfulness of their past existence. I find it interesting that opium was at the entrance, signifying its essential effect: oblivion, facilitating the forgetfulness. The thought of forgetting all the painful episodes in this life is tempting, while losing all the memories of life and love along with them is abhorrent.

In the first several months after our son's death, I would weep as I listened and sang along with "Ghosts That We Knew" by Mumford & Sons: "So give me hope in the darkness, that I will see the light..." A lot of spiritual thoughts and honesty about faults and choices and forgiveness. It caused me to wonder: Why were we, and our son, not given the chance of his surviving an overdose, like other families we know, along with the hope of a life that was brand new and even helping others find their way out of addiction? Why are we still living with this pain? Why are so many other parents living with this same pain? Was his death the inevitable end anyway? Will we find hope in the darkness someday?

September 11, 2014
JL,

Mom here. *This, in Gold Cord, reflects how we feel now: "Where were our hopes? Dead...with our dead babies (son). We were sorely tempted to discouragement but then a "word" that was given to us held us in confidence, some word that was life to us and that we keep in our hearts. When all looked hopeless we looked back to it." That "word" for us was the word and picture Heather had in July while praying for your oral surgery, that now gives us peace: "JL will be Victorious" and the vision she had of you standing in bright white light next to the Lord. What she didn't tell us in July was that she has only had this experience two other times in her life and each time it was right before that person died.*

Kyle also said he had a supernatural peace and sense of you smiling down on him from heaven. Johanna said that she had a dream about you after she returned to Oz. What she remembered when she awoke was a strong sensation that you had hugged and said goodbye. When we both feel like we failed you, we remember that what really mattered to us as we raised you and Johanna was that you would grow up to know and love others and God and serve him and this world, and then be together with us for eternity. This is the hope we cling to in dark times even though we did not receive all we prayed for.

We knew what our hopes and dreams were for our son. Nothing out of the ordinary—a healthy, productive life, contributing to the well-being of those he loved and the world.

But what about the hopes and dreams he had? JL was a human being and would naturally have hopes for his future. But that is one of the soul-robbing aspects of addiction of any sort: the need for instantaneous gratification for pleasure that sidelines future aspirations and hopes while that insistent, always present, urgent need for immediate satisfaction is a mirage they head toward. All plans beyond the present compelling urge their body is clamoring for are pushed aside until they finally disappear, out of sight, and ultimately out of reach. Acquiescence to the fate before them. I saw this many times in the last few years of JL's life, and it was torturous. In conversations, I would try to give him a picture of what his future could be like once he was clean and sober, to remind him of *his* hopes and dreams, the ones he had when he was young, and again, as an engaged university student. I could see the absence of hope in his eyes. It was, and is, devastating to think of someone I love living without hope. It was so hard to watch, and must have been even more devastating to bear. I know I couldn't do it.

My oldest friend, Elizabets, was the first person to help me see into my own soul by reflecting back to me how I viewed the world and the people in it. Something she said decades ago, a new insight to me, was, "Your doors and windows never shut." Yes. I have always had a hard time shutting down my mind and closing out the stimuli around me. Curiosity about everything has distinguished my life, searching out interesting facts about all sorts of subjects: this world, life, people, but there many times in my life I have wished I was not always thinking and questioning, that I could just *accept* things as they appear on the surface, because it causes so much turmoil to be wondering why something is the way it is, or how it happened, or how something could be improved. This "defect" is not limited to things in the natural world, but extends to people as well. What motivates them to say and do and be the way they are? When I am finally alone (which having grown up in a large family was usually only when I was in bed and the lights were out) is when I think about all the things I am trying to understand, projects I want to do, or people and situations I am concerned about. It creates anxiety and makes falling to sleep very difficult.

John Leif was very much the same, which is why he was attracted to opioids. They were a way to have peace and quiet and not have to deal with incessant thoughts and ideas. Our modern culture dishes up continual stimuli from the time we are born, which doesn't offer much help for personalities like ours. Had I not learned the spiritual disciplines that have been part of my life since I was a teenager, I would have walked down the same path as my son. Prayer and meditating on God's words brought peace and hope and a sense of place in this world for me that have kept me sane. How is it that for all my hopes and prayers, desires and effort to pass on these spiritual practices to our son so he could cultivate a fruitful and joy-filled life on this earth, I am now having to accept that they were not able to outmatch "the joy plant" as the ancient Sumerians called opium?

October 19, 2014
JL,

Mom here. *I am still dealing with gloominess over your death and feeling like I don't know where God is. Maybe as new disturbing information comes to the surface, I don't want to accept it and accept that you are gone. I think that what I want now is comfort—but maybe not, since we are receiving comfort from people who knew you and they remind us of what a wonderful person you were. I guess it's wanting you here and also wanting the answer to whys—those "whys" that come back again through my tears: Why did this have to be the answer to all of our hopes and dreams and prayers? Why couldn't we have our miracle? And why does our family so rarely have the miracles that others receive? Answers to which I will never get on this earth. These verses that Jeremiah wrote in the Bible come to mind today and they do bring comfort and hope for the future:*

A voice is heard, lamentation and bitter weeping. Rachel is weeping for her children and refuses to be comforted, because they are no more.

Restrain your voice from weeping and your eyes from tears, for your work will be rewarded and your children will return from the land of the enemy.

And there is hope for your future and your children will return to their own territory.

December 14, 2014
JL,

Mom here. *We are in Melbourne with Johanna, Gerard, and the girls. Being here is wonderful in so many ways, but hard in others. I woke up feeling weepy and sad about you. I had an email from our older friend whose son committed suicide and she is reeling from it, at 81. Her therapist said that she is grieving hope. She had spent decades hoping things would get better for her son and then with his sudden death, hope died, too. Yes. That is exactly what I had written to some close friends. Dad and I are grieving all the hopes we had for you.*

As I sat in our caravan crying (our one-bedroom trailer), attempting to encourage myself, I read notes about how the Christian faith has a strong and focused sense of future hope. But instead, it was discouraging, because it felt like God took that hope away from you and from us in allowing your death.

John and I have put our hope *in the eternal God* for what we trust will be in our future, not in a nebulous and dying universe. But, that place of hope is so far beyond our limited, finite, human comprehension that we regularly cast the shape of our expectations from what we have experienced, from what we think would be the best for us and our family. We are disappointed when our hopes and expectations don't agree with what actually happens.

While we were with our grandchildren in Melbourne, although having fun, I found myself at times overwhelmed with activities and interactions. I didn't realize this aspect of loss, the need for time to be alone and continue processing my grief. Some people thrive on activity in order to avoid dealing with issues that are painful, even after loss. Maybe they do it in an effort to forget, or to move it off in to the future, or to dull the pain. I don't want to dull the pain because I don't want to lose any connection to my son. I was continuing to grieve the permanent loss, the negated dreams, and the ruined hope that he would one day be clean and happy here on earth.

I have wondered about the role dreams play in the process of grief, in our grief. Are they reflections of our wishful thinking? Our dashed hopes trying to resurface? Unconscious attempts to resuscitate our hopes, our son? If so, I would have thought that we would have had more frequent and vivid dreams about JL early on after his death. I was wishing I would have them. As I look back through our journal, it seems that the dreams that were more like visitations came only after months had passed. They felt like gifts given to us to assure us of his well-being. This seems to be fairly common from what I have read. Joan Didion writes that when her husband died, she stopped having dreams. It was half a year later when they started again. I remember C. S. Lewis saying in his private journal *A Grief Observed*, written after his wife Joy had died of cancer, how "passionate grief does not link us with the dead but cuts us off from them." This would explain why we didn't have encouraging dreams during the first weeks and months of grieving. Our grief was very strong, and bitterly passionate.

October 11, 2014
JL,

Mom here. *You were in a dream last night—one of those mixed-up dreams. We lived in an unknown city and house and you had friends stopping by. The familiar aspect was that some statues outside had been broken apart and you said you didn't know how it happened, but I felt that you did. Somehow Dad and I had access to* *your computer and there were pictures that showed the before and after. I think this came because I've been thinking about some of the times when unexplained things happened that you either really didn't remember or know about because you were high or drunk—or, you were not owning up to them in order to protect yourself or your friends. Most of the time I didn't believe you and Dad would get mad at me for not trusting you.*

My brother Joseph had a very vivid, visitation like-dream with JL. He was at home in the living room and JL was next to the front door and heading toward the staircase leading up; interesting how these scenes always have JL going up. He asked JL "What's up—what are you doing here?" JL turned and hugged him and they spoke a bit, but it seemed more like communicating by thought. My brother said the feeling was that JL was in a different world now and just going about his business but had an errand here on earth. JL was doing fine but had a degree of sadness and regret while he was on this plane of existence. The dream ended and my brother was left with a positive and peaceful feeling.

As the months progressed, John and I were both having more vivid dreams about JL. They did seem more like visitations, and they brought comfort, as our journal entries describe:

December 18, 2014

JL,

Mom here. *When I woke up at 3 a.m. urgently needing to go to the bathroom, I was in the middle of a very vivid dream about you, having a very different experience than any previous dreams about you—I would say it was a visitation. John and I were in a home somewhere, it was very white and light, and all of a sudden you came in. We were so glad to see you! You were very normal. But when you went into another room it hit us that you were alive and we kept saying to each other, "We know he died, we saw his body in the casket, how can he be here?"*

We went to find you and there were a bunch of your friends in the room with you and you were all looking at your phone and computer trying to erase things you did not want us to see, but realized they were already removed. I had to go to the bathroom, and you headed up a steep white ramp into very bright white light, saying you had to go. I awoke at peace.

My dear friend Ann L. shared this with me: "I dreamed of you last night. We were together and joyous. No tears. I sensed a true experience when we were together. I imagine that's exactly what you felt about being with JL in your dreams." Yes, that is what we felt, it was a true experience. I found my journal entry from November 2001, a year after my brother JD entered the ICU unit and 10 months after he died there from AIDS. It is interesting to read my thoughts and feelings from that time, many of which I had forgotten. One paragraph was about dreams:

During JD's hospitalization, death, and the months following, I had not dreamt about him. Others had and I really wanted to have a dream in hopes that it would help replace the looks on JD's face that I remembered from those months in ICU. Those looks were of pain, sorrow, deep regrets, shame, and the bitterness that comes from poor choices and a prematurely shortened life. They were hard memories for a very visual person like me. I had been struggling with believing what I had always believed: that God is good. I knew I had a decision to make: He either is or isn't. No middle ground. The day after I renewed that decision, I had a dream about JD. It wasn't anything earthshaking or spiritual per se, but it brought comfort to me. He came by our house and we went to see a landscape job he was working on in a rural area somewhere. He introduced me to the older man who was the owner and then showed me with great enthusiasm all they were working on. Then I said I thought we should be going because of his illness. He agreed amiably and we left. That was it—just a normal scenario that left me with a sense of peace. I felt blessed and was thankful.

On Grief and Grieving has a section on dreams that is beautifully insightful. The thought that dreams help our souls deal with an incomprehensible reality while we are asleep, and aid the grief process, absolutely rings true for John and me. The authors tell us that most dreams are hard to understand with unclear messages, but after a loss, the messages are much more to the point and they hold reassurances of the continued existence of our loved one, and that they are *not* the body we saw at the funeral home. "Our loved one is healthy and intact, the person we knew, and who we now long for." John and I know JL still exists and the dreams we have fortify our fluctuating hope. John took some photos of JL's friends surrounding his casket at the viewing before the memorial. We later sent the photos to those friends and they were so grateful. As odd as it may seem, we also took some of him in the casket when John, Johanna, and I did our private viewing. I've looked back at those photos a few times and I was reminded of the internal conflict I felt between wanting to touch and hold on to our son while also knowing he was no longer in that cold, waxy body.

February 24, 2015
JL,

   Dad here. *I had a wonderful dream last night. I saw you standing at the memorial service—arm in arm with your friends as they stood around your casket, your arms around their shoulders, smiling. It was another gift showing me that you are alive and well in heaven—and not bound by time or this world—and that you were at the service and were pleased.*

Do we have dreams of reassurance because we want them? Do we have any say in what we dream? From all I've read and all I've experienced and all I've heard from others the simple answer is

"No." They are involuntary because they arise from deep within when we are in the not-conscious state of sleep, REM, beyond deep sleep. This is the time when the most vivid dreams occur, because the brain is so active during this stage, increasing to levels experienced when a person is awake, even though we aren't awake. We supposedly have three to five REM cycles each night. Did we dream of JL during all those cycles, every night? I wonder why we awoke after some dreams and not after others? I wish we had remembered every one of them.

January 16, 2015
JL,

Dad here. *I continue to dream about you. In this dream, you and a group of your friends were at Casa Mexicana (our home) for a party. That was it, but I am glad for even the slightest peek of you. I remember some of the bonfire parties in the arena and meeting Kyle for the first time and thinking, "Who is this? He must be 25 with that heavy beard. If they wanted to buy alcohol he would be the go-to guy." Little did we know that you and he would become such great friends and alternately help and support each other over the years.*

We had a riding arena behind our home, and after Johanna's horse was moved to a stable, JL was able to use it for a variety of things over the years: a go-kart track, paintball field, occasional fireworks launch site, and bonfire pit. John's entry reminds me of one weekend night in late winter when we let JL and some friends amass a giant pile of debris (our large dead Christmas tree was included) and make a bonfire. They set it up in the middle of the large cleared dirt area, and we had the hose ready just in case. It turned into a *huge* fire with flames that went 30 feet into the air; it seemed that more friends showed up as the fire grew in size. All of a sudden, we heard fire engine sirens in the distance, and everyone went into action trying to put the fire out. Just as the sirens slowed down around the curve near our property, the flames were out, we turned off all the lights, and everyone hid inside, trying to keep quiet but laughing 'til we ached. We weren't sure if having a fire was illegal, but we knew someone had called the fire department at least out of concern. We were a family of pyromaniacs for sure.

January 23, 2015
JL,

   Dad here. *I had a vividly realistic dream. I saw you through a large sliding glass door. You were real, happy, alive, smiling, talking— although I could not hear your words. We were separated by that clear but impenetrable barrier and I could not reach you. I dreamed that I was sobbing, heaving in tears. Will there be no more "Tears in Heaven" as Eric Clapton sang following his four-year-old son's tragic death? "Beyond the door, there's peace I'm sure, and I know there'll be no more tears in heaven." I am longing and waiting for that day.*

February 12, 2015
JL,

   Mom here. *I had a dream with you in it last night, one which I can't remember now, but when I woke up enough to know I had dreamed, I realized that you were in it but were not the focal point. And even that saddened me. As I think about it, and you, this morning once again the truth smacks me between my eyes that the world moves on, our world moves on, regardless of your not being here. And I know from feelings like this in the past with JD and Susan that the fear C. S. Lewis talks about after his wife Joy died is that you will gradually fade from the vivid presence and remembrance we have had. I don't want that, but it seems it is not within my power to stop it.*

May 13, 2015
JL,

   Dad here. *I continue to have dreams about you. Some very happy—some very, very sad. It's like a video of your life plays in my head when I close my eyes to go to sleep. I see you as a little child, as* *a young boy, as a young man. I see you healthy and sober. I see you tormented and sick. I see your beautiful face, playing with Anaëlle and Zaria. I see your anxious face, stressed, preoccupied.*

While we were in Australia in 2014, after Christmas we spent a week at the beach with our little family on Phillip Island. It was bittersweet—playing in the water, building sand castles, collecting sea shells with our granddaughters, while we carried our son's death within our hearts. We brought some of JL's ashes to cast into the ocean there, to leave some of him close to where Johanna lives. Why is this significant? Perhaps the physical act reflects the words "dust to dust, ashes to ashes." Closing the lid to his casket was a similar commemoration for us, our last goodbye to his physical body, although it was just an empty shell. The first goodbye was holding onto our son through The Body Bag on August 2nd.

On New Year's Eve, John and I drove to Woolamai Surf Beach. It was a beautiful evening with enormous, wild waves and huge, rocky cliffs. It feels like the edge of the world. We walked alone to a rocky place where we threw some of my sister Susan's ashes five years previously, just after her death. As we took photos of us tossing JL's ashes into the tide pools and the sunset, a seagull flew by and small rainbow appeared, the symbol of hope. Hope will return to us someday.

Hope is like the sun, which, as we journey toward it,
casts the shadow of our burden behind us.
–Samuel Smiles

19

SONGS FOR BROKEN HEARTS

Where words fail, music speaks.

–Hans Christian Andersen

Children. I love how they look at the world, at life, at ordinary things. It is so straightforward yet profound in its simplicity. I remember some of how I thought as a child, living in the present, optimistic, carefree. I believe that being child*like* is a virtue while being child*ish* as an adult is indicative of immaturity. The great authors, like Andersen, who write for children must be childlike. I wish I was. My husband and favorite friends are.

Our granddaughter, Anaëlle, at age six was driving in the car with my daughter, listening to Adele sing "Set Fire to the Rain." She started tearing up. My daughter asked her how she was feeling, and she replied: "Sometimes songs make your eyes wet." She may have had an incomplete idea of what the words meant, but she could feel the intensity and passion in the words and music. I just loved hearing this, the beauty it conveyed, the sensitivity it reflected. Music reminds us that we are not just physical beings. Eric Clapton put it this way: "Music will always find its way to us, with or without business, politics, religion, or any other bullshit attached. Music survives everything, and like God, it is always present. It needs no help, and suffers no hindrance. It has always found me, and with God's blessing and permission, it always will."

Songs have been part of our salvation since John Leif died. We have gone back to them repeatedly, listening to them to steady ourselves, to bolster our failing resolve, to soothe our broken hearts. Clapton's "Broken Hearted" is one of our best-loved at this time in our lives. We know we share broken hearts from the loss of a son to a tragic death: "Who alone will comfort you? Only the broken hearted."

We are told in the Psalms that "A broken and contrite heart, O God, you will not despise." We can't manufacture broken hearts, because they happen on their own, unpredictable, unbidden, and definitely unwelcome. But, as my friend Annie Herring sings in her song "I Cry for Mercy," "Sometimes it takes a broken heart to see the light of day." This was the song I listened to, sang with, and cried through while my heart broke at my brother JD's bedside for the months he was in ICU dying of AIDS, and it was the theme song at his memorial service. Yes, a broken heart can help us see what is really important in life, the intangibles, if we allow it to. Conversely, I have seen a broken heart close up and scar tissue form that creates hardness to any signs of love, goodness, or mercy.

August 13, 2014
JL,

Mom here. *When I hear "Yesterdays" by Switchfoot, it causes my heart to physically ache for you. All we have left of you now are yesterday's—no tomorrows. It's literally a deep, physical ache—a dull, persistent, lingering pain. I shared this with Linda and Dad as we drove home from dinner and a movie tonight—an attempt to give ourselves some momentary relief from the pain—it was, sadly, only momentary.*

While we were all at dinner, John expressed anger towards me over some things that happened in the previous 10 days—those first, excruciating 10 days. Later, when Linda and I were talking, I shared that John tried to call her to apologize for being angry at me so many times while she was with us. "I don't want to hear an apology because anger is part of grieving and I wouldn't want either of you to hold it in." She felt John had to express anger with me over irritations and little things while a safe mediator was with us because *"The Big Thing"* was too painful to even mention. JL's death was unspeakable, to the point that if John or I uttered the words, it would make all of it real and too unbearable.

Aug 14, 2014

JL,

Mom here. *I am so sad—so very sad—things couldn't have been different for you. You struggled and suffered daily because of your addiction. Because of your early exposure, heroin was the only thing that would ever spell pleasure for you here on earth. Addiction is such a lonely state—particularly opioid addiction—it is not a party drug. I think of the opium dens of the 1800's. It caused you so much shame and guilt and kept you from feeling the joy of living openly with others. We really did not fully understand this. My heart is broken and disintegrating into a million tiny, hurting pieces, leaving a trail behind me wherever I go.*

Sadness. Such an inadequate word, but the one that persistently comes to mind as we think about our son. It is a heaviness in our entire beings, lead in our shoes, dragging us down with each step as we attempt to move forward. Like Herman with those giant shoes on the TV show *The Munster's*, or the weighted metal boots worn by early deep-sea divers, as in Jules Verne's *20,000 Leagues Under the Sea*. Perhaps it is God's grace that has outfitted our mourning clothes with these lead shoes that keep us grounded and upright.

C. S. Lewis, in consoling a friend on the death of his young wife, said: "How you reassure me when, to describe your own state, you use the simple, obvious, yet now so rare, word *sad*. It suggests a clean wound—much here for tears…And I'm sure it is never sadness—a proper, straight, natural response to loss—that does people harm, but all the other things, all the resentment, dismay, doubt, and self-pity with which it is usually complicated."

Sadness along with anxiety have been part of our storehouse of feelings since the summer of 2005. My birthday that year fell a few weeks after we first discovered JL was using heroin. We were in the midst of his withdrawal and simply putting one foot in front of the other as we searched to find the next step in the long uneven path ahead of us. No one in the medical profession we contacted had ever heard of BT and had no places to suggest for us to find help for JL. As we were going to sleep that night, my heart began racing and pounding as though it was going to burst out of my chest. After an hour or so, we realized we needed to call 911. I was taken to the ER and given tests to see if I was having a heart attack. I was given morphine and was able to feel my heart rate slow down and rest. Early in the morning we returned home. Diagnosis: extreme anxiety—deep, un-verbalized, foreboding. Who else but our children can affect our hearts at such a fundamental and unconscious level?

October 6, 2014
JL,

Mom here. *Dad and I made the decision to go to Oz to be with Johanna and family for December and January. We bought our tickets last night. I thought of you, and the anxiety and apprehension we had on previous trips leaving you, not knowing how you were doing while we were so far away. Also, the desire we had for you to go with us and to be with Johanna and her family and to experience Australia, even to checking out the Law School there in hopes you might consider going there.*

Now I feel a sadness over those lost hopes. I also felt a heart-pain because we can no longer do anything for you the way we can for Johanna and her family. We will never again experience the joy of giving to you—birthdays, Christmas, gifts, trips. We always loved you and Johanna equally and now it feels unfair somehow.

Heart-pain. Again. This experience is unconscious. It is definitely a real, physical pain that I feel in my chest, just like the night of my birthday in the ER, sometimes with my heart skipping a beat then pounding out the next one. Our bodies are like barometers that respond to our mind and emotions, subconscious or conscious, regardless of any attempt to control it. Sometime after JL's death, I woke up seeing a picture in my mind's eye of tears flowing, not from my eyes, but from my heart, only they were not tears of saltwater but of blood. Similar to the Mexican Milagro symbol of the burning heart of Jesus with a crown of thorns and blood dripping down. That is where I see my tears streaming from now, my heart. Leonardo da Vinci said: "Tears come from the heart and not from the brain."

We took a short trip to California a few months after JL died to visit very dear friends and also John's cousins. I think we needed reassurance from people who knew our son, to reassure us that we were not total failures as parents. As John and I walked through his cousins' front door, they were overcome with tears. Tears for us, feeling what we must feel after our son's death, and tears for him and the loss of his life at such a young age. It is every parents' nightmare, to lose a child, especially in a sudden death.

All Terry and Ronda could do was hold us and sob and tell us how sorry they were, tears rolling down their cheeks. We are so thankful to God to have these types of friends and relatives that love us, and loved JL, so unconditionally, and feel free to express it to us. It's almost like we don't need to continually have "liquid moments," as another grieving friend calls her spontaneous, unpredictable tears, because our friends are releasing those tears for us. Washington Irving said it so beautifully: "There is a sacredness in tears. They are not the mark of weakness, but of power. They speak more eloquently than ten thousand tongues. They are the messengers of overwhelming grief, of deep contrition, and of unspeakable love."

For months, I wasn't able to watch the memorial service or tribute video, I just couldn't. I was afraid of falling apart entirely. John and I differ in this. I knew I would not be able to function if I wept as much as I knew I would, I would become drained of energy and get a headache. Several months later while reading back through *On Grief and Grieving*, I came upon a section in Chapter Two on "Tears." It is a story about a couple facing death and the wife holding back her tears, fearing if she started, she would never stop. The truth is that uncried tears have a way of *filling the well of sadness* even more deeply. I think I knew this intuitively but have not lived it. Looking back, I should not have been so concerned about being able "to function" and allowed myself to weep without the fear of not surviving it. I would have felt release sooner.

My dear friend Ann D. remembers coming over to see us around this time. John was in his office watching videos of JL and crying and I expressed my anger at him. Anger because he was causing himself misery. "I saw you holding in your emotions, holding it all together and not giving yourself permission to cry more often." Ann was amazed at my strength but knew that controlling emotions takes much more effort than releasing them. She didn't feel free to share this with me until recently, and how I wish I would have been able to "hear" this from her at the time. I deprived myself of some physical and emotional healing I could have experienced sooner rather than later. I see now that tears are a nonverbal way of expressing sorrow, and they can speak for us when words would be too much or too frightening.

Memories of JL surfaced again when John and I got home from our trip to California, sadness resurging in my soul. Needing encouragement, I listened to the playlist of songs I've made from different artists that over the years I would listen to and sing as prayers for our son. God used them to speak to my heart about JL's desires and struggles, increasing my empathy. Though I still had a hard time coming up with any other descriptive words about how I felt except sad, when music was with the words, phrases came to life: "Everything is Broken," Bob Dylan. "In this life, you're the only one…You're everything I'd ever hoped for." Switchfoot.

Music is the universal language because it is the language of the soul and spirit while it also engages our minds—all of us— uniquely. John will listen to songs that remind him of JL's death and our separation, or songs from JL's playlists, as he plunges into and lingers with the pain. I look for relief from the pain as I listen to songs that bring me hope for the future while they echo the cries in my heart. Somehow, both methods work for us individually to help heal our sorrow. For Johanna, there was a song that resonated with her after her brother's death by singer/songwriter Vance Joy, from Melbourne: "Think you're in control until you're not. And we all die trying to get it right. So, aim high, and aim true."

September 7, 2014
JL,

Mom here. *Since your death that Saturday morning, weekends continue to be grueling and emotionally punishing for Dad and me, like we are punching bags at a boxing gym. We are occupied all week with work and interactions, which distract us somewhat. Yet even then, you are still always right there below the surface, a low bass note constantly playing beneath everything, an "ohm" from a deep meditation. How long can we listen to it? Will this ever change? How will we feel if it does?*

As we approached what would have been JL's 26th birthday on March 11th, once again in the first year, we felt that yesterdays are all we had left of our son. Memories of events, interactions, and words from the past. No more future birthday celebrations for our son, or his future children. "Yesterdays" by Switchfoot was written about their friend who died, and we used it at JL's memorial service, also listening to it repeatedly during that first year. It was balm: "Every lament is a love song. Yesterday, a love song. I still can't believe you're gone..."

Music has always been an essential and significant part of my life. From the time I was a child, my mother would sing songs as she went about her day being custodian to five kids. Sometimes it would be songs from the big-band era that she and my dad would go out and dance to. Or songs from World War II that gave courage to the boys fighting overseas and their loved ones waiting for them at home. Her music was almost always cheerful and upbeat, sung with her beautiful voice, smile, and facial expressions. My father had a more serious, introspective taste in music. He listened to intense jazz and big bands from the 1940s and '50s along with classical music. I remember hearing Beethoven, Mozart, Holst, Vivaldi, and Italian opera streaming out from his study as he worked at night. They both played the piano; my mother from sight, my father by ear.

My mom knew the words and melodies to hundreds of songs—she had a gift for this. She taught us funny little tunes from her childhood in the 1930s, or story-songs from Burl Ives or Disney stories. Now suffering from dementia, songs and poems are what she most easily remembers. We had records with a huge variety of songs including ones in foreign languages—traditional folk songs for children. When my sisters and I were in our twenties talking about this one day, we hit upon one record that had given all of us the same recurring nightmares during our childhood: *Peter and the Wolf.* We had a record of the music by Tchaikovsky, which also had a narrator telling the story. My mom would play the record and we would act out the story with our stuffed animals. Little did she know, cheerful soul that she was, that it was the source of nightmares for us all. Our little minds turned the story into frightening dreams of being chased by a wolf from our home and not being able to get back. Mine also had our house on fire as I tried to run to it for protection.

Beethoven said, "Music is the mediator between the spiritual and the sensual life." It permanently cements words into our psyche. Listen to the jingle for any product being advertised. Even if you don't want to remember it, you do. That is the power of a hook. I still remember songs from commercials while growing up in the1960's and 70's. Brylcreem, that waxy stuff men used to put in their hair so they looked like an FBI agent, "A little dab will do 'ya." "Hot dogs, Armour hot dogs." "Coke, It's the Real Thing." The list is endless.

Likewise, John Leif and Johanna grew up with me singing around the house, and both our kids sang or hummed to themselves when they were alone playing, which was such a joy. I have a video from my recent trip to Melbourne of our youngest granddaughter, Zaria, as she improvised words with melody to accompany a puppet show she and her sister were doing for her parents and me. No self-consciousness at all as she sang from her heart. It's priceless.

August 28, 2014
JL,

Dad here. *We have decided to keep your Toyota 4Runner. It is beautiful and clean, not to mention the killer sound system you have in it. I am listening to London Grammar a lot. Mostly dark songs about love and loss—very appropriate for me now. I think you would have liked it. When the sub kicks in on their tunes it is incredible—I know you loved that bass. We will try to take good care of it for you. I wish you could have enjoyed it a little longer. I love you.*

One regret and sense of failure that surfaced after JL died was that John and I didn't have him and Johanna take music lesson while they were young. It is odd to our friends that John and I are musicians and always so involved with music but that neither of our children were. One reason was my experience of not having had music lessons and learning to play by ear as a young adult because I wanted to express my heart and soul. It didn't matter to me that I couldn't play other people's compositions. Many of our friends who had been classically trained seemed to lack the emotional element I admired. Looking back, some musical training would have given our kids a skill that could have been a family bond, would have brought self-confidence, while nourishing their souls, as opposed to all the physical activities that John did with the kids. With JL and his friends, John taught them dirt bike riding, paintballing, shooting, swimming. Johanna loved horses and became an accomplished rider through US Pony Club. Yet even with all the physical skills our kids learned, the influence of music on their lives was inescapable. JL was learning to deejay and Johanna always loved being immersed in live music, from her very first concert at age 13, to meeting her musician husband at a live music festival and now playing ukulele with her daughters.

Every Baby Boomer remembers where they were sitting when the Beatles first appeared on *The Ed Sullivan Show* in 1964. My parents' generation remembers the songs that marked the various events of World War II. We all remember where we were, who we were with, and other sensate things around us when we first encountered favorite songs. I was reminded of this, while at the wedding of young friends, the bride began her slow walk up the garden pathway. As I heard the first few measures of the tune, a song I haven't listened to in decades, it rustled memories of the song we began our wedding with: "The Wedding Song," by Noel Paul Stookey. Instantly, I was back at the day, time, and setting so many years ago, a garden wedding too. These music memories are non-erasable, deeply ingrained. They are, I believe, humans' link to the eternal, transcendent, non-tangible part of our lives.

I would be lost without being able to express the feelings I have that won't fit into words without music, especially now. I wish that our society wasn't so performance-oriented so that regardless of "talent," we could feel comfortable enough with our own voice to just sing, whenever and wherever. It is how millennia of families used to be, and still are in traditional societies, singing and playing instruments together in homes and community gatherings. My Italian grandparents played violin and concertina and my English grandparents played the piano. A highlight of some of my favorite movies is where a group of people break into song and dance. It is good for the soul and brings health to our bodies. It's the main reason many attend church.

Who would have guessed that singing releases positive neurochemicals like endorphins and oxytocin, the same ones responsible for the pleasure center and reward system in our brains, the same ones that opiates affect, the same ones that relieve pain, reduce anxiety and stress and boost our immune system? One of JL's friends from high school is a singer/songwriter and was struggling with pain over JL's death. Someone suggested that the cure for his pain was the pain itself; not running from it but embracing it. So, he decided that instead of writing out the positive thoughts he wished he had, he wrote about the tragedy he felt over JL's death, turning his pain into a tribute song. With it, the healing for his broken heart began.

April 1, 2015
JL,

Mom here. *Dad and I talked about how it is always songs that mark times and places in our lives. They are indelible parts of our memories, reminding us of joy, love, beauty and sadness, too. There are songs we would sing as prayers for you, hoping they would define your life and future. Ultimately, our confidence of your being in heaven now should bring us hope and joy, which it does, but it is mixed with the pain of not having you here on this earth, whole, well. We miss you.*

Music is God's gift to man, the only art of Heaven given to earth,
the only art of earth we take to Heaven.
—Walter Savage Landor

20

SHAME ON WHO?

Shame is a powerful force in our life.
It is the trademark of dysfunctional families.
It is an overwhelming negative sense that
who we are isn't okay.
Shame is a no-win situation.
It can propel us deeper into self-defeating
and self-destructive behaviors.

–Melody Beattie, *The Language of Letting Go*

Yep, my family had the trademark. From what I have learned in recent years from friends, we weren't that different from many of the families in America during the 1950's and 60's, but our family has suffered extreme consequences of that dysfunction: I believe that shame lies at the root of both of my younger brothers' deaths.

JD's death from AIDS at 40 could have been averted, or at least delayed, had he gone to the doctor and gotten treatment when he first suspected he had HIV. I don't know when that was, whether in the early 80's after he had Hepatitis C from IV drug use in college, or the early 90's after a decade of partying and sex, or a few years before his death when he must have started feeling he was sick. After his death, I found a lab report among his papers that showed he had a complete panel of blood work done 2 years previously. Whenever he knew, he hid it from everyone who knew and loved him. Why would an intelligent person who loved life and had everything to live for behave in such a self-destructive way, unless they had something to fear? A fear of how his family, friends, and clients would view him, which would cause him to feel shame. During his entire life, JD had always seemed to be a being a well-balanced and self-confident adult who didn't take enjoying life to the extreme. It was that image and his desire to protect my parents from any dismay that caused him to continue to keep secrets right up to the end of his life.

After his death, when we were trying to figure out how he contracted HIV, we talked to many of the women he spent a lot of time with. We always assumed he had intimate relationships with them, but we were wrong. Every one of them said that although they had wanted a relationship with JD, they never had more than a platonic one with him. So, it seems that not only did he use drugs, but he was most likely homosexual. I have always felt that he was sexually abused for a period of time by an older male neighbor, at exactly the time when his sexuality was developing. My parents were in a rented house while they built a home and JD was around 12 years old. He spent quite a bit of time after school at this man's house and when I met the man later, I knew he was gay. My mom described Mr. X as "such a nice older man." She was so believing of people, many times the very people she should have been wary of and kept away from her family. There were lots of them in our lives while we were growing up. Maybe that's why I found myself at times singing the refrain from The Doors song, "People Are Strange."

My youngest brother Joe's suicide in 2017 was the result of an entire life dominated by shame: the overwhelming negative sense that who he was would never be good enough. Born into our family when dissention was becoming increasingly common, I don't think Joe ever felt a sense of security or peace. My mom became involved in radical right-wing politics as my sisters and I entered our teen years, so her ideologies didn't really affect our thinking while it absolutely negatively impacted our lives with more rules and restrictions during the time when we should have had increasing freedoms. My father's temper increased in response to our push-back against the increasing restrictions. JD and Joe grew up with mom's fears and conspiracy theories which permanently affected their world view and view of life, but unlike JD, Joe took the brunt of my father's anger and abuse and my mother's enabling. As he got older, and we three girls had married and left home, Joe was the subject of the tension between my parents. He became the "Whipping Boy." JD went to college and Joe spent his teen years with my father's anger and mother's fanaticism: cure-all diets and supplements, politics, religion. (She started storing food for the coming economic crash.) I think Joe always felt alone in our family system.

Joe was different from JD in almost every way: he was very much like my mom in that he did not have a mean bone in his body and was very compassionate and loving. Like her, these traits also seemed to endow him with a lack of discernment. He had relationships with women who were very much like our mom, in that they were controlling while many times lacking her kindness; Joe was constantly in enabling relationships which caused resentment. He didn't know how to say "No" until he got pushed to the limit and became angry. That's when his temper, like my dad, would surface. It stemmed from his sense of powerlessness, helplessness, an inability to change the dynamics in his relationships. In his 20's, while in one of these relationships, a woman became pregnant while she had assured him she was on birth control. What is telling about this is that our family never knew about his daughter until she was an adolescent. Although he loved and supported his child, between shame and the angst of his relationship with the mother, this was one more episode in his life that spelled failure to himself.

Joe was an extremely gifted guitarist and songwriter and if he had been given any encouragement or sense of confidence, he would have been successful making it his livelihood. As it was, since my mother was convinced that rock music was of the devil, and my father thought it was not even music, it was one more polarizing factor in their lives. He was in a band during and after high school and also when he moved to Seattle a few years later. He worked in group homes for dual-diagnosed patients with mental/emotional illness along with drug abuse, gravitating to people with emotional and mental turmoil, something he could relate to.

My brothers' deaths make me feel frustrated, and angry, at my parents, mostly. Yet, when I pause to remember they had none of the self-help books and relationship classes that were accessible to us, I have compassion on them. They were just duplicating the family systems they were raised with like so many other parents. They did the best they could with the tools they had been given. For my sisters and me, there had been different dynamics than for my two brothers. We were like a separate family during our early years, when my parents were young and optimistic, before their lack of relational skills fully surfaced. I have happy memories of my childhood. I never felt any sense that who I was wasn't good enough, and I don't live with a sense of shame.

What I have always admired about John's parents is they made *conscious decisions* to change the family dynamics they grew up in and they were enabled to follow through, breaking the cycles and starting new ones because of their strong faith. John's father grew up with a strict and emotionally inexpressive Norwegian immigrant father, and Leif vowed he would be a kind and affectionate father. Which he was. John's mother grew up with an alcoholic father and the tensions that creates, and so she never drank alcohol and made a warm and accepting home for her family. John grew up in a family with healthy relationships that extended throughout his life. His sense of self is balanced and other than a few residual shame-based beliefs from early teaching at his parents' church, he just doesn't operate with blame and shame. How refreshing it was for me when we met.

When we raised Johanna and John Leif, we tried to not use blame and shame as parenting tools. We focused on responsibility and choosing to do the right thing even if it wasn't easy. And any attempt at not taking responsibility for one's own choices and actions was quickly exposed, especially by me. My fierce determination to not have any dishonesty in our relationships seems to be in direct opposition of my upbringing. I should have found kinder ways to elicit that honesty, as I've said. What we didn't realize until after JL's death was how our strong desire to please God translated into an unattainable goal post for our kids which then led to their sense of disappointing us.

September 26, 2014
JL,

Mom here. *I am so sorry that Dad and I over-spiritualized, once again, and made you feel "less than" if you needed Suboxone and that you just had to "try harder." Of course, you wouldn't feel you could tell us of the overpowering craving you were giving in to because you felt shame. I am left so disheartened by this recurring thought.*

Shame is a predominant emotion among addicts and alcoholics. And it is the least understood by those around them. It was for us. It is probably because neither John nor I carry it around. Shame lies at the heart of many of the behaviors that addicts have, internal conflict and confusion being just two of the many "shame-full" emotions warring inside. It is the reason, I now understand, they have such a hard time escaping the whirlpool of their disease. Shame is the current that keeps sucking them back into the center vortex, as it did for JL—I could see the dejection in his eyes even while I was unable to understand why. It is the conflict between what he knew was good for him, listening to that voice of self-preservation we all have built into our DNA, and the pull of the self-destructive behavior he was engaged in. He wasn't able to resolve the dichotomy of who and what he wanted to be with who and what he was while addicted. Yet, in order to not constantly feel lower than dirt, a person has to compensate for that feeling. JL (and many others I'm sure) have used common strategies like these when pulled in two directions, such as attacking others, seeking power or perfection, blame-shifting, being overly kind or self-sacrificing, or social isolation and withdrawal.

I have an email from JL dated August 2011. He had relapsed and was using BT again and after talking with us and John Leggio at the Mark about it, had a plan to just quit on his own by tapering off by using some benzodiazepines and return to a young men's group there for support. He started back to the U of A. His email is hard to read now as I see his strong desire to be free of the life-draining burden of his addiction while he, and those around him, thought he could just stop. *"I realize that I do not have the power to do this alone and I am not in control of this disease as much as I have tried to convince myself and everyone else that I am strong enough...I need to say that I am so grateful for all of your help getting going in school this semester as it gives me a goal to aim for in life which I need, so I don't feel like life is one big waste of time. I guess I'm writing all this to you because I am embarrassed about thinking I had control over this disease...Thank you for all your support—you guys are awesome parents and I hope my failures don't make you think otherwise. I love you lots."*

People, Places, Things is a play about addiction by British playwright Duncan MacMillan. At the center of the play is the 12-step process. For those who have trouble with AA and "surrendering to God" it shows that perhaps it is easier to understand it as acknowledging that you can't have control over life. We are all powerless over *People, Places, Things*. It is literally one day at a time. The crew visited a recovery center in London to get insights for the play, trying to find a way to accurately and respectfully represent the day-to-day struggle and work of living in recovery. After witnessing the daily life-and-death struggle that addicts fight, MacMillan said: **"One day at a time. And life has to win every single day. Death only has to win once."**

Many years ago, while studying personality traits and human behavior, I wondered about the difference between shame and guilt. Historically, the word shame seems to have been used interchangeably with guilt. In older writings, shame was the appropriate pang of conscience that followed doing something wrong. In reality, there is an important distinction. Shame is about *who you think you are*; guilt is about *what you have done*. John and I both have healthy guilt consciences and being a part of a community of close friends really helps, and is another example of why AA is so important for addicts. We all need encouragement from others who know and love us to help change patterns of unhealthy behaviors.

March 4, 2015
JL,

Mom here. *Dad and I and others thought that with all the groups and meetings and 12-step work your willpower could beat your addiction. But we were wrong. I feel the pain of the shame you carried because this thinking made you feel inferior. Your defensiveness was only logical and natural, especially with us. As David at In Balance recently told us, "Parents do not realize how much their young people want to please them and not be a disappointment." And how much they feel guilty for all the money spent on them and trouble they cause us. What a revelation this was to us.*

JL lost a lot more of the things that mattered most to him, more than we realized. He lost his self-esteem, self-confidence, and self-respect. We didn't understand how to help him express those losses without feeling shame. He was well aware that he was way off course for his life, surviving not thriving, without those "self's" that could accomplish the change. He needed to know that there was actual, practical help to get back on course, that he wasn't lacking character or failing morally because he needed medication to fight the cravings in his body and brain.

April 6, 2015
JL,

Mom here. *Thinking about how hard you worked led me today to tears, for the first time in months, over how stupid we were and how much of the recovery community hasn't gotten it yet either: most of you who started these new very strong and potent opiates* *as young teens, cannot beat the physical and mental addiction with willpower and support groups alone. It's not an excuse, but a reason. Why didn't we see and acknowledge how hard you were trying and how much you deeply wanted to be free? We have such regrets and sadness because we know we, and others, made you feel that you were not working hard enough, negating the strong pull back to using that you lived with on a daily basis. We didn't understand. We hadn't walked a mile in your shoes. We made you feel ashamed.*

Stigmas are linked to shame. In the Greek and Latin worlds, a stigma was a mark or brand, especially for a slave, identifying the person as "inferior." Later, in English language, its use became known as a mark or stain we can't see with our eyes: social stigmas that are based on perceivable characteristics, associated with certain behaviors that distinguish a person from other members of society. They convey disapproval and disgrace.

We experienced this with our son. Off opioids, he was his real self, the son we had loved and raised, a young man of integrity and compassion, someone who could have been a blessing to the world had he lived long enough to become free of his addiction. If the current statistics for how many recovery attempts it takes before an opiate addict can stay clean and sober had been available, we hopefully would have embraced MAT, which could have helped JL get through further attempts and come out on the other side.

For generations, the combination of personal shame and public stigma has produced tremendous obstacles to addressing the problem of alcoholism and drug addiction in America. Addiction stigma prevents too many people from getting the help they need.
—Hazelden-Betty Ford Institute for Recovery

21

THE RESCUERS

"Letting go" helps us to live in a more peaceful
state of mind and helps restore our balance.
It allows others to be responsible for themselves and for us
to take our hands off situations that do not belong to us.
This frees us from unnecessary stress.

–Melody Beattie

Historically, "enabling" referred to facilitating or empowering someone in order to help them accomplish something. By teaching children to read, we enable them to develop their intellect and further their learning, or, as in 1933 Germany, "The Enabling Act" gave Adolf Hitler the power to enact laws without the involvement of the legislative bodies: he was enabled to become a legal dictator. Even in modern psychology, enabling can be positive, but it is also used in a negative sense when it encourages dysfunctional, unhealthy behavior and habits, as it is used in addiction and recovery vocabulary. Rescuing and caretaking are terms that mean what they say. They are closely connected to enabling: *we* rescue people from *their* responsibilities and *we* take care of people's responsibilities for *them*. Melody Beattie refers to the "Drama Triangle" roles of victim, persecutor, rescuer, first described by Dr. Stephen Karpman in the 1960's and says "Rescuing/caretaking looks like a much friendlier act than it is. It requires a 'victim' who is actually capable of taking care of themselves even though *we and they* don't admit it…After we rescue, we will inevitably move to the next corner of the triangle, persecutor. We become resentful and angry at the person we have so generously helped…Then *we* move to the 'victim' corner of the triangle, at the bottom, the predictable and unavoidable result of a rescue."

In my family, I watched as an alcoholic cousin was constantly propped up, first by his mother and then, after her death, by my mother. My parents gave him handyman jobs and a place to live, in the name of helping him because he was in need. One can only assume these sisters learned this behavior from it being modeled in their home when they were young. I asked my mother if she ever thought about offering him work with pay only if he would attend AA meetings. She said she had suggested he try AA, but he said he didn't want to, that he liked his life as it was. He was a career alcoholic, so the help continued. The last time I saw him a few years ago he was homeless, had lost all his teeth, was as thin as a rail, and was riding a bike to and from his "office"—his favorite bar. He may be dead by now.

The "Kindness Rule" that I grew up with was never referred to as such by my mother, but it was what beat at the very core of her philosophy of life. I grew up hearing her mantra: "If you can't say something nice, don't say anything at all." Wisdom from Thumper in *Bambi*. This moral became so pervasive it now has its own name: "The Thumperian Principle." And my mother *is* very loving, kind and self-sacrificing, like many women of her generation. Her children, grandchildren and great-grandchildren adore her.

In my immediate family, this dynamic was at the core of the un-health we grew up with and suffered from. Over the years, the dissonance between my parents increased as the pressures increased from raising five kids with very little in way of assets or extended family and community. My father responded to provocation with outbursts of anger. My mother believed that "a soft answer turns away wrath" was not just a proverb, but an unequivocal response to my father's volatile temper. She was mistaken. It was not the loving thing to do for healthy interpersonal relationships. The damage done by her not setting a boundary against his lack of self-control perpetuated strife and turmoil in our family. When I married John, he began to witness my father's selfish demands or outbursts of anger at family gatherings or when it was directed at waitresses. John took my father aside and told him that if he behaved in that manner again, John and I would get up and leave. It took several times of repeating this warning, and sometimes acting on it, before my father changed his behavior, but only *when we were present*. The behavior continued at times until well into his old age with my mother and the rest of the family. Boundaries were not set or enforced.

After I became a Christian and had some years observing people in churches, particularly women, a growing discomfort began roiling deep inside me, lava just under the thin crust covering a volcanic crater. I felt there was something that didn't *ring true* about how the injunction to "Love one another" was interpreted and applied to interpersonal relationships, and church politics. A lot of dysfunction was being assigned to Paul's New Testament teaching to be "kind to each other, tenderhearted, and forgiving one another as God, because of Christ, forgives us." C. S. Lewis wrote that love and kindness are not coterminous because "love is more stern and splendid than mere kindness."

In 2015, *NBC Nightly News* began to air their series, *The Heroin Epidemic in America*. Its journalists interviewed families who are keeping naloxone on hand for their heroin addict children. Naloxone (Narcan) is a drug that blocks the effect of an opioid quickly and helps restore breathing for up to an hour, giving time to get the addict to a hospital before the effects of the opioid can resume. It is not without some potentially serious side effects. When I watched the interviews and heard the desperate parents almost unanimous desire to have this magic bullet so they could save their children from death by overdose, I was frustrated and baffled. Does this mean that these parents have their addict children living at home while they are *actively using*? Were none of them part of a recovery process and program with their kids?

More significantly, why do parents think the "kind" thing for their child is to allow them *to merely exist* as an addict at home? What quality of life does an opioid addict have? As C. S. Lewis said: "It is for people whom we care nothing about that we demand happiness on any terms: with our friends, lover, children, we are exacting and would rather see them suffer than be happy in contemptible and estranging modes." Is that the existence they want for their children? For us, the answer was, and would remain, no. Naloxone should not be used as an alternative to treatment for addiction. Historically, most people addicted to opioids overdosed while they were alone. But as this dynamic changes, as more addicts are coming out of the shadows, having naloxone available wherever opioid addicts may be could be life-saving and hopefully life-changing. Using medications for an emergency is *not* the same as enabling or rescuing.

And where does "Empathy" versus "Tough Love" fit in, opposing approaches now being discussed for the millions of families and friends with loved ones who are addicts. *NPR* recently published an article about families who choose empathy over the tough love approach that has failed them. In the article, a couple tried tough love, believing that letting their opioid addicted son "hit rock bottom" was what would do the trick, but because of this era of opioids, including fentanyl, **"The concept of letting their children hit bottom is not the best strategy,"** says Dr. Nora Volkow, director of the National Institute on Drug Abuse. **"Because in hitting bottom they may die."**

The parents in the *NPR* article went through Community Reinforcement and Family Training (CRAFT) program, where an emphasis on authoritative parenting created a sense of responsibility in the child, while at the same time saying "I am here for you. I love you. I'm going to help you." Things shifted from chaos to calm in this family as they went from enforcing punitive consequences to supporting their son as he faced the challenges of recovery. *NPR* reports that studies show a compassionate approach and voluntary treatment are the more effective ways to engage drug users in recovery and keep them alive. As John and I look back over the decade that JL battled his addiction, we see that we had some of these principles in place, but not others, and so wish we had this training to help us navigate such troubled waters. It was always hard for us to find a balance between loving JL unconditionally (which we did) and enabling (which we also did). We tried to have tough love as we swung between feeling pity and wanting to offer him grace, while having to do the hard things to actually allow him to suffer the consequences of his addiction. As our journal entries show, much of the time we were confused as to what to do and when.

January 25, 2015
JL,

   Mom here. *Dad I flew home from Oz and now, 9,000 miles from our only child, Johanna. We both watched the movie The Judge in flight, and both wept because it reminded us of your death and the imperfect love that parents have for their children. His "tough love" ruined the relationship with his son until just before his death, but it gave his son back his life. Sadly, we did the opposite. Another reminder of being flawed and fallible parents—humans.*

For John's and my generation as parents, our relationships with our children are significantly different that the ones we had with our parents. Baby Boomers were born to parents who had grown up during the Great Depression and World War II who are sometimes referred to as "The Silent Generation." They knew hardship and it had made them resilient. They resisted giving in to their feelings and expressing them. How could they? When humans are faced with external difficulties, it is not by being in touch with themselves that enables them to fight against all odds and overcome. It is by focusing outward on the task at hand and giving sacrificially. When I was growing up, I watched my parents as they would run into a wall of difficulty, back up, and run at it again with more force. Persistence was deeply ingrained. But one thing they didn't do was to seek advice or counsel. They just kept trying harder. I believe that my lifelong desire to learn from other people's mistakes, avoiding unnecessary pain (especially emotional pain), came from watching their approach to problems. However, there are situations where all the advice in the world can't keep us from experiencing pain.

As a result of the dynamics from our parents' generation, we young adults of the late '60s and '70s left home as soon as, or even before, we graduated from high school. It was expected. You figured out how to make it in the world on your own. You went to college (or not) and supported yourself. If you were from an affluent family, they supported you while you went to college, or you went into the military by draft. You were independent and naively confident because of that independence. Consequently, most of our generation did not have close emotional connections with our parents. And that was something, because it was missing for us, we held as a value to have with our own children. Thus, began one more cycle of children doing things differently than their parents. Not necessarily because it was better, but because it is an important step in becoming an independent adult. In having closer, more emotionally intelligent relationships with our kids, Baby Boomers are also more prone to enabling. Certainly, there is nothing wrong with having your adult kids live with you during or after college, and it is what the majority of the world does. It is economical and relational, but since it is new to many Americans of our generation, there are issues related to boundaries that continually arise. I think this is why JL kept his friends more to himself. He had enough "family" involvement, both nuclear and extended, and needed a separate identity, which I think was healthy.

There is a balance, of course. I have peers whose parents encouraged and supported them, while they may not have been their *friends* per se. They had a more human, *humane*, connection with their kids and less authoritarian approach, which was common in the parents of Baby Boomers. There were also lenient and/or uninvolved parents of those decades. Fathers, climbing the ladder of corporate success or building their career, were too busy to connect with their kids, or be home much of the time. Many times, this led to an over attachment by the mothers to one or more children. We all have "family of origin" issues, although the issues of our generation and the families we grew up in were different than those for our children. JL's generation family of origin issues (growing up with so much encouragement, opportunity, and available resources) caused them to expect the world to be generous and kind to them. I believe this has caused many Millennials to be woefully unprepared for the real world.

Enabling occurs in the best of families, by the most caring of parents. I know, because we were some of them. How I wish we had heard about, and read, *Codependent No More* by Melody Beattie when it came out in 1987. I believe our lives would have taken a different course. John and I have learned so much from her writing since John Leggio first introduced them to us in 2005, when we began attending meetings at The Mark. I have given many copies to friends and addicts. We read these "Daily Meditations for Codependents" as they are meant to be read, daily. As part of our son's addiction recovery plan, Leggio required parents or partners to attend group meetings with their addicted family member where we gained information, had discussions, and went through training scenarios together to practice new behaviors and responses. Being part of a 12-step family program such as this, or Al-Anon, is imperative in order to help bring health to the ones addicted and to those who care for them—the entire family system.

What is interesting, and at the same time sad, is that I was well aware of and loathed unhealthy "kindness" from having watched it in the dynamics with my mother and brothers in particular. And even though John and I did not replicate those dynamics, we, in different ways, were still enabling. It almost seems genetic, but not quite. These are the learned behaviors in families of alcoholics and addicts of every ilk. Even if there were not genes for addiction, the learned codependent and enabling behaviors would carry families a long way down that road. It did ours.

March 29, 2015
JL,

Mom here. *I was randomly thinking about scorpions and the one time I have seen a scorpion in the house. It must've been the fall of 2013 when you came back from Prescott and were living with Dad and me, trying to find a job and using BT (unbeknownst to us) again. We were trying not to enable you and give you time to get a job etc. One night in the early morning hours you came and woke us up because you had been stung by a scorpion in the shower and didn't know what to do. I remember your disorientation and being scared. We told you to take a Benadryl and probably to elevate your foot and put some ice on it. I was frustrated with you because you were living the "stay up all night and sleep all day" lifestyle while we had to get up and work. It was the struggle we constantly had— living between a rock and a hard place.*

February 5, 2015
JL,

Dad here. *I think about you all of the time. I see your face in my mind when Mom and I are falling asleep and when we are waking up. As a little boy, happy, smiling, bright, hopeful eyes. As an adolescent, with the sparkle still in your eyes. As a young man, happy at times, but sad or discouraged or frustrated at other times. I am so sorry that I did not understand or reach out to you in more intelligent and compassionate ways when you were a young man. How could I be so insensitive and callous to your feelings when I was so fearful as a child myself? Why did I not encourage you more with the truth, with reassurance and confidence as God does, because he*

knows our fears and our frame—that we are like dust? I hope you
are soaring in complete freedom even as we wait to see you again.

Six months after JL's death, John continued to feel responsible: responsible for his perceptions of his poor parenting, for letting JL down, for not being a perfect father—or anywhere near perfect. I have always told him he was a better father than almost any other man I know and a much better father than I was a mother— more self-sacrificing, more encouraging, more fun. But it is what you believe about yourself that ultimately matters. This is where John's personality as a perfectionist is self-defeating. When our friend Heather shared her thoughts at JL's memorial service, her primary topic was how, over the years, she witnessed John love JL *very well,* the way God loves his children: compassionate and gracious, slow to anger, abounding in love.

It's funny that John feels so bad about his parenting in an area where he behaved opposite to the perspective he holds about himself. In many ways, it is this very love in excess that we have consistently argued about over the years. Even though John can agree when counselors encourage him to be less indulgent, in his heart he just can't accept that as good or right: "How can you give too much?" But we are all flawed humans, even in our love, and can do even good things to excess. This is where we differ so much from God. In his wisdom, he loves perfectly. We simply can't love the way He can.

In recovery teaching, we learn to discern the difference between healthy giving and caretaking. Melody Beattie writes that *healthy giving* holds the giver and the receiver in high esteem, gives with no strings attached, and is based on a contract with expectations and conditions clearly understood. It is not done from motives of obligation or guilt, shame, or pity. Caretaking is at the core of codependent behavior. Beattie writes that caretaking "involves caring for others in ways that hamper them in learning to take responsibility for themselves ... We have been doing the *wrong* things for the *right* reasons." We need to ask ourselves if our giving prevents others from facing their true responsibilities. With hindsight, that accuracy of vision that is so precise, we can see how many times, due to our generosity (which was caretaking) we prevented JL from facing his responsibilities as an addict—those real-life consequences that may have caused him to have a wake-up call and have helped him to actually embrace a recovery plan.

Caretaking generally causes *us* to feel victimized and the receiver to feel resentful. For John, he rarely, if ever, felt victimized. His giving sacrificially is a source of joy for him and is part of who he is. Once he makes a sacrifice, it usually doesn't matter to him how the recipient reacts, which is both a virtue and a weakness. It causes John to be unable to see how his generosity could negatively affect the receiver. Even though I don't think JL felt resentful, I think that much of our giving (to both of our kids) cultivated a standard of living higher than they could hope to achieve early on in their own lives—like many of their contemporaries. More importantly, in some areas, it did not help to cultivate confidence in their own ability to take care of themselves. When you are on your own and run into obstacles, it is the very need to dig deep within yourself to find and work through to a solution that builds self-confidence.

For me, I can say that at times I felt used, which is like feeling victimized. I knew that our kids didn't really know that we were sacrificing our time and money to give them so much of both of these limited resources. Having educated them at home in their early years, they were both very self-reliant regarding taking care of their own laundry and rooms and helping around the house. It was in the many extra things we bestowed on them that bordered on indulgent. In this, John and I both were not unlike many of our peers. I was usually a willing partner in those decisions, even though I would later have second thoughts. With JL and his addiction and recovery cycles, I enabled him in ways that John would feel were not healthy, such as making meals, helping with errands, and the biggest one, paperwork and calls. Every time JL relapsed, there were consequences involving the university, doctor and therapy searches, appointments, insurance changes, and I was without hesitation willing for us to cover the associated expenses. It was our son's life, what else would we do? I think this is why, when we were making the decision about Suboxone in January of 2014, I did not want us to pay for it or be involved monitoring it any longer. I was worn out. John and I both were.

What is the solution to break the pattern of the codependent Drama Triangle? *To detach.* We were the perfect models of parents who were unable to detach and let go from trying to control people and/or outcomes, to step back from our son and his journey toward sobriety. Beattie uses the 12-steps for her teaching foundation, which are integral to recovery from codependency as well as substances. They are inextricably intertwined. I have many notes referring to JL in the margins of our copy of *The Language of Letting Go*. The notes were things John and I needed to work on or that I wanted JL to understand. One of the areas I noted related especially to JL and one of his girlfriends. It was hard for us to watch them interact, feeling sorry for both of them for different reasons. They had the typical complex relationship that seem to characterize alcoholic/addicts and codependents. She was a strong, intelligent young woman who was attracted to JL because he was smart and charismatic and confident, and he was a genuinely wonderful guy, except for his addiction.

This is a dynamic I have seen with many young women, and it can also be found in men, though not as often. They become involved with someone who is an addict or alcoholic without realizing it, causing them to not see the telltale signs or to ignore the ones they do notice. It's odd to see young women who come from seemingly solid and stable families, become entwined with alcoholics/addicts and turn into the perfect enablers. I believe it goes back to the dynamics of their family of origin and what type of "system" they were raised in along with the particular role women have historically had in the family. Having come from a dysfunctional family system myself, I had to work to learn how to relate differently to people. After many decades, my antennae are up, recognizing similar interactions happening in others, such as patterns of denial, secrets, and covering up embarrassing behaviors in the spouse.

It seems that many women have an innate need for someone to take care of and nurture, while men can have a need to "fix" things which can reveal itself in the form of enabling as well. When given to someone addicted to drugs or alcohol, someone who is *needy,* they believe they can make him or her a better person and they may set out to do so, but trouble will always follow. There is also the dynamic for many to be kind and "the good one." I refer to it as the "Mother Teresa Syndrome" after hearing my father use it to describe my mother. They genuinely want to do good and be good, but it can lead to self-righteousness, to feeling better about themselves compared to the addicted one they love. They confuse being good and offering kindness with "being better *than,*" which is ultimately an unkind way to view yourself compared to those around you, especially those you supposedly love.

July 12, 2015
JL,
   Mom here. *A year ago, dad and I had no clue that we had only three weeks left with you alive on this earth—three weeks in which you were tumbling down a hill that you would not be able to climb up because there was a bottomless cliff at the end. We knew it was risky having your wisdom teeth out with pain meds afterward, and should have insisted on none, especially since we were paying, but it seemed cruel to do that since your wisdom teeth were impacted and pressing on nerves in your jaw. One more time where our "compassion" was shown in the wrong way at the wrong time.*

Aside from all the normal tendencies of dysfunction we had, I think an important element of *our particular dysfunction* with JL was the fact that we had such a good relationship with him that he didn't feel the need to be a part of a recovery community. We gave him too much support, but not the *particular* kind of support an addict really needed. He needed others who were addicted who knew when he was dishing up bullshit and would call him on it. He needed others who were addicted who knew when he was on the edge and needed someone to stay with him. He needed others who were addicted who could encourage him to take the next step regardless of how hard it seemed because they were living testimony that it was the only safe path to take.

We continued to booby-trap and undermine our most sincere and deep desires for JL by not understanding early on how desperately he needed to be fully immersed in an AA community. We accepted his excuses—they were very rational which, of course, worked on us. Then, as the cycle of relapses grew shorter, and together we tried more serious options like rehab facilities and sober living programs, he had a pattern established of starting out in the 12-step programs and benefitting from them, but gradually, as he left the sober homes, his attendance and involvement quickly subsided.

JL had many good strong relationships with lots of friends who did not struggle with addiction. These are the majority of the sixty or so young people who were at his memorial service. JL loved them and had fun with them and vice versa. This was a beautiful, admirable aspect about our son and about his sister Johanna: they both have the ability to make and maintain great personal relationships with friends. We as a family always focused on having good close friends, but as a friend once told me, surface relationships have their place too, and in our particular situation, they could have helped us know more of what was going on in our son's life by at least knowing who his friends' and their parents were.

As an addicted individual interacting with non-addicts, it was a problem because his clean friends had no clue when he was using until he was in serious relapse. And JL did not really want other *addicted* friends for several reasons. In his desire to be clean, he didn't want to be drawn back into using. But another one was that he did not like viewing himself as "an addict." He knew he was smart, and he knew he should be accomplishing so much more than he was, and being reminded of his failure was hard, very hard on his self-image. But embracing his addiction, his "powerlessness," would have changed his life. Eric Clapton shares in his autobiography that his family now brings him the greatest joy in his life, and if he were not an alcoholic, they would be the number one priority. But he knows he would lose it all if he did not keep his sobriety at the top of the list. If we could have actually accepted JL's powerlessness over his addiction, it would have caused *us* to be more supportive of his being on medication while also holding *him* accountable to be involved with a 12-step group. "Powerlessness" is not the same as "helplessness." We are not helpless and we can learn how to live differently by making better choices and building healthy relationships, without trying to force or control people or things in our life.

July 11, 2015
JL,

 Mom here. *Today was JD's birthday. Another beautiful, brilliant, winsome guy who died too young. JD had so much to offer his family, friends, and society. It is just so sad to think that aside from his own choices, a big part of his demise was the family genetics of addiction, along with the associated behaviors of my dad's favoritism, and denial and enabling behaviors that my mom learned in her childhood. Denial is such a destructive force, not only for the one engaged in it, but for those surrounded by it.*

I think when most of us picture denial, we see an ostrich with its head stuck in the sand, refusing to see what is happening around itself. In reality, ostriches stick their head in the sand because that is where they lay their eggs and they need to regularly turn them. Yet, while they are about their business, they are not able to see what is happening around them with their head buried. The image is still one of the best visual images for denial. Denial is the refusal to accept reality or fact, acting as if a painful event, thought or feeling did not exist. It is said that children frequently engage in denial because they do not have other ways to handle painful events, but as we mature, we are supposed to learn that it is actually self-destructive. Supposedly like "shooting oneself in the foot." Denial rarely causes immediate consequences and sense of pain. It is more like hiding in a closet when a fire starts in your home. You momentarily escape the heat, and while getting out was possible and would save your life, the longer you stay hidden, the more certain is your fate. The reality is that denial works by sheer virtue of the delaying of consequences. Which is why once it has become an integral part of the way a person, family, or organization deals with problems, it is very hard to change.

A codependent person is one
who has let another person's behavior affect him or her
and who is obsessed with controlling that person's behavior.
–Melody Beattie

22

AUTO-PILOT

*The condition upon which God hath given liberty to man
is eternal vigilance; which condition if he break,
servitude is at once the consequence of his crime.*
—John Philpott Curran

The computer system that can fly an airplane after takeoff up until, and sometimes through, landing is called "Autopilot." Airlines generally use this automation for most of the flight, although the pilot and co-pilot must stay at the controls to keep an eye on the computer to make sure everything is running smoothly and remain absolutely aware of everything the autopilot system is doing or is not doing. When it is working correctly, the autopilot will disengage itself in the event of extreme turbulence and the pilot will be alerted to take over control of the plane.

After returning home from a recent flight, I was thinking about how habits are similar to autopilot. Through proper programing (that's repetition for us humans) we can acquire a skill or behavior. When the circumstances call for it, we can rely on an automatic response. When children learn to play catch, they are taught to keep their hands out and their eyes on the ball. If they drop their hands or look away, the ball may hit them in the face. When we learn to drive, we need to know where to keep our feet so we can step on the brakes quickly for an unexpected danger. We must always remain at the controls, alert and present, watching and vigilant for unanticipated problems. With chemical addictions such as taking drugs or drinking, the human brain is on autopilot, but the person who is supposed to be on duty at the controls is gone. The chemicals have hijacked the cockpit.

June 19, 2015
JL,

Mom here. *I have been wondering if you had been trying to let go of your addiction while heroin wouldn't let go of you. I believe it's true and it is so, so heartbreaking to think of you and the thousands of young people whose lives have been ruined by this deadly drug. Opiates, then heroin, derailed your entire life. Freedom has a price—in any setting, in any context, in any situation. Freedom from opiate addiction is so hard and rare. It takes "Eternal Vigilance" —I've been thinking about that famous quote—which is why AA and the 12-steps are so important in conjunction with medication. Community is needed to support the huge effort of eternal, persistent, vigilance. For anyone.*

For our kids' generation, fighting drug addiction that started so young, is like carrying a weight on their backs along with shackles on their feet while dragging a weighted cart behind them through life. They need help to stay vigilant and encouragement all along the way, and if they dismiss the support of the group and decide to try it on their own, enslavement to the drug is at once the consequence. Without continual vigilance, "servitude" to any unhealthy habit is the inevitable result. This is what happened to our son.

I heard a saying: "The chains of habit are too weak to be felt until they are too strong to be broken." And some habits are more deadly than others. As we share what happened to John Leif, at least half of the people we talk with have a relative or friend who is struggling with heroin or opiate addiction. Many of them have the same sad story of being introduced to it while they were young and naïve, and then it became too late to break "the chains of habit." Opioids are a physical habit that the body can't just stop on its own. Regrets come again for not being more aware of what the world was like that we untethered our son into at seventh grade for public middle school. We had been so involved in what we refer to now as the "Christian Ghetto" that when we stepped out of it, we were woefully unprepared and sadly unaware of what the world was like.

As our kids grew up, I spent many, many hours thinking about spirituality and religion. I never wanted them to be inoculated against knowing God intimately and enjoying having relationship with Him, like so many kids who are raised in and around Christianity, or any religion for that matter. Or, mindlessly on "auto-pilot," just going through the motions without their heart and without passion. John and I both intensely dislike *religion:* man's idea of "spirituality" turned into sets of rules and regulations. Having your own faith, freely making the choice for a relationship with God, and not having something imposed from the outside is what we believe ultimately matters and brings spiritual freedom.

Yet, I saw John and a few other friends who had grown up going to church with truly Christian parents, honest souls with integrity and not hypocritical or bigots, who were actually real believers. What then was the road map we could follow through all the ups and downs and twists and turns in life? We knew there was no formula for parenting or spirituality, because formulas offer control, not relationship. But there are basic elements, truths to live by, that we hoped to make appealing to our kids as they became young adults.

As a young teenager growing up in a spiritual void, when I heard about God, the Bible, and Jesus, it immediately struck my heart and mind as true. So perhaps my ease in believing was in direct proportion to the void I grew up in. I knew I needed something beyond myself, even at that young age. I never looked back on the decision I made that day, even though I would continue to question the decisions God makes and how He interacts with us, this world, and wickedness.

I feel that accepting God's role as Father in our lives is first modeled and learned in the context of our families, where there are consequences for actions which can affect relationships negatively, a fact of life. Viewing God as a genie to be called up from his lamp when we want something seems to be a by-product of the "God loves everyone" mantra of the 1970's Me-generation, which morphed into the "Name-it and Claim-it" self-centered Christianity of the 1980's, which is still a snowball that is rolling even now, gaining girth and momentum to this day. And why not? That's the kind of God we all want. I love the song "Laughing With" by Regina Spektor. It expresses the idea of God as someone who is laughed about at parties and presented as someone who grants our wishes like a genie if we just pray the right way. But *"No one laughs at God when the cops knock on their door, and they say we got some bad news sir…"* No, we can testify that you don't laugh then.

For all of our habits, there is a cycle starting with a craving that is triggered by a cue, then the routine we have to satisfy that craving, which leads to the reward we get. This is why AA has been one of the most successful methods of wide-scale habit change. Their techniques help alcoholics use the same cues, and still get a reward, while shifting the routine that are built into the AA system of meetings and companionship which forces members to do something in place of drinking or using every night.

Mitchell's message in *The Big Fix* is that "In the end, I found that, for me, there was no Big Fix." Her life changed incrementally as her behaviors changed and new habits were formed. The beginning of those changes started for her in prison through a forced period of detox and sobriety. If we do anything for a long enough period of time, it becomes a part of who we are, not just what we do. But, when people begin forming or changing habits, they are inevitably surrounded by temptation. So it is *essential* to create an environment that is supportive of the new, healthy routine. This is where a 12-Step group is so important—as other sober addicts all testify. Being part of, and accountable to, a community of like-minded people is what will help with our vigilance in fighting our demons, whatever they may be.

Creating habits of relying on community and the 12-steps is the "autopilot" for people with addictions. When stress or catastrophe happen, the learned response for seeking support and help will get them through. But alcoholism and certain drug addictions are also more than a habit—they are physical *and* psychological addictions. For opiate addiction in particular, there is a very prolonged physical addiction that has links to predisposed genetic traits. Modifying habits is therefore *only part of* the solution and is best used in conjunction with MAT.

Some of JL's friends who are addicted have had experiences that have left them permanently changed and scarred. They are still alive, but they walk with a limp through this life and carry a weight on their shoulders. They have to remain forever vigilant against the physical and psychological pull back into addiction, like a giant magnet constantly drawing them towards itself. That is why their support groups are so important to them. They know they can't do it on their own. But full recovery is possible, even to those who have been close to death, and many have found joy in embracing the freedom of abstinence and living without addictive behaviors and substances in their lives.

One of JL's closest friends miraculously escaped from his kidnappers in Southeast Asia after he was abducted and assaulted and was being prepared to have his body cut up for parts to be sold on the black market. He had relapsed and was drunk when he was drugged and kidnapped but finally sobered up enough to escape. Oddly enough, that horrific experience did not bring about an immediate recovery. Rather, his experience prompted him initially to begin a recovery program, but soon afterwards, he sank into several years of alcoholism before finally becoming sober. Now he knows he can never let down his guard or disconnect from his AA support group as he walks through this life, even as he lives with scars in his soul.

Another one of JL's friends has had to protect his identity because not only did he abuse opiates, but he was involved with dealing Oxy. The people he was involved with are constantly trying to pull him back into the business while he works hard to continue in his recovery. They are also concerned about all that he knows about them. Drug dealing is a cutthroat world. A friend we knew had a child with a young woman while they were both using. Now that he is clean and sober, he is trying to navigate the intricacies of a relationship that could start the cycle all over again, while he wants to be father to his son. For these and countless others in JL's generation who were snared into trying opioids or other drugs while they were so young, the remainder of their lives will be an uphill struggle. This is the sad truth for them. They need all the support and encouragement we as individuals and a society can offer them.

Great effort is required to arrest decay and restore vigor.
One must exercise proper deliberation,
plan carefully before making a move,
and be alert in guarding against relapse following a renaissance.
–Horace

23

SHREDDING YOUR LIFE

When you lose a parent, you lose the past.
When you lose a child, you lose the future.

–Anonymous

While getting ready for our first trip to Australia after John Leif's death, I had to update our passport contact information and house sitter contacts. There was an abrupt halt for a moment, an eraser paused mid-air, before I removed his name from the front of our passports as the emergency contact. Then removed him from our contact list. Deleting our son from the land of the living. A shove back into the real world, our new world, the world where he is no longer here.

In the Spring following JL's death, John and I set aside a Saturday to sort the closet in the guest room where we stored all JL's clothes. Friends were arriving to stay with us for a few days, so it was a deadline that made us move ahead—there had to be some outside impetus to force us to face the task. His clothes were all cleaned and packed in his suitcase and a plastic bin—he had just moved them to Cory's the night before he died. I knew it might be hard to go through his things, but I did not know in what way. I made a pile of things to give away and washed them to freshen them up. The first impression I had was a reminder of how neat JL was, even having moved so many times. He both liked and needed order in his life. One thing I had hoped to find and was longing to read and keep, as I sorted through his things, was the birthday card he said he had sent me last July but which I never got. It wasn't there.

February 16, 2015
JL,

Mom here. *I started sorting all your logo T-shirts to see which ones John wanted to save and then decided to pick some to give to your close friends. I took photos and sent them so they could choose the shirt they wanted that best reminded them of you. As the evening progressed, I felt a heaviness and sadness. This morning, John asked if I was mad at him because I was snapping. I left to do errands and think about it. Of course, I was just upset and mad from these vivid reminders of you. Touching the clothes you wore, remembering some shopping trips buying them with you, memories of seeing you walk into the kitchen wearing various ones at random times, helping you get a stain out before washing. All of these normal trivial actions and interactions that have now become magnified significant memorials of the lives we once shared here on this earth.*

Nine months after JL's sudden death, we were "gradually unearthing" our grief, as we gradually unearthed pieces of his life. We were miners searching for something precious, digging through the layers of years as if through layers of rock. Or perhaps we were more like survivors of an earthquake. Our entire earth, with everything we had built on it, was suddenly shaken to the point of collapse, and we were sifting through the remaining buildings and rubble to see what was left. Deciding what to keep and what to dispose of. "Dispose of" has new and unwelcome meanings now. Clothing, personal belongings, furniture, files, photos, childhood toys, memorabilia.

As I was sorting JL's T-shirts for his friends, I had the idea that instead of just giving them a shirt that would get stuck in a drawer and forgotten, we would make them into pillows so they would be displayed, used, and seen: JL would be remembered and not forgotten. Linda lovingly agreed to take on the project to make them. We wanted to give them by the anniversary of JL's death, with the hope that the recipients would feel the love that went into making them—an expression of the mutual love we all have for John Leif.

April 2, 2015
JL,

   Mom here. *I finally went to the storage shed to sort your camping gear, motorcycle gear, furniture, etc. I hadn't been in there for at least a year—not happy memories of you having to move out of the poorly maintained place where you and your girlfriend lived. Seeing your possessions stacked up and gathering dust and cobwebs like orphans, things that were once purchased from saved up allowances or jobs, part of a full life of activities for a young adult, now being given away or sold for pennies on the dollar. It made the investments of time and money feel futile. Life is feeling futile. Sadness once again. Will we ever get beyond this sadness?*

April 9, 2015
JL,

   Dad here. *Today we had the yard sale at the sheds. We brought some of your things home—a jar of bottle caps, camping gear and clothes, the big chest of motorcycle gear with helmets and boots— lots of memories, lots of Saturdays together, lots of life experiences shared—now lost.*

   One of JL's t-shirts had a logo for Killswitch Engage, a band we were unfamiliar with. We looked up the band and again were impressed with the music he liked. They have significant words, not twaddle. We wish he had felt free to share these things with us and that we could have *heard* his feelings without editorials. We could have seen a bit more into his soul and the struggles he faced. "Always" is one of their songs, it is so powerful. "In these moments of loss and torment, when the weight of this world bears down...I am with you always...from life until death takes me."

May 12, 2015
JL,

   Dad again. *We are going through more of your things and I spent a half-day shredding old papers and notes. It is so odd that much of our lives comes down to boxes of paper to shred. This is very, very hard for me. Shredding your life.*

July 5, 2015
JL,

   Dad here. *Today we are going to go through some more of your things. We found boxes of shot glasses, beer glasses, throwing stars, blow darts etc. We will check with Johanna to see if she wants anything then offer the rest to your friends on August 1st at your Remembrance Gathering. We decided to do this for your friends—and for us—as a way to remember you and celebrate your life. I think I am not looking forward to that weekend—I am kind of dreading it—I think it will be too hard. But I also know God will be with us.*

   With the physical motions of mourning we were going through, having to sort and separate and make decisions on what to shred, get rid of, keep, we had a strong desire to preserve as much of JL as possible. To not lose him by losing memories, by losing the things that connected us to him in this life, the only "shreds" of connection we have left. We didn't want others to forget him either, although we know that no one can truly sustain the intensity of emotion that closely follows a death. There is a fairly normal timeline for grief and grieving, although some people and cultures do have ways in which they attempt to prolong it. I think of the ancient Egyptian tombs and mummies.

   Our culture, our Northern European heritage, tends to want to get it over with as soon as possible, to "look on the bright side of things," to "put a good face on it," to just "move on." We heard all of these comments and more and had to just ignore the advice and understand the source is the discomfort people have with the whole subject of death. My personal feelings are that the less spiritually aware a person is the more the subject of what happens after we die creates discomfort. Understandably so. Being unsure of what lies beyond this world or the concept of Nihilism—where belief itself is rejected—is not a very comforting thought.

We have two memorial areas to JL in our home where some minutia of our mourning are visible. One has the large photo we had at his memorial service, along with the guest register and a photo of the group of all his friends who came that afternoon. The other area has framed photos of him from throughout the years along with lots of memorabilia: some of his childhood toys, his first pair of shoes, a bib his sister made for him; his AA/NA/HA tokens for 30, 60, 90 days; his work name badges from his various jobs; his stainless-steel water bottle, etc. We were cleaning one day and these areas really needed dusting, as it had been at least a year since we moved anything on those shelves. So, we moved everything off and cleaned. As I began putting things back, I wondered, *How long do we leave these photos, the memorabilia, on display?* It had been four years by that point. Just the thought of packing those things away— or worse, disposing of them—filled me with dread, and some anger, and deep sadness. I thought about the hallway photo galleries many of us have, with sepia-tone photos of our grandparents and some great-grandparents. Hallways are a good place to display them, kind of like a history museum for our ancestors. But for our son?

I don't ever want to disassemble these shrines. I don't have to. I don't ever want to move him to the hallway.

Then, there is the CD from the Sheriff sitting in the office. John and I still have not inserted and looked at the photos of JL when he was found in his room—in his boxers and white T-shirt, bent in half and slumped over to the floor, his head swollen from the blood pooling there when he died instantly before he could even enjoy his shoot, his belt cinched around his upper arm and the needle still in his vein, bent at his elbow. We will never look at them. I have a pain in my chest just thinking about it now. Why did we get them? I guess so that we would have everything we could surrounding his death. All the documentation.

Who will we pass all these shards and remnants of his life on to when we die? Johanna wants the things that remind her of her brother as they were growing up. This is one of the saddest aspects about a person when they die, and they do not have any children: no one beyond their parents and siblings and a few friends will be interested in having their possessions or remembrances. This was a hard truth to face when my brother, JD, died as a forty-year-old with no spouse or heirs. Even the things that meant something to me or my family after he died have no future life except a few pieces of information of interest to family historians. I still have a few boxes of his papers and school records that I never got around to sorting after his death and wonder why I still have them, but it somehow feels like throwing things away after a death without sorting through them is invalidating that person's' life and expunging them from our world, from the world.

Every form of addiction is bad,
no matter whether the narcotic be alcohol or morphine or idealism.
—Carl Jung

24

TIME AND ETERNITY

Life is the fire that burns and the sun that gives light.
Life is the wind and the rain and the thunder in the sky.
Life is matter and is earth, what is and what is not,
And what is beyond is in Eternity.

—Seneca

John and I frequently discuss time and eternity and the many and various theories we have heard over the decades, both Christian and non-Christian. We have both said that we could picture ourselves as quantum physicists. It's fascinating to us and, we believe, where science "proves" that there is more than what our eyes, or any physical tool, will ever be able to see. I am curious about quantum physics and there are parts of it that I actually *get*. John, as a scientist, understands theoretical physics much more than I do. Of all the sciences, there is an intuitiveness about physics that appeals to us both, probably linked to whatever makes us both musicians. Albert Einstein said that if he were not a physicist, he would probably have been a musician because he thought "in music" and lived his daydreams in them. The meeting of Art and Science. We continue to read books on the subject, by Stephen Hawking, Carlo Rovelli, and others, even though we don't agree with all their conclusions to the unanswerable questions. For some scientists, like Einstein or Polkinghorne, quantum physics explains that there is another dimension we cannot access, and which represents our ignorance. Blaise Pascal concluded in the 17th century that in our finite thinking, the last step is the recognition that there are an infinite number of things which are beyond reason. This is where we believe science and faith meet. It takes the ability to admit one's ignorance to "keep asking, keep seeking, keep knocking."

One day when JL was a little boy, about 5 years old, he was riding in the car with me and singing along with a CD that was playing: "Mysterious Ways," by Kim Hill. I thought I heard him singing something different than the actual words, so I turned the music down a little and listened. "God wants us to be his slaves" was the line from the chorus he was singing along with—or so he thought. The actual words were "God works in mysterious ways." I put my hand over my mouth as I laughed so hard I could barely control myself.

The more I thought about it, however, I realized that JL's interpretation of what he heard was coming through his filter of what he probably felt about God: an unknown entity, very large, out of sight, and someone who wanted him to do chores, like his mommy and daddy. We talked about what the words were and what they meant, and over the years we had more conversations about the mysteries of the universe, science, and spiritual realities.

Death naturally brings up thoughts and questions about existence beyond this life, this earthly existence. I love how John Milton said it: "Death is the golden key that opens the palace of eternity." For us, after a death so intimate as our son's, one can imagine how often we thought about it, particularly in the subsequent months.

August 25, 2014
JL,

Dad here. *Another Monday. It is just impossible that time is moving forward and you are not here in it with us. We wonder if you—and all our deceased relatives—are able to observe us in time since for you "time" has stopped. It is truly a mystery. We are looking forward to the day we can all be together again and there will be no more wondering—and no more tears.*

We have more work, more email, more things to do around the house, which is really good. When I stop to think, it is not good. So many people with sons, daughters, brothers, sisters, struggling with addiction just as you struggled. So many with heroin, the cancer of addictions. So many young people dying in the prime of their lives. It was your day, your time, and it has been taken away from you. How unfair. How wrong. How sad.

One thought that continues to captivate John and I is the possibility that others can look into our time while they are in eternity, in heaven, like someone looking into a cell under a microscope at us, the human specimens. Or are they frozen in time, like being in a time capsule?

September 17, 2014
JL,

Mom here. *I've been wondering, and wishing I knew the answer for sure, if you and others who are gone can hear us and are conscious of what is happening on earth and in our lives. Can you hear when Dad and I talk to you? If you can, I think you would be crying for us many times as you see and hear our pain. I hope we are not causing you any more pain...*

Dad and I went out to dinner and talked about this. What he brought up was that eternity, by definition, is the absence of time as we know it here on earth. So, if those of you who are dead are also in "no time," even though present with the Lord, you may not experience any consciousness between death and the final resurrection we believe in—it may just be a flash. Hmmm...I don't like that concept. I want to know you hear me and my apologies and love and thoughts towards you.

These feelings of mine express (once again) one more painful aspect surrounding the tragedy of a sudden death: all the unspoken words and unshared gestures of love. They created frustrations that greeted us every morning and kept us awake at night. We wanted to finish the conversations, say our "final words," give our last hugs to our son because we would have known they were our last goodbye.

September 20, 2014
JL,

Dad here. Oh, to be 25 again. But perhaps it is a blessing for mom and me to walk through our separation from you at our age. I don't think I am that far behind you now. "Trang's Second Law" is definitely catching up with me: Time passes more quickly with every passing day, week, month, year, as each moment becomes a smaller fraction of our total existence. Saturdays are still very hard for me. So painful, weird, surrealistic. How difficult it is to imagine what you now know as "reality."

We have no real frame of reference for what lies beyond our consciousness, beyond this physical world. Even as people of faith, we can only try to create a picture from what we have been told by Biblical writers over the millennia. However, the awe-inspiring photographs from outer space that we in this generation are so privileged to see, the other solar systems, wormholes, black holes, create a physical rush in my chest, a sense of connection with eternity. Someone has "put eternity in the heart of man" as Solomon said—I agree with him that someone is God.

January 7, 2015
JL,

Mom here. Dad and I are rereading A Severe Mercy by Sheldon Vanauken, about the third time since we first read it in the late 1970's when it came out. After Sheldon's young wife died, he was talking with C.S. Lewis about awakening after death: "Whatever it would be like, we thought our response to it would be 'Why of course! Of course it's like this. How else could it have possibly been?' We said it would be a sort of coming home." I hope, and feel certain, that you have had the comfort of "coming home" in heaven.

In The Chronicles of Narnia, C.S. Lewis wrote true allegories, vividly portraying what lies beyond this world, which Aslan said was not the real world. You loved the Chronicles and hung on every word when we read them aloud in front of the fire every winter when you and Johanna were young.

One of our favorite quotes from the Chronicles is in *The Lion, The Witch, and The Wardrobe* when the children had been taken into shelter by Mr. and Mrs. Beaver as they are being hunted down by the White Witch's wolves. The Beavers are telling the children about Aslan and trying to explain who he was. When the children heard he was a lion they asked: "Is he safe?" "Oh my no," said Mrs. Beaver. "He's not safe. But he is Good." If, as the foundation of our faith, we did not believe that God is good, but rather that he is contrary and arbitrary, we would have no hope for a future joyous reunion with our son. Then, I would not only fear the process and physical pain of death, I would fear death itself.

January 4, 2015
JL,

Mom here. *When dad and I were going to sleep last night and praying, as we always have, the same thing happened that has happened many times since your death. That is, you and Johanna have always been foremost in our hearts and so also in our asking God to be with you and help you with your present needs. And last night, as before, we forgot and started to pray for you. A reality check, again. But, maybe instead you are praying for us now, asking God to comfort us? Maybe it is not so odd, since we believe that you still exist, as we are told: "To be absent from our bodies is to be present with the Lord."*

For death is no more than a turning of us over from time to eternity.
—William Penn

25

MEMORIES

*I've never tried to block out the memories of the past,
even though some are painful.
I don't understand people who hide from their past.
Everything you live through helps to make you
the person you are now.*

–Sophia Loren

Memories are strange things. How much control do we have over them? What triggers bring up which memories? How do triggers differ with each individual personality? Does grief affect memory? I know it does mine because I continue to experience new associations and memories being formed from what were once familiar items with no particular memory attached before—which now, after my son's battle with addiction and death, have a specific memory related to him.

Like aluminum foil.

I can't recall ever having a memory associated with it. It has been in my life since I was a child, used for baking projects and science projects and art projects. When I saw little wadded up balls of it in our son's closet, I assumed it was from his fireworks projects. Who could imagine that coming across a bit of foil now, laying on the ground in a parking lot or sidewalk or garden, could bring up a pang of anxiety and grief and regret? It does. Ever since June 22, 2005 it does. Ever since finding out that day that there was Black Tar Heroin residue inside each little wad. There does not seem to be any way I can change or delete this new association.

When I was at the dentist recently, there was 70's muzak playing. I think the era of music reflects the age of the clients. I was able to sing along with most of the songs. When *The Chain* by Fleetwood Mac came on I had an instantaneous memory of JL and a deejay mix of it that he had given to us on a CD, along with other songs. I thought of him during the entire song and beyond. I had never given that song a second thought before.

A few weeks after JL's death, we drove to the mountains to spend the weekend with Curt and Heather at their cabin. We needed time away where we could feel free to express, not hide, our feelings as they went up and down without rhyme or reason, and our friends were a safe place. For John, he was also anticipating a connection to our son by returning to a place where there were specific physical connections of past moments in time with JL, reminiscences of life together.

August 30, 2014—End of Week 4
JL,

Dad here. *We are in the White Mountains now and it is beautiful here. I decided to try to get to Patchita Creek from here—to revisit a place of treasured memories. I drove until I found the tracks that led to the very first campsite we went to when you were 10 or 11. It hadn't changed a bit. It was great to find these spots, to remember you and your beautiful smile and laugh. But it also made me really sad. I miss you so much. My heart feels worse than broken—it feels crushed. As I drove back across the Bonita Prairie, I saw some rusted-out trucks and a beautiful sunset—but no you.*

Years ago, I purchased a leather belt with JL; it was the belt he used for the tourniquet on his bicep the morning he died. I can now wear it with my jeans. It took a very long time before I could even look at it, because it was no longer just another belt. It had a new, painful memory attached to it: I would immediately visualize it on his bicep, wondering what he was thinking as he cinched it tightly on that pre-dawn August morning.

September 6, 2014
JL,

    Mom here. *Once again, I woke thinking of you. Today it was an image of you sitting on the side of your bed, with your belt cinched around your bicep and the needle in your hand—all alone—and the unintended events that followed. All I can do is ask: Why did you overdose? Were you so drunk you weren't thinking clearly and then used too much heroin? What happened? Was there something else in the heroin or was it unusually strong? The visual memory with so many unanswerable questions attached.*

As our close friends continued to keep tabs on us, a few asked what they could pray for us. I asked that we might have a better, less melancholy Saturday. They had been so painful since that day with new and awful, embedded memories. Our next Saturday, and most of them since then, have been much better. Yet, we would never ask, and it wouldn't be possible anyway, to have our sorrow removed entirely. I think it is in our grieving that we will best remember JL, and we don't want to avoid or bury our feelings and leave a messy, unhealed wound in our hearts. We know that the sadness will gradually diminish as we give it the time and space it needs.

There are more memories than that Saturday morning's knock at the door or memories connected to a specific tangible item. Some are very difficult because they are not from pleasant experiences. Others, like weights on a hot air balloon, anchor us down because they represent hopes that will never be realized. Still others are bittersweet because they are fond recollections that are now memories detached from a living person.

November 2, 2014
JL,

Mom here. *I found your travel alarm in among some of your things that Dad put into bins the day you died. I decided to put it in our travel bag to use as a reminder of you on the trip. What I wasn't expecting when I opened it up the first night we were away as I pushed the button through the settings, was to find the alarm set for 10:25 a.m. As we found out the morning of your death that is the time your alarms were going off on this clock and your phone. You had no intention of dying. You had every intention of attempting to control your relapse and continue on with life: wake up, go to work, pretend everything was normal. Cory heard your alarms and broke in through the patio door and found you dead. As soon as I saw 10:25 a.m., I remembered all of this—a painful new memory from a black travel alarm clock.*

My mind wants to have the rest of the story, the clock rewound back to when? When would be far enough back in the story of JL's life, of our lives together, for this scenario to have ended differently? I just can't seem to get that image out of my mind, my son, all alone with only the sound of that ticking clock, ticking out the minutes until he would be found at 10:25 a.m., as he sat slumped over, dead.

December 11, 2014
JL,

Mom here. *As we prepared for our two months in Oz I had many memories from previous trips with concerns about you while we were away. I will never have those anxieties again, because you are not here to be concerned about, or to hope for. While Dad and I lose this day as we fly over the Pacific, I feel a sadness leaving all the physical mementos of you behind. Once symbols of our life, now of our grief. I don't want to leave all that we have left of you on this earth.*

February 19, 2015
JL,

 Dad here. *Well this is kind of a weird entry. Last night when mom was reading to me, I looked up at the recessed light bulbs above our heads, without my glasses, and you will never guess what I saw in the light bulb reflection—you! Clear and no question—just like your recent picture with me and mom out front, beard and all. Of course, when I put my glasses on, it was just a lightbulb. But without them again, it was you! Very cool. Another one of God's little mercies and compassions for me. I love you and miss you.*

 I was listening to *Science Friday* on *NPR* and the guest scientist, Dacher Keltner, shared some significant facts about memories: our emotions are powerful drivers *and* effectors of our memories. When we pull out memories from our past, we always pull them out altered. There is no way around it. So, in that sense, there are no pure memories. It's interesting to think about. I wonder if memories we frequently recall are more altered?

 Since we are constantly pulling out memories of JL, will they be altered in some way? If so, that makes me not want to pull them up for review, but of course, I can't control that. Perhaps that is how the process of grief works to help us deal with tragedies. If we had the vivid first-moment feelings exactly as they were over and over again, we could not stay sane, so is it by slowly and gradually and repeatedly drawing memories up, and therefore altering those memories, that we come to not feel the pain as raw as we once did? If so, then it is compassion from God. Yet, there is a part of me that does not want to repeatedly drag up memories because they won't be honest, real, true. It is how many people, from family to politicians, seem to regularly deal with "the facts" and it is what I resist constantly. Changing history. David Carr's memoir, *The Night of the Gun,* is his story gathered from the people around him because, "Memories, even epic ones, are perishable from their very formation, even in people who don't soak their brains in mood-altering chemicals … old memories are prone to replacement by newer ones. The power of a memory can be built through repetition, but it's *the memory* we are recalling when we speak, *not the event.*" I think that writing things down, documenting events, right after they happen helps keep them honest and unadulterated, which is probably why I have journaled all of my adult life. I wonder if some people are less prone to alter memories than others? I think I am incapable of altering them, but I may be wrong. Maybe it is because my memory is visual and I remember the snapshot, the View-Master. Click, click, click. I think it's why I deliberately shut out the "snapshots" like the day the sheriff came to the door. The picture never changes, the frame gets stuck, and so neither does the memory—or the pain.

As the first year progressed, it seemed that as each day, week, month arrived, we were drawn back to what happened at the same time the previous year leading up to, and ending with JL's death. There were memories of "events" that would never have been considered events if there hadn't been *"The Event"* of August 2nd, just a daily occurrence in the course of our lives. I don't think we humans do this under normal circumstance. It seems to be a particular ritual that occurs without planning or forethought after someone dies. Normally we only revisit past events on specific anniversaries, to reminisce in an ethereal, "wasn't that wonderful" sort of way. Death changes that, though. Death changes everything.

April 12, 2015
JL,

Dad again. *We are both in the middle of a deep blue funk. When we re-read our journal notes, we often see that we've been feeling similar things and written them to you, even though we may not have talked about our feelings. There it is—the feelings—every memory, every photo, hearing your voice on a video, seeing your face and your smile in our mind's eye—all of the memories are just memories now.*

Sometimes just being in a certain place will bring a sudden memory, a flash that eventually leads to other remembrances, as if you are sorting through a drawer and find a piece of cherished family jewelry that has a story attached to a person or an event.

July 1, 2015
JL,

Mom here. *One night as we were getting ready to go to bed, as I closed the media room drapes, I looked out of the glass door at the dark back patio and I remembered many times you sitting out there late at night. You had your hoodie up over your head, sometimes having a smoke, doing something on your phone. Were you playing a game? Texting someone? Sometimes you were just staring off into the dark night. I can see you now, but it is just a specter, while the overwhelming anguish remains of how defeated you seemed. And how we never realized how hard you and Johanna always tried to be perfect and please us—and how you both just sort of gave up on it. If we pressured you to be perfect, it was definitely not intentional.*

What causes children to feel the pressure to be good, or excel at something, or everything? Is it always pressure from parents? We had seen that scenario in many families over the decades, children with every kind of anxiety disorder, and it was something that John and I wanted to avoid like the plague. We had been around neurotic or highly competitive friends enough to see that their relationships were strained, and their lives were not enviable.

I have spent a lot of time thinking about the differences in how we were raised and our family dynamics. Neither of us came from homes where "performance" was important. John's family stressed excellence but not to the point of neuroses, just doing your best to honor God, and his parents gave the encouragement and support to help achieve it. I think John worked hard in order to please his parents because he had a good relationship with them and loved them and wanted them to be proud, and John has an inborn desire to please anyway.

My family had very little in way of expectations, with a mindset more in line with "just do your job." I never thought about pleasing my parents, sad to say. I did not have a close emotional tie to them growing up—thankfully, that has changed over the past several decades. I just felt a sense of self-determination and desire to accomplish the things I was interested in. I think that is why four of the five of us were under-achievers. Only my younger brother JD really excelled early on in his career, which we attribute to his being the long awaited first son in the Italian family. So, there was pressure on him, but also all the support too, albeit in some very dysfunctional ways. As my youngest brother, Joseph, said about his years growing up in the shadows of JD, the dysfunction with my parents was like a decades-long train wreck at home. After JD died, Joseph said to me, "They put all their eggs in one basket—and then it broke."

After much self-examination and reviewing conversations with both Johanna and John Leif, we have come to realize that they wanted to please us because they loved us. How amazing. It is the loving relationship we always aimed toward and longed for while raising them.

May 10, 2015 – Mother's Day
JL,

Mom here. *I have gotten several sweet texts and emails from family and friends who are remembering me today and trying to imagine how I feel without you this year. Oddly, I have not had any real feelings—which is probably because I've just shut out thinking about you because it is too painful—so I go numb. I just do not want to be sad all the time, and if I look at your photo and into your eyes, how else can I feel? When asked, I've said, "I'm used to being without our kids on Mother's Day since 2008 when Johanna moved to Oz and many times, sadly, my memories of JL were of him not being emotionally present."*

Being a mother was never something I spent time thinking about as a young woman. Maybe it was the times I grew up in—women's roles were changing, and motherhood was no longer a primary or sole vocation. Maybe it was my personality—I was always living in the future and had a million things I wanted to do in life. Even when I was a teenager, friends said I was 14 going on 40. And I am not a nurturer by nature. But once I had Johanna and allowed myself the time to slow down and experience the total trust from that new little life, I wanted to have more children as soon as possible. It took almost six years before John Leif was born and it was a long, hard road with a second miscarriage along the way. I was ready to have a hysterectomy when I "miraculously" got pregnant. And although having young children was not easy—"Mother-work" is relentless—there are precious memories that surface and bring me joy.

One such memory came to mind when I was looking through photos of JL as a baby. He was probably two years old and I had recently weaned him. I had put my long hair up in a clip and then picked him up into my lap before bedtime. He looked at me, clearly distressed, his chin quivering as he started to tear up and he put his little hand up on my neck. He was looking for my hair and thought it was gone. He had always taken a strand of my hair and twirled it in his fingers while he was nursing. When I realized what was wrong, I removed the clip and showed him it was all still there. Peace returned to his little eyes.

Some memories are realities,
and are better than anything that can ever happen to one again.
–Willa Cather

26

REGRETS

Make the most of your regrets; never smother your sorrow,
but tend and cherish it
till it comes to have a separate and integral interest.
To regret deeply is to live afresh.

–Henry David Thoreau

Regrets seem to be a natural part of loss, at least for John and me. When John's mom died at 58 from a heart attack, I experienced more grief and remorse than he did, and wondered why. For John, although he was very sad, especially for his dad being left alone, he accepted her death. He had an open and honest relationship with his mom, few regrets, and had peace in knowing he will be reunited with her someday. It was different for me. Through some honest soul-searching, I realized my regrets were due to guilt over how I felt about his mom and how I had behaved towards her. Ours had never been an easy relationship for many reasons, not the least of which was the polar-opposite cultures we came from. And there was the normal scrutinizing from his mom toward the young wife of her only son, to make sure I would be up to par. For my part, I was critical of her and did not enjoy our times together. I was young and not very mature.

Regrets surrounding my brothers and sisters deaths related mostly to wishing I had made better use of the time we did have together. With JD's and Susan's drawn out deaths, I regret not taking advantage of opportunities as they were dying to freely express myself to them regardless of family taboos on speaking directly about their pending deaths. When my brother Joseph died by suicide, not only was there the shock and pain of not realizing the desperation he felt, but re-thinking everything that we might have done to prevent him from getting to that point. The loss of our son from a sudden and tragic death brought even more intense regrets—since regrets are matters of the heart, not the head—and he was literally a part of our hearts in every way. Death is cruel in how it focuses our attention on any and every past thought and action where we cannot change a thing. With a sudden death, what is even more excruciating is the feeling that things were left *unfinished,* things we did not do: words of love left unspoken, hugs terminated too quickly, smiles not bestowed often enough. Unfinished business that can never be finished. As Sidney Harris said, "Regret for the things we did can be tempered by time; it is regret for the things we did not do that is inconsolable."

August 22, 2014
JL,

Dad again. *Mom and I are trying to move on, to move forward, but it doesn't seem like there is any forward—the lead shoes. For me, it doesn't seem like there is a point to anything. Still, we eat, sleep, work, swim. Swimming is becoming a problem for me. Every time I swim I have time to think—not really a good thing for me now—I always seem to think about all the things I wish we had done differently.*

The pattern of blaming ourselves for so many things was set from the moment our son died. John and I kept wondering why we did what we did, rethinking every decision we made over the past decade. We have so many regrets, so many things we wish we could go back and change and have been told this is very common for parents of addicted and alcoholic children; there is always a swirling storm around your loved one, and there is no way to ever get it right. John and I are both perfectionists, although in different ways and areas. What we have in common is the self-imposed desire to do the best we can for the people we love, the world, and our God. So, we struggle with our humanity.

September 15, 2014
JL,

Mom here. *Dad continues to beat himself up and said again: "Why couldn't it have been me who died instead of JL?" All the "Why's" we have. A new one pops right up after we deal with the previous one—little prairie dogs popping up in another hole in the yard after you think you've plugged them all up and seen the last of them. We just want to understand, and we never will. I guess at some point we will stop asking and accept what has happened...*

Our desire for perfection caused us bitterness with many Christians and organized church systems and hierarchy. The more we became involved, the more impure, nepotistic, and partial we found them to be. We were in good company, as many spiritual pilgrims throughout the centuries observed similar contradictions. Gandhi marveled how Christians could be so *unlike* their Christ. It took years for us to finally realize that the only thing we were changing as we tried to work within the system was ourselves: we were angry and bitter and hurting ourselves and our children by carrying this in our hearts. Removing ourselves from the situation was the best solution for us; relinquishing the bitterness in our hearts, however, took years.

Regrettably, our open conversation regarding organized Christianity and our unhidden contempt for those tarnishing the simple teachings of Jesus undoubtedly shaped the version of Christianity that Johanna and John Leif knew while they were growing up. How sad that in our passion for truth and justice, we weighed ourselves and our kids down with a burden too great to bear.

During JL's high school years, I was working on a book that was to be titled *Devolution*. It was an expose-type book on the sad state of American Evangelicalism, the prosperity gospel, the personality-driven church, etc. I worked on it for several years, but in the end decided no one would be interested: non-believers could care less and believers who were part of the problem wouldn't want to hear anyway. I put it down and realized I was repeating some of my mother's misguided zeal while JL was struggling. Instead of spending my time getting to know the parents at his schools and being involved where it might have actually benefited our family and possibly others, I was zeroing in on the hypocrisy we had witnessed for decades and which we hated. A worthy cause, but one that was dealing with an intangible and ideated peril when there were tangible and real perils right at our door.

JL's death caused me to ponder how we raised Johanna and JL— why we made the choices we did. Everything we did in our lives, including raising our kids, was with eternity in view. Of course, Fanatics and Zealots can be the most misdirected and misguided people, as both history and my family confirm. I remember so vividly the frustration I had in the late 1960's when my mom became very politically involved with right-wing extremists and was also part of a group fighting against sex education being taught in public high schools. Meanwhile, she never taught my sisters and me a thing about reproduction or sex, and she never saw the contradiction. Were we equally blind?

John Wesley, commenting on fanaticism during the 18th century, uses the word *enthusiasm* in referring to fanatics and zealots:

Enthusiasm is undoubtedly a disorder of the mind: and such disorder as greatly hinders the exercise of reason. Nay, sometimes it wholly sets it aside: it not only dims, but shuts, the eyes of the understanding. It may, therefore, well be accounted a species of madness; of madness, rather than folly. Seeing that a fool is properly one who *draws wrong conclusions from right premises*; whereas a madman *draws right conclusions, but from wrong premises*. And so does an enthusiast. Suppose his premises are true, and his conclusions would necessarily follow. But here lies his mistake: his premises are false. He imagines himself to be what he is not, and therefore setting out wrong, the farther he goes, the more he wanders out of the way.

Were we "so heavenly minded as to be no earthly good," especially with our own children? A. W. Tozer said "The deeply religious man is far more vulnerable than the easy-going fellow who takes his religion lightly. This latter may be deceived but he is not likely to be *self*-deceived." I hope all we have believed and staked our lives on is true, because *if* there is no God or life after death then, as Paul said "We of all people are most pitiful." Even with this sure hope of being with JL again, how I felt, in those first months especially, is that I didn't want him **then** (in the afterlife), I wanted him with us **now** (here in this life), whole and healed. Why not? Was that too much to ask for?

October 21, 2014
JL,

Mom here. *It seems I receive the most comfort from friends of dad and mine who knew you the best, friends like Linda and Heather. They objectively watched you grow up from a nine-year-old in fourth grade and prayed for you all these years—just as I prayed for their children. I shared my tortured thoughts with Linda from the weekend and my asking God for some comfort. Her message to me was: "Be kind to yourself."*

I continue to struggle in the space where perfectionism affects me most, in my inner world, my spiritual life. I am exacting and critical of myself, as I am of others, too. I never thought of my self-criticism as a negative trait until several close friends over the years have all given me the same advice: "Don't be so hard on yourself." Our kids also experienced my exactitude toward *their* character. Looking back with the clarity only hindsight offers, of course I wish I had learned how to walk more gently with them. In so many areas, this specific regret will now surface when I remember John Leif.

One time in the midst of raising our kids, and regretting yet one more mistake, John was talking with our friend Wally about why we just couldn't seem "to get it right" with our parenting. We always seemed to go overboard one way or another. The response was: "We all love imperfectly, John."

November 10, 2014
JL,

Mom here. *Elizabets called and shared that she felt John and I need to settle once and for all that there was not just one cause for your death, not one thing that determined your life's course, but many things. Most of which had nothing to do with dad and me, or even you. It wasn't just our decision to not send you to the private high school and the bitterness we had, or just you being indulged. Rather, it was a combination of who you became friends with at such an impressionable age, our family genetics that would have snared you sooner or later into addiction, where we lived in the drug corridor from Mexico and the center of the BT market with easy access, and the specific drug you were addicted to with impossible odds against beating it. We need to remember that bad things do happen to good people on this earth, this fallen earth.*

As far back as Job, two millennia B.C., one of the ever-present questions of thinking people has been: Why do bad things happen to good people? I remember hearing an interview with Rabbi Harold Kushner, sometime in the 1980's after his book *When Bad Things Happen to Good People* was released. His son had died at 14 yrs. old of a rare genetic disease. Naturally, his thesis tops the list for grieving parents. He was seeking to bring comfort to others who are grieving and believes that God is with us in our suffering, but that He is *unable to* step in and prevent tragedies. I agree wholeheartedly with his first premise. I absolutely disagree with his second—the book of Job, and the Bible in its entirety, supports my beliefs. That is, there is an evil, intelligent super-human being named Satan who hates mankind, and especially those who follow God. He is intent on destroying them and their faith. I understand that this sounds spooky, but as I tell my friends: if we believe in the God of the Bible, then we must believe in the Satan of the Bible too. That God can step in and avert disasters on this fallen earth is well-known and accepted by the majority of people. That He chooses not to do so is what causes us to falter, to question, and for many, to lose faith.

November 14, 2014
JL,

Dad here. *I am sitting at my computer and staring at your beautiful face and clear, bright eyes, and crying. I am so sorry that I was not the dad that you needed. I think we were friends, but you needed so much more. You needed a wise father who recognized your incredible strengths and showed compassion for your weaknesses, not the contempt that I felt for my own and projected on to you. There were times you needed mercy and I gave judgment. I hope that you now know and feel God's mercy triumphing over my judgment. I love you more than I can express in words. I miss you and carry a profound, deep sadness through each day.*

"Accept life, and you must accept regret." Henri-Frédéric Amiel, philosopher and author, said this in the nineteenth-century as he struggled with his own slowly encroaching death. There's that word again, *accept*. Have regrets but accept them because they are part of being imperfect and human. We were struggling with having tried so hard to make perfect decisions after much thought and input, and those decisions turning out to not only be imperfect, but terribly wrong. In the spring, more than six months after JL's death, I realized John and I were still unable to get past all the regrets we had. What would change this dynamic that kept us awake at nights and that tortured our still moments in the days?

When our kids were young, we built lots of puzzles together. Their Nonna especially loved building puzzles with them. JL also really liked those 3D puzzles where you try to figure out how to get rings off of a closed loop of rope or unlink chains that have no apparent opening. And all of us loved the art of Dutch mathematician and artist M. C. Escher: the buildings that opened into themselves, the school of fish that become a flock of birds, the circuitous stairways that went up and down throughout multiple buildings without an end point. Yes, stairways that never get you where you want to go, but keep you endlessly retracing your steps. They are no longer interesting art to wonder at. They now mirror how John and I have felt many times since August 2nd—regrets—retracing the steps of our entire lives.

Regrets were not new to either of us regardless of the varying reasons for them. On my maternal grandfather's ninetieth birthday two decades ago, I was curious and asked him about his life and if he could do any of it over again, would he do it differently? He responded without hesitation: No. He had no regrets. I was surprised as I thought about some of his legacy. No regrets? In my continuing quest to understand how to get past regrets, I asked some of my mentors to share their thoughts with me about how they handle them. Two women, whom I admire and look up to spiritually, said the same thing: they don't have regrets because they are pointless. You can't change the past. It is a waste of time and energy. And it is a matter of trusting God and his plan. At the end of these conversations, I felt like a spiritual pygmy, and moved forward with even more regrets.

Now that John and I were facing regrets every day, I asked the same question of two of my close friends. The first friend totally empathized because she deals with regrets herself, albeit in different ways than we do, but she feels it is a normal part of life and being human, and imperfect, while also knowing there is a Perfect whom we strive to emulate. My other friend is a therapist, intimately acquainted with our struggle while also insightful into the larger picture. She said she doesn't dwell in regret because it is a dead end. We have to accept that we all suffer from others, and our own, mistakes—and our kids suffer from our mistakes.

She said it all comes down to control: It is a terrifying feeling to not have control and not be able to go back and change the outcome. Being angry at ourselves points to a belief that we *think* we can control more than we can or could have. It always feels better to *think we could have* done things differently. In recovery, JL was working on the realization that he had no control over his addiction. We, as his parents, were working on realizing that we had no control over his addiction and recovery. Regrets are our mind's way of getting some control in an out-of-control situation. If we would have done this, then that would have happened. So, why haven't we been angry at God for JL's death? She said when we are stuck, we avoid the thought: What kind of God allows these horrible deaths? As believers, rather than accuse God, we are angry and blame ourselves and regret decisions as if *we* were in control.

I believe there is another dimension to regrets. After my initial foray years ago into understanding regrets, I remember reading where God has regrets too, and sorrow when he has to allow hurtful things to happen, because he will not violate human choices. I have always felt that if God has an emotion, then we can follow his example. The emotion itself cannot be wrong, but of course, the degree to which we allow it to affect us and our actions can be. As I continued reading, I saw God changed his mind and his future plans in response to urgent prayers, even while it could not change the past. Agathon echoes this truth: "Even God cannot change the past."

I think that it is also just how some of us are wired. John and I are self-doubters, apologizers, re-thinkers, and we believe having regrets does not *necessarily* mean we are struggling with control issues. It seems to be a struggle with the areas of our responsibility where we, not God, made choices to the best of our abilities at the time. They are common areas where we as humans make choices and mistakes and learn from them. Our goal is to not allow our regrets to cripple our present life while helping inform our future decisions. Unfortunately, we do not have the chance to "do better" with our son. Some mistakes are fatal, and what we can learn is only useful in future decisions, other relationships, or for others' lives.

June 21, 2015—Father's Day
JL,

Dad here. *Another weekend, another Sunday. This time it is Father's Day—I am very happy I am busy. When I think about Father's Day and I think about you, the overwhelming feeling is failure: Not trying harder to understand the world from your perspective—your normal childhood fears. Not providing more guidance to you as a young boy, giving you clearer direction you could use. Failing to pass the baton. Failing you.*

I was working under the philosophy that by spending time with you, lots of time, and by doing fun and interesting things, the values Mom and I had would be best "caught not taught." But I needed to be more intentional with my words, too. Not sharing truthful wisdom with you as a young man, giving you words of life, more consistently. Not responding more appropriately and aggressively when you began using as a young man. Believing when I should have questioned you. Doubting when I should have believed you—like when you were only four or five and Mom had gone out one evening. I was getting your bath ready and you said you already had one. I didn't believe you because I thought you were trying to get out of taking a bath in order to have more play time. Because I didn't believe you, I forced you to lie by badgering you until you said that Mom hadn't already given you a bath—when in reality, you had already taken your bath. This is such a painful memory for me—projecting my own capability for deceit onto an innocent child—my child. Mom says I place way too much importance on it, but it still haunts me. So basically, this Father's Day was about you, missing you, loving you and being sad—deeply, profoundly sad.

Do your best to make peace with as many regrets as possible.
Forgive yourself.
Isn't it true that if you could have made better choices,
you would have?
You did the best you could at that time of your life.
—Elisabeth Kübler-Ross, On Grief and Grieving

27

GRIEF PART 3: ACCEPTING THE MYSTERY

But now, oh Lord, these things are past and time has healed my wound. Tell me why weeping should be so sweet to the unhappy. Have you dismissed our miseries from your concern? Yet unless we wept in your ears there would be no hope for us remaining. How does it happen that such sweet fruit is plucked from the bitterness of life, from groans, tears, sighs, and lamentation? Is it the hope that you will hear us that sweetens it?

–Augustine, *Confessions Book IV,* "My Friend Died"

For the previous several years, I had increasing premonitions that JL would not survive his heroin addiction. Christmas of 2013 brought foreboding of his death as a real possibility. After his scare that same New Year's Eve with his friend's overdose death and JL's radial nerve palsy, then our finding he was an IV drug user, I had a very real sense of evil stalking him like a tiger, waiting patiently until its prey was in its most vulnerable position before it pounced, tearing apart his life.

Looking back now, it seems we were all given seven months' grace, extended life for JL. What did we do with it? What did he do with it? How do we recognize Grace when she shows up? I have found that she rarely comes with a loud voice or trumpets blaring to announce her arrival. U2 did a beautiful job describing Grace in their song of the same name: "*Grace, she takes the blame, She covers the shame, Removes the stain, It could be her name.*" I think it was actually too late in JL's life as an opiate addict for anything to change, except with continual medical intervention. And it was too late in our tenure as parents of a young addict to really alter our interactions with him *significantly* enough to climb out of our skins and look objectively from a broader perspective. We were fatigued emotionally, and truthfully, our particular mode of dysfunction with JL wasn't changing quickly enough for us to understand what to do or not do differently. We are grateful for those months with our real son back, wishing it could have lasted.

What is hard about the presentiments I have frequently had in my life is I never know if or when they will occur. My brother, JD, was rushed to the hospital the night before Thanksgiving 2000, and we went to see him. We had no idea what was wrong with him other than he had pneumonia. We had no idea that my parents had been finding him passed out at his home in the middle of the day many times in the months leading up to this emergency. They kept it secret as they made excuses and kept his business going. Thanksgiving morning while I was praying at home for him, I had a very clear, complete sentence "appear" in my heart and mind: "*JD will not leave the hospital.*" I was taken aback, then overcome with grief. I told John so there was someone who could validate what I said and when. We carried this *knowledge* with us for the next two months while we also prayed for him to get well and visited daily. He had a tracheotomy inserted Thanksgiving Day because his lungs were failing, and was put into a medically induced coma because of his inability to tolerate it. It was only after several weeks and many tests that we were told what the doctors suspected: JD had HIV/AIDS to such a degree that they had never seen a person still alive with the Western Blot count he had. The diagnosis for AIDS is a count below 800, a severe case at 200. JD's count was 8. He died in the ICU January 2001. Afterwards, we put some pieces of the puzzle together, although we could never be certain we had the whole story due to the secrets. He may have been self-medicating with opiates in the preceding months due to physical pain from his illness or emotional pain—and addiction may have been the source of his AIDS. We will never know for sure.

When my sister Susan called in October 2007 to say that she had found lumps under her armpit and was going to her doctor for exam and tests, the same thing happened: When I was praying for her the next morning, I "heard" that *Susan will die from this.* I didn't know what "this" was. As the subsequent weeks unfolded, she found out that she had stage 4 cancer, two different but very aggressive types, one in each breast, and that more than twenty lymph nodes were already involved. This led to radiation, chemo, and surgeries over the course of the next several months. Then a short reprieve after the doctors hoped they had gotten it all, until early 2009 when debilitating headaches began and they found the cancer had metastasized to her brain. They tried to remove it surgically, but the majority was deep in her brain.

In May she was put in hospice as she became unable to eat and speak. That is when we flew in to Seattle from Australia. Then in June I moved in to take care of her during her last five weeks. I went with the hopes of nursing her back to health, as she had rallied and been put back on home health. But the rally was short-lived. She lingered a long time, unable to get out of bed or eat or speak, because she was in such good overall health and she had no major organs that were failing. Regardless of all the prayers from the myriad friends who believed she would be miraculously healed, deep inside I carried the *knowledge* that these were her last days. She died July 2009.

I had no idea the few weeks before JL's death that I would soon be experiencing what I had felt would one day come to pass, (possibility had not moved to probability in my mind). Desperate hope was still present. I think it was a blessing, a protection really. Otherwise, if I knew exactly how and when he would die, I would have been so full of anxiety, and attempts to change the future, I would have been driven mad.

July 2014, John planned a birthday party and dinner for me with our friends. He outdid himself and our friends made it a memorable evening in every way. It was two weeks before JL took his last breath on this earth. As I thought back on this, I find it startling that life was just going on as usual for us, while our son was spiraling down to a place of no return. I guess most deaths occur in these types of spaces in our lives, during the routine and daily living of life, particularly unexpected or accidental deaths. Could we have at least gathered hints about our son's true condition if we had not been preoccupied with our life?

Pondering JL's death and the weeks leading up to it, and having the presentiments I had, leads me into forays of being angry with myself for not acting differently when we thought he was abusing Percocet, not realizing he had moved to heroin after that, not being more empathetic with him and understanding the shame and fear he felt as he relapsed. Not *lovingly* asking him if he wanted help instead of confronting him about his relapse with alcohol in June. So many things we could have done differently if we had only understood more. If we had truly realized we had so little time left together.

What I was experiencing is referred to as "Anticipatory Grief." It is the beginning of the end in our minds and places us in two worlds: the real and present one we live in and the world where a loved one might, or will, die. Those with a long, drawn out terminal illness live in this nether-world along with their loved ones. Opiate addiction is very much a terminal illness unless there is, and even at times with, the help of medication. The anticipation can help brace us for a death, but it can also be as intense as the death itself. The uncertainty causes this grief to be separate from the grief we will feel after the loss.

After the first four stages of loss and grief—denial, anger, bargaining, depression—comes acceptance. Acceptance is not an end point but a process that we each, in our own time, use to reintegrate the pieces of our life without our loved one's presence. Kübler-Ross tells us that acceptance *does not mean* we are okay with what has happened but rather it is about *accepting the reality* of what has happened, that our loved one is gone, and that we have a new reality which is permanent. We slowly transfer our energy from our loss and re-invest it in our life. For those of us who experience complicated grief, the readjustment to life without a child is understandably harder because it increases the sense of unfairness. Accepting that it was our son's time to die while we, and others, live on will never seem fair. But we know we cannot change it and that it is now our time to heal. The healing process can actually bring us closer to our son as we begin a new relationship with him, plodding ahead in more uncharted territory.

Acceptance cannot be rushed, and it cannot come before grief is fully experienced and processed. Regardless of the non-linear moving in and out of the first four stages of grief, acceptance necessarily comes afterwards. In reflecting on my journal entries from the first weeks and months after JL's death, it seems I felt some pressure to accept, to move on. Was it self-imposed from my own impatience, trying to escape the pain, or was it pressure (either real or imagined) from the world around me?

October 13, 2014
JL,

Mom here. Although I cannot really know if my thoughts and feelings about you, and what you were thinking, in the weeks before your death are true, I do feel it was a mercy that you died suddenly—for Dad and me, too. I know you had lots of fears, like a lot of people in our family. There are healthy fears and destructive fears: Healthy fears help us see the red flags clearly and avoid danger. Many people in my family seem to be fearful, but of many things that don't really matter in the end—fear that is destructive and keeps them paralyzed from moving forward, or worse, retreating.

Anyway, it has been hard for me to accept—I don't want to accept it—even though I feel it is true: your sudden death was a mercy for you because the path you continued to get sidetracked onto would ultimately lead to your separation from all who loved you. It was a mercy for us because any more ups and down, closer and closer together, would have drained us emotionally and physically. I don't want this to be true, and I will continue to feel protective of how others remember you, because I just wish we had the real, alive, walking, talking, John Leif back. I want to live in my wishes—I don't want to accept that you are gone—it feels traitorous.

In the fall, John and I met with JL's addiction doctor and program director. What were we after? More pieces of the puzzle to work with and hopefully some answers, or at least some understanding. This was one additional step we needed to go through to bring some order to the disorder that was plaguing our minds, unable to incorporate the finality of his death into our lives. We discussed the medical answers about what ended JL's life but there could be no answer to the constantly nagging "Why?"

October 28, 2014
JL,

Mom here. *I remembered the story about Jesus weeping at the death of his friend Lazarus, and some of the people looking on asked why he didn't do something to prevent it if he loved him so much? In a few lines that sums up my feelings today: Why wasn't your death prevented? This is where trust comes in and I'm lacking it today—again.*

What I failed to remember as I thought about this story, was Jesus' response: "Did I not tell you that if you believed you would see the glory of God?" I was having a hard time with trust in God's ultimate goodness and that we will see his greatness somehow displayed—understandably so, less than three months after our son's death. I was focused on the past. Faith focuses on the future, where anything is possible. It was hard to see beyond the pain of the moment, with each and every emotion, repeated or new, as they rose up to the surface and we were forced to face them. I was in suspended animation, living every minute on hold, waiting for the next tragedy to pop up, the next assault on our lives, wondering where it might come from, and ultimately, how, or if, we would survive when it came. I was overwhelmed with pain, afraid of it, unsure of how much more I could bear.

November 20, 2014
JL,

Mom here. *I am still amazed at the direct answers that come when I am puzzling over something and searching for answers. I woke up early this morning and read a parable about a blind man and various opinions as to why he was born that way: he was innately bad, his parents were bad people, and so on. Jesus responds to all those opinions: "You are asking the wrong question. You are looking for someone to blame. There's no such cause and effect here. Look instead for what God can do." We need to look for the good that can come out of your death, even though I can't see any now—we need new eyes.*

Surrendering is the act of trust, faith, confidence, that we will, eventually, be enabled to fully accept what we have had to experience. Our son's death was a tragic reality, one we had to find a way to accept so that we could move forward and realize growth in our lives. On reflection, what made acceptance more difficult for us, is the lack of ease in first accepting our limitations and what we did not do better, which is one of the struggles of perfectionism. Letting go of even thinking all of our best planning and effort would not be fraught with *common* human failures. "The best laid plans of mice and men *often* go awry."

January 12, 2015
JL,

Mom here. *I was reading in Gold by Moonlight, in the chapter called "Snow." Amy writes that at times we have hopes for something and then snow falls and covers everything, and we are discouraged.*

The only solution is to accept: "Accept the unexplained in our lives… Time as it passes makes a clear glass. We look through it and see things less as they appear while in the midst of them and more as God sees them from Eternity, timeless." There's the rub: accepting the unexplained. We are not there yet.

Numbness, like how your face feels after novocaine at the dentist, existed in my heart and soul frequently in the 6 months after JL's death. It's like submission: Lying prostrate on my face before an enemy with his boot on my back, in utter subjection, and then being led away in chains. I have found myself at this place many times in my life when facing an extremely difficult or confusing situation. I submit, but acceptance along with true peace are both elusive, and seem to be connected. I wonder if and when I will be able to *fully* accept what has happened to my son?

January 26, 2015
JL,

Mom here. *Home from two months in Oz Your absence is present here. We are both sad—our entire beings heavily weighed down. I read this quote: "When things seem all wrong, trust God anyway." Things seem all wrong with you being gone. I thought about "whistling in the dark"—pretending you are not afraid when things go wrong and doing something physical to help bolster courage. But I think that "singing in the dark" is a step further than pretending—it is trust. It's why songs are so much a part of spiritual practices and have meant so much to us. There was a crucial moment in The Lord of The Rings trilogy where Sam has to keep moving forward in The Quest, even while he thought Frodo was dead. In the midst of his desperation and depression, he summoned up his courage and broke into song— attesting to his wavering but deep-rooted faith—and he was enabled to move forward and carry on. I need a song to sing.*

I was reading about Job's trials—the guy referred to in the old saying "like the patience of Job." The real point of the story wasn't his patience; it is that he had to get past trying to make sense of the loss of all he had to the place of *accepting* his finite mind could never understand God's dealings. He had to trust until he got to the other side of them without an answer to the "Why?" This is where I get stuck so many times in my life, trying to make sense of the insensible. The path of JL's life and his death doesn't make sense, and I realized I would never get to acceptance trying to make sense of it. It was a question of trust, something I didn't have at the time, but it wasn't entirely a lack of trust. The truth is, I was disappointed with God...

He could have done something to avert this tragedy, but he didn't. Regardless of our continual prayers for our son and our cries for help, we still got "No" as our answer. Most Christians—or adherents to other faiths—would find it bordering on blasphemy to admit being disappointed with our almighty God. I think if we are honest with ourselves, the word "No" is unwelcome to most of us, whether to a toddler who wants his sister's toy, a teenager who wants an extended curfew, or an applicant who hopes to land a new job. "No" is not what we want to hear in response to our requests, especially when we're hoping for at least a "Maybe," or even better, a "Yes." But, when something sudden and horrible has happened, if you lose your spouse suddenly to a heart attack, or a sibling in a car accident, or your son dies of a heroin overdose, facing that sort of trauma it is like hearing "NO!" shouted at your face from 3 inches away, a STOP sign that suddenly appears out of nowhere. Regardless of how and when the "No" appears, we have a choice to make: to accept and move forward, or to resist and reject. The first choice brings inner quietness and peace; the second perpetuates the anger and the agony. This is the bottom line for all of us in the matter of acceptance. If we remember our childhood experiences, I feel pretty certain that most of us will confirm that when we accepted the "No" from our parents—if we had good, trustworthy, non-abusive parents—and willingly obeyed, there followed peacefulness and abatement of anger and resentment.

Since becoming a mother, I have more easily envisioned myself in God's place, with my child asking me why I won't allow her to do something, asking why I won't say "Yes" to her request, and the subsequent petulance or tantrum when I hold fast to my answer. I may not be able to help her understand my denying her request, or why I won't change my mind, but there is one thing I would never do: I would never reject her or withdraw my love from her because she was upset and disappointed. *Never.* As an earthly parent, I know how much less capable of perfect love I am than our heavenly parent. So, I express my disappointment to Him without fear, all the while knowing that ultimately it is me who is going to have to adjust and accept, probably without ever understanding. And really, who am I to be questioning someone else's life-path, even a child of mine, as if I am in control?

April 25, 2015
JL,

Mom here. *As we think about vacation plans for the summer, our minds are jumping ahead to August 2nd: What should we plan for the anniversary of your death? How can we know how we will feel about something we have never had to even think about before? Will it be similar to your birthday and not feel very emotional? I don't think so, since even thinking about August 2nd now gives me dread inside, remembering that morning, remembering everything that followed. I wonder how dad and I ever got through those days and weeks. And how about your friends? What are they feeling now? What do they need?*

John was thinking of visiting *altars*, significant places we could revisit to honor the memory of JL, places like Garage-Mahal, Joshua House, In Balance, Prescott. I did *not* want to do that. I felt anxiety just thinking about them, and still do, but perhaps time will cause the dread to fade and I'll eventually be able to face those places. I just wasn't ready then.

May 14, 2015
JL,

Mom here. *We discussed what we want to do to remember you on August 2nd with Linda. She said we should not be alone—it is a significant mile-post—it needs to be commemorated. If we do an open house, we shouldn't feel we have to invite everyone, especially difficult or needy people. We'd like to invite your friends, but now that we've read about how young people are affected by a death, we may not. It's not like when you are older and usually have experienced more loss. But what do they need? Maybe your friends need something to help with closure. I will write a few of them and ask.*

I have read that more courage is required for a walk downhill into shadows than for a plunge into darkness: you know it will be hard when you start off down a hill as you make the choice and have to set your determination to do it, but being plunged suddenly into darkness is nothing you can plan for, and so your survival instincts take over and you do somehow manage to handle it. JL's sudden death was a plunge into darkness, landing us deep in a tangled, old wood forest. As the months passed, the path forward was a continual walk downhill into shadows of grief, where we made the choice to not go back, but go forward, down into a ravine. The bottom was probably reached by early summer and John and I were likely meandering slowly up a switchback trail out of the ravine but didn't yet realize that we had actually started the ascent.

May 20, 2015
JL,

Mom here. *Since your death, I rarely feel fear any longer. It is as if the worst thing that could happen and every parent's deepest dread has already happened. Of course, losing Johanna would be just as catastrophic—but I don't go there. How did we survive? I know the prayers, compassion, and acts of love of our many, many loving* *friends played a big role. Since God carried me, carried us, through this and we did survive, what could happen that we cannot handle with Him?*

Yes, I think the worst thing that could ever happen to a mother has happened, so everything, big and little, pales in comparison. Fear of what could happen to my kids has always been part of my mothering world. Most of the fears were founded in reality: they could get seriously sick or have an accident and have to go to the hospital, which happened to both our kids, and was traumatic for me as a young mom. They could be seriously injured in an accident while active in any number of the high-risk sports they were involved in: horseback riding, dirt biking, surfing, rock climbing, shooting. They could be in a car accident as young drivers, driving with other young drivers, or they could become victims of some random act of violence. The list was endless.

Things in the past that would have caused me anxiety, typically about an imminent event or something with an uncertain outcome, have become non-issues. At times I wonder if is it fatalism: why bother investing emotions into anything since so much goes wrong on this planet? Or is it acquiescence: most things that happen are out of my control anyway, right? At other times, is it a form of acceptance? Acceptance of tragedy in life, in my life?

Through everything that happens now, I do see the world through different eyes; somehow, I am now seeing through lenses that focus on things beyond what is first apparent or on the surface. Right after JL's death, John and I made it through each day with a glaze over our eyes, a film of some sort, like temporary cataracts. A blessing, especially for someone like me, historically viewing life through a microscope and wanting to know the true nature and source of all I see. I seem unable to view daily events of life through a kaleidoscope, multiplying even the most common item so that it takes on beautiful form. John and I tenuously went through the motions of living each day without really seeing further than the next step in front of us. We were just existing. I think this might be how the struggling millions, in war zones and refugee camps, in prisons and in poverty, look on their world. How do they go on? What essential element causes humans to forge ahead through life-crushing experiences? To take the next step forward? Ultimately, for me, for John, it is hope, based in faith. Faith that there is more to this world than what meets our eyes. That when a life ends here, this is not the end of the story.

June 25, 2015
JL,

Mom here. *While I was driving to a client's house this week, I was thinking about you, as usual and I see that my feelings have changed over the past 10 months, in subtle ways, not consciously or with effort. I have said how I felt so happy and content in the past two years, mainly since our move from our historic home, Casa Mexicana, and all its projects, and since I started doing landscape design. But I also feel more at peace than I ever have—and I realized where you come into that. I am no longer worrying about you— concerned for your life—wondering how it will go—anxious for your life and your future. There are no more conscious or subconscious thoughts in my daylight or nighttime hours where I am trying to figure out what, if anything, could help you overcome this disease, help you find a once-and-for-all solution so that you, and we, could begin to move into the future without constantly looking over our shoulders at the beast that was stalking us. All that is gone now— gone with you. Your death closed the door on any and all options.*

This is what the recovery community calls "letting go." It is too bad that what it took for me to learn it completely was a forced and final letting go. I had no control over the circumstances of JL's death and what John and I were gradually learning was that we had no control over changing his life. We understood it in theory, but we had a hard time getting that knowledge to drop from our heads into our hearts and actions, where our intense but misguided love for our son outweighed everything we heard. It was a gradual process that had started a decade ago. We wanted so much better for our son, but we couldn't make it happen for him, and there were few safety nets in place to help him or other opiate addicts achieve long-lasting sobriety.

It dawned on me one day, after our son's death, when we knew we would have to finally get to the point of acceptance, that we were facing a similar challenge as those who are learning acceptance in recovery—addicts and their codependents. The goal of letting go and turning over control, accepting our place in the scheme of things, in the Big Picture, in the Universe, in order to have sobriety, to have peace, is the same for us in the grief process. How ironic that we were again facing a challenge that we and our son had been facing in the years before his death.

June 26, 2015
JL,

Mom here. *I think I am finally coming to accept that you are at peace from the war you fought so hard and for so long. I am accepting that it was a mercy to us too, even though I hate saying that because it feels like we are saying that we are glad you are dead, but it is not that—never that. Rather, it is accepting we could never feel at ease as long as your struggles were going on, they would have been lifelong, because eternal vigilance is not only the price of freedom, it is the price of true peace, too.*

July 4, 2015
JL,

Dad here. *Oh boy, another Saturday, another week, another month—eleven months now—still hard to believe—still all of the same feelings.*

Less intense, but still there.

We had several sweet emails from friends after the July 2nd Facebook post.

God continues to encourage us—still.

I love you—still.

July 9, 2015

JL,

Mom here. *I am taking private lessons to learn how to take clips from your memorial service video to post on Facebook for the one-year remembrance of your death. While editing one section, the young woman teaching me said she was so impressed with what Kyle said about you and his love for you. A sweet and unexpected reminder: You had good friends and good relationships—and that is something dad and I worked hard to have and to model and teach you and Johanna.*

Kyle was one of JL's closest friends and fellow companion in the struggle for sobriety. He shared at the memorial service that when he heard that JL had died, although he was devastated by the news, he had a feeling of indescribable comfort, peace, and serenity that continued on with him and he felt it was "God's way of telling me that JL was alright and in good hands." He ended his sharing by saying "JL, I love you and I'll see you on the other side."

It is always interesting to me to observe the different responses people have to disasters and pain. Why are some of us focused on what lies beyond this world and the physical universe we live in while others seem to not sense, or perhaps ignore, the temporal nature of this world? There is a great gulf fixed between our reality and whatever the reality is for those who have died and "gone on before us," which I think *everyone* knows deep within themselves. Charles Dickens wove this thought in *A Tale of Two Cities* when Charles said to Lucie: "We shall meet again, where the weary are at rest."

July 13, 2015
JL,

Mom here. *The approaching anniversary of your death is bringing up all the memories from last July. Dad and I did not expect this but on reflection, it is logical. All the things we wish had happened differently, that we had known and done differently. Your dad is really having a hard time, blaming himself again. I can say that even with the hard, sad memories, I feel very different than 6 to 10 months ago, more accepting now of what is, and of mercy. We are blessed.*

"Blessed are those who mourn, for they *will be* comforted." Will be. I think the Beatitudes hold a promise for both the present, here on earth, and for the future, in eternity. We mourned and we were comforted, receiving so much love, care, and support from friends and family here on this earth, where we are and where our son is not. If we believe the promise, we *will be* comforted when we see JL and all our loved ones face-to-face someday.

As we begin to accept reality, ultimately, we are accepting our mortal-ness, our human-ness, our limitations, knowing that we will always make mistakes and that some of those mistakes lead to unforeseen disasters. This is where forgiveness and grace come in, towards ourselves and others. It is a process, and it takes time, as our journal entries clearly record. Time to become willing to even *want* to accept our son's death. Accepting it even though we don't like it is the first step. Accepting it fully as best for some unknowable reason lies in the spiritual sphere, where we can each choose to go or not. What I do know is that when I fully accept, I move myself from the ever-elusive realm of wishful thinking into the domain of reality of life here on earth. What propelled us forward and enabled us to fully accept the tragedy of our son's death is our hope in a future understanding, a joyful reunion in eternity together, anchored in our faith and trust in God and his promises.

As the anniversary of JL's death drew close, John worked on the patio, sorting, cleaning, listing, taking photos of JL's dirt bike gear. It was time to sell or give it. This process was hard for him, having so many memories of enjoying times with JL riding the motorcycles. As I watched him take pleasure in putting the helmet on a little friend who was visiting, I was impressed again at how loving, patient, and fun a man he is, and how different from other fathers I've known. He actually *enjoys* being with young children. He enjoyed being with JL. I cannot conjure up even one memory where he and JL were not smiling while playing or doing a project together. The same with Johanna. Our children brought him so much joy.

July 18, 2015
JL,
   Dad here. *I have been having a really hard time for the past few weeks. I still think about you all of the time, and this month my thought turns towards the things we were doing and what you went through last June and July. It is very painful. Thinking about the struggle of your last few weeks—after having done so well for months. In the midst of a bright sunny summer, it is a very dark time.*

It seems women in general are somehow given the inner strength to deal with death more easily than men. Perhaps it is having to contend with the entire process of pregnancy and birth that enables us to somehow also accept the pain of death. I don't know. But I have seen this unexpected phenomenon and wondered at the paradox of physical strength but emotional weakness in men. Mary Karr shared her observation upon witnessing this after deaths from a hurricane: "I could tell by the moans and bellows those grown men let out that their grief had absolutely nowhere to go...The mothers cried too...but they seemed better equipped for it." John sorting JL's belongings, especially the things related to what he and JL did together, were more acts of mourning that were keeping all the memories alive, present, and raw. He was having a hard time thinking about giving them away and losing those tangible connections, as he took one more step in the grieving process that would drive home the reality of our son's death.

July 25, 2015

JL,

Dad here. *Fifty-one weeks. Still the new reality. I have written my close friends and asked them to pray for me—I said I do not like the new reality—and I am dreading your remembrance gathering next weekend. Mom asked if I could explain why I am so anxious. I said I am not anxious, I have dread. She said, "What do you think dread is except extreme anxiety?"*

John needed encouragement, so I suggested he call a few of his "soul-mates." He has a significant number of close male friends, guys he has known for decades and whom he shares his most intimate emotions and thoughts with, even though most of them now live in other states. He is wonderfully gifted in relating on a deep personal level because of his emotional honesty. It is what drew me to him when we met—it was so different than what I had grown up with. To this day, it is John who will turn conversations from the surface to the depths; not by some clever psychological tool, but by his own transparency. Because of this, his friends were diligent to keep up with him after our son's death, and we were strengthened and comforted because we knew they were praying for us.

July 26, 2016

JL,

Dad here. *Last night mom and I met your good friend and fellow IV opioid addict, Bart, and his parents for dinner. He was in town and we had not heard from him since your death—mom had tried to contact him but to no avail. We were both anxious because we didn't know what to expect. We prayed.*

We had a powerful and painful time over dinner. Bart was clearly very troubled and struggling with the reality of your death. He had been holding it in for almost a year. Was it "survivors guilt" or fear or? We hugged and wept, and his parents wept with us— painfully aware that our places could easily have been switched. Although obviously hard for him, it was a very healing time. He loved you very much.

John and I have kept in touch with Bart, along with many other friends of our son. He is doing well, although he has not embraced a solid recovery plan. We worry about him.

July 29, 2015
JL,

Dad here. *I am in the middle of a long run of extreme emotions. Pretty hard for mom or anyone to take. Really angry over little things and then happy over washing and brushing the dogs. Crazy. At mom's request, I called David at In Balance. I shared the dread that I have about this coming weekend—he assured me that it is completely natural. I shared the anxiety I have about the Saturday evening gathering—he assured me that it is going to be a wonderful, terrible, silly, and sad time that will be of great significance for us—and for your friends. He shortened his vacation to be able to attend.*

He also shared something that really touched me. He said, "John Leif was a real warrior." That you fought a hard and serious battle with one of the worst opponents that life has for us to face—and you had many successes, including the seven months prior to your death. Yet, this was not the outcome that you or we had hoped for. Yes, it was not.

July 31, 2015
JL,

Mom here. *I was thinking about the upcoming anniversary of your death, and how different our feelings are now compared to on your birthday. It seems logical that someone's birthday would be the* *hardest time annually after they die, but it is not for us. I thought about JD and Susan—it is the same for their birthdays too—it's true for others I've asked. I wondered why? I think the reason the day of a person's death has so much impact on our memory is because it is a tearing away of a person we are connected to and suddenly there is an unbroachable barrier between us—a veil that lies between our world and the eternal—that we cannot get through. Death marks a moment in time when the clock stops, and the veil appears.*

That veil is not one of a bride: sheer, lightweight, gossamer, obscuring her enough that we can see her, but only just. When it is pulled back, we see her in all her beauty. The veil between us and those who have died is opaque, unyielding, leaving our loved ones hidden; not just from our sight but from any contact, like a concrete wall. Weighty and grave. Joseph Lightfoot said: "The future is hidden by a dark impenetrable veil, and yet we struggle to pierce through it."

Sunday, August 2, 2015
The One-Year Anniversary of John Leif's Death
JL,

Dad here. *Wow! Mom and I are overwhelmed at God's goodness and at the deep love and respect of your friends. I have already shared my dread at this coming weekend—I was anxious about who would come, how many would show up, what it would be like, how it would go. Well, it was amazing!*

Twenty of your friends came and they all loved seeing each other and seeing us and reconnecting. Some of the guys brought gifts: a beautiful orchid, cake, roses. Very sweet.

The meal was perfect. Our caterer knew there would be hungry young men and made meatballs, cheesy baked potatoes, coleslaw, dessert treats, sodas. They all loved it—and thanked us over and over.

Then we gathered in the living room and mom led the giveaway time—they loved it—so fun! Everything from sunglasses to shot glasses, blow darts to Billy clubs. Then I started the sharing. This was another first for us in our walk with you: the first and last one-year celebration of your life and commemoration of your death. Amazing. Everyone shared, some several times. It was great! Lots more funny stories: Richard shared about blow darts for body parts, Parker said you were always the voice of reason and very persuasive, David was amazed that you would complete assignments from 3 to 7 AM after you were all drunk and they were all crashed in your dorm room your freshman year at the U of A.

Then the serious stories. Violet shared how you, she, and others would stay up talking about the deep things of life and that she could tell you anything. Others remembered watching many sunrises together with you. Justin wished he had been more involved during your last two weeks because he could tell something was not right—being a recovering addict himself. Richard, David, and Cory had no idea you were still struggling. Andy wished he and you had reconnected. Ryan wished he had stayed in touch as you always did with him. Tears of sadness and joy mingled together, offered up to you.

Mom here. *When friends ask us how the weekend went and how we feel, all I can say is we had great joy. All anxiety and sorrow were gone. The sum of my thoughts is how much we have been loved and cared for by our friends, and your friends, and how much they loved you.*

And I wonder: how have these dozens of friends remembered us and you and offered true comfort in a world with so much going on? It is a marvel to me. I can easily forget others serious problems when I am so absorbed with my own. There are so many families losing children daily to drug abuse. Amy Carmichael says: "God comforts us so that we can comfort others." May this now be true of us.

The feelings of joy and encouragement we experienced during the one-year Remembrance Gathering did not remain constant throughout the second year following John Leif's death. We continued to have times of profound, painful sadness and regret from a young life stopped dead in its tracks. Even now, there are days we still feel that we failed JL: not in the depth or quantity of the love *we* gave, but in the timbre and quality of the love *he* needed. When JL died, it was as if all three of us were in the county morgue, on the medical examiner's table, under the lights, where everything was laid open and bare and secrets don't survive. All we did, every thought we had, every choice we made, every word we spoke, was under scrutiny, and not by others, but by ourselves. We knew all too well our flaws as parents, yet even when those feelings resurface, there is now a sense that the ground beneath our feet has settled, that the shaking and surging that we lived through the first year after his death has subsided—we will, and we now want to, survive. Acceptance has made this possible: surrendering *to what is*, not to how we *wish* things are.

And though there are many days when we don't want to accept what has happened, either the events of August 2, 2014, or the events leading up to that day, we know by experience that in order to be sane and at peace, we must *choose* acceptance. John and I knew that we needed to take a drastic step of faith to accept what had happened to our son, to our family, to us.

Now, several years after our son's death, we are still learning acceptance and the truth that it is not accomplished in one step. Rather, it is a process, one that for us started in June 2005. A chance note that surfaces in our files, a photo we come across while sorting, a memory that suddenly pops up. At each of these moments we are faced once again with JL's life and death and the hurt and sorrow they revive and challenged to embrace acceptance over again. It is not closure. There is never closure on the death of anyone. Accepting our humanity, accepting reality as complicated and mysterious, is part of living in this temporal world. John and I have come to understand that Perfect Love is neither indolent nor indulgent. And regardless of how much we wanted to be perfect parents, we are ever so slowly accepting that we are human with all its inherent foibles and frailties. Healing, peace, and freedom are within reach—every day.

> *He said, "I will accept the breaking sorrow*
> *Which God to-morrow will to His son explain."*
> *Then did the turmoil deep within him cease,*
> *Not vain the word, not vain;*
> *For in acceptance lieth peace.*
> –Amy Carmichael, "In Acceptance Lieth Peace"

28

STORIES OF HOPE

Hope is being able to see that there is light
despite all of the darkness.

–Desmond Tutu

As we have continued to seek to understand more about the drug epidemic of our son's generation, our nation, and the rest of the world, we have learned so much. One sad but significant truth is that the majority of people who become addicted to drugs had their first experience with alcohol and drugs when they were very young. Statistics show that now *preteens* are the perfect target for drug dealers, and this is usually the age when future drug addicts start drinking alcohol then experimenting and consuming drugs. Statistics also show that one third of us have our first exposure to opiates from the dentist, mainly during adolescence—a perfect set-up for seeking a repeat of that same euphoric feeling.

In the final analysis, there are no formulas for raising kids that will not use drugs or abuse alcohol. But we have seen that there are common threads and risk factors in families with addicts and alcoholics, which, if understood and taken into consideration, might help avert tragedies such as the one we experienced. As we shared, there are strong genetic tendencies and also behavioral patterns of family dysfunction that play significant roles in addiction and alcoholism. There are also specific geographic danger zones that lead to easier accessibility, which leads to more peer group experimentation and use.

Just as there are no formulas for parenting, neither are there formulas for gaining and maintaining sobriety for those who are trying to be free of addiction. But, again, there are common threads that we have seen in the stories of recovering addicts and alcoholics—principles for being successful in returning to life and freedom.

During the past several years, we have continually been encouraged and supported by many of our son's friends—many of whom have awe-inspiring recovery stories. We have asked several young friends to share their stories in the hope that they will give insights for parents and encourage others to know they can be sober and have a meaningful life full of joy, love, and hope.

Hank's Story

My name is Hank and I was a close friend of John Leif—and I am an alcoholic. I was born the youngest of seven in a devout Catholic household and was raised with positive family values and was provided all the love and care that a child could ask for. Although there are no alcoholics in my immediate family, my mother's side of the family consists of proud Irish New Yorkers where alcoholism runs rampant. Even though I grew up across the country from my extended family, I observed their excess drinking during my summer east-coast vacations and idolized that lifestyle. Throughout my childhood and adolescent years, I developed a great sense of pride in my heritage where I developed a *pseudo American-Irish* identity which embraced the culture's negative stereotypes.

I experienced my first drunk at the age of 13. A friend and I stole a bottle of Jameson Whiskey and I poured myself huge glass. In hopes of impressing my friend, I chugged the entire glass. After all the gagging and coughing I was able to keep it down. And then the magic happened: the warm sensation of the whiskey going down my throat into my belly, and, since I drank so much with no tolerance whatsoever, the instantaneous effect that it had on me was incredible. I felt perfect. All of my self-esteem issues and insecurities associated with teenage angst were gone and I felt one with the universe. For me it was the spiritual experience I never got from church, sports, friends, or anything. It felt as if "I had arrived." I remember that night like it was yesterday. From that day forward, my life changed forever. Whether or not my genetics predestined my abnormal affinity towards alcohol, from that point on I wanted to drink whenever I could.

In the beginning of my drinking career, my drinking was confined to the weekends with my friends. It didn't take long for me to discover my father's liquor cabinet where, by the time I was 15 years old, my drinking patterns quickly progressed to the point that I had developed an affinity for drinking alone.

As a teenager, my drinking completely stunted my emotional growth. I quickly began to develop a low self-esteem about myself along with an array of insecurities and antisocial tendencies. During my adolescent development, I not only I used alcohol as my social outlet but also as my coping mechanism for dealing with my emotions. Why deal with all my problems when I have a solution that not only allows me forget about them, but I get to feel perfect in the process? Dealing with life this way, and learning to drown all of my insecurities and resentments down with booze, I started to develop some pretty crippling social anxieties. I do believe that many of my insecurities and self-esteem issues were merely growing pains but instead of growing out of them, my alcoholism made them worst and would cause some to persist throughout my adulthood.

Also, in the beginning stages of my alcoholism, I started developing some pretty severe changes in my personality when I drank. I think that although I used alcohol as a coping mechanism to repress my feelings, many times it would magnify the problems in my head and I would act out quite severely. There were other times when I would become terribly depressed and there were many instances when I would become violently angry, where I had no boundaries on people I would attack.

During one of my drunken nights as a junior in high school, I was so drunk that I took on a group of macho guys solo—I thought I was invincible. I ended up in the emergency room with a broken jaw that had to be wired shut for two months with my only source for food being liquids that could pass through a straw.

Another example of my severe personality change was when I was 17 and I was drinking with two of my brothers. Once I blacked out, I became extremely violent to the point that my brothers had to hold me down until I passed out. According to my brothers, later that night I sporadically got up from where I passed out, walked to the balcony, and finally flung myself off. I landed 18 feet straight onto my head, severely injuring myself. Needless to say, that experience really scared my family and they suggested I stop drinking, which I agreed to. Temporarily. Within months, however, I was back drinking exactly how I used to. My drinking morphed me into Dr. Jekyll and Mr. Hyde—when I blacked out, I never really knew which Hank I would be for the night.

The summer after high school, I went on a service trip to a third-world county. It was an amazing experience that caused me to feel good about the real me. I stayed sober for the entire time. But to celebrate on the last night, I went to a bar with some friends and got drunk. Somehow, two men drugged me and hours later in the dark hours before dawn, I woke up in a body bag, hours away from being prepared to be cut up and have my body parts sold on the black market. I was able to slowly move the zipper and realized I was in the back of a pickup truck. I rolled out while my guards were sleeping and found that I was on an island somewhere with all of my identification gone. I saw lights in the distance and swam towards them, finally hitting the mainland and getting to the police. It was a very traumatic experience physically and mentally, but even more so emotionally. I entered rehab after I returned to the States, but amazingly, I didn't stick with it.

By the time I entered college, I had already acquired all the tell-tale signs of an alcoholic. I was a blackout drinker, I drank alone, and I had severe personality shifts when I drank.

So without that parental supervision holding me back, during college my drinking and alcoholism escalated extremely quickly. As my alcoholism progressed, so did my insecurities and self-esteem issues. By 20, I was drinking almost every day, usually alone or with my one friend (JL), who drank exactly how I did. I started suffering from the shakes, insomnia, depression, and barely sliding through school. I was very unhappy with who I was and what my life had become. Throughout this time, I had a few more violent episodes, which scared my family and friends, so there were times I would go to AA to do some "research." They were always just half-hearted attempts. I would only go a few times after a crazy event. I never, however, really wanted to stop drinking.

I tried to move away, to Flagstaff, thinking a geographic change would help me escape from my alcoholism. A new start. The second night after moving in, I woke up to a trashed apartment, bruised and bloody. During my blackout, I must have called my brother, who drove from Tucson to pick me up and take me back. This event was the final straw for my family who decided to send me to a rehabilitation facility that would help me deal with my alcoholism.

All in all, rehab wasn't the magic remedy for fixing my alcoholism that my parents or I had hoped for. I do, however, credit rehab for keeping me from hurting myself and others while trying to fully come to terms with my alcoholism. I also credit rehab for "planting the seed" of Alcoholics Anonymous. This was very important later on in my struggles with alcoholism when I was finally ready to seek help outside of myself.

After treatment, I lived with my parents for a few months but I wasn't fully sold on the AA idea so I began white knuckling my alcoholism (staying sober without a support group). I eventually convinced my family—and myself—that I was safe to enter the "real world" again so I moved back to Flagstaff to "finish school." Once I settled in Flagstaff it wasn't long before I started drinking again.

I tried to drink "socially" but after a series of violent outbursts, I eventually confined myself to drinking alone, which lasted for about six months. At this point my life became very small—school, library, and drinking alone. I have never experienced the immense loneliness that I felt during those months. Participating in college, surrounded by cheerful students and campus energy, while living in complete isolation is the loneliest existence I hope I will never have to experience again.

Through a series of hospital visits and other close calls I finally walked back to AA. Still not fully sold, I sat in the back, never participated, and for the most part, I was invisible in AA. Sick and tired of drinking but resentful for being in AA, I went through a series of half-measured attempts at sobriety for 2 years. I thought the steps were bullshit, God was bullshit, sponsorship was bullshit, and I resented everyone in the room. I judged everyone's sharing and I always looked for a way to excuse myself due to special circumstances. During this 2-year period I experienced what a lot of struggling alcoholics endure: admitting my powerlessness over alcohol but too selfish and prideful to embrace a Power greater than myself. In my experience, the half-measured "one-door-in/one-door-out approach" to AA only led to chronic relapse and more resentment. Needless to say, my insecurities, self-esteem, and self-hatred magnified during this period. This downward spiral made each relapse, and the consequences, more severe.

On October 30th, 2011 (my sobriety date), I woke up on the floor of Coconino County Detention Facility after another damaging drinking spree of several days. I felt all of the usual emotions after a relapse—humiliation, regret, guilt, fear, anger, confusion—but to a level I had never felt before. It was truly pitiful and an incomprehensible demoralization. It was also the emotional bottom I needed as I felt truly hopeless. I got on my knees and said, "God, I'll do anything." That prayer marked the beginning of a new life. I was finally willing to believe that a power greater than myself could restore me to sanity.

Once released, two of my siblings—who flew from across the country—greeted me and brought me back to Tucson to recover. Although still numb from my relapse I knew where to go. With my tail between my legs, I quickly walked back into AA, got a sponsor, and started to work the 12-steps.

Since my sobriety date, my participation in AA and approach to staying sober was completely different from my previous attempts. In my newfound willingness to believe in a higher power who was greater than myself, I began to take suggestions from my sponsor as well as other AA peers. Equally as important, I began to be honest with myself and others. As I progressed through the steps, I started to understand my part in my alcoholism. I became aware of my character defects and various shortcomings that influenced my drinking habits. Once aware, I slowly learned how to untangle my habitual toxic thinking.

I think the biggest realization was that my "self-will" will never keep me sober. Throughout my drinking career, I thought I knew all the answers. I thought that my intellect alone would deter me from drinking. My pride and my ego built many barriers from truly seeking guidance or perspectives outside of my own. Paradoxically, it was myself-will that always led me to relapse. I have come to realize that all the knowledge in the world won't keep me sober. My self-will is fundamentally flawed and unless I embrace a higher power to guide my thoughts and actions, I will eventually pick up a drink. There is a saying in AA that the day will come when the only thing standing between me and a drink will be my relationship with my Higher Power. My experience—and continued sobriety—is a testament to this.

It wasn't until around a year of sobriety that I recognized how selfish and self-centered I had been. Throughout my alcoholism and the chaos, I put my parents through, I never thought about the pain and worry that I caused my family. During my drinking career, I thought that I had everyone fooled. It was only later that I realized that they always saw through my lies and deceit. But it was their unconditional love for me that gave them hope that I would change into the man they knew I could be. Recognition of the pain I caused was difficult to accept. I know that I cannot change the past, so the only way for me to honor my family is to love to my full potential. Even with all the damage I caused, in time I was able to restore my relationships and trust with my family. I am there to celebrate the good times, such as officiating my brother's wedding—while also providing support, such as donating my kidney to another brother—during the bad. These are memories and experiences that I would never have been given had I continued drinking.

Having had a spiritual awakening as a result of working the 12-steps of AA (and great sponsorship), my perspective on life has completely changed. AA is still a big part of my life, where I now practice the principles I have learned in all areas of my life.

One of the biggest accomplishments in applying AA principles was my ability to move back to Flagstaff and to finish college. Since the majority of my struggles getting sober occurred while I was living in Flagstaff, the city represented relapse and loneliness for me. Therefore, I had a lot of fear and doubt in my decision to move back. Once resettled in Flagstaff, however, I immediately became an active member in AA where I was able to maintain a fulfilling, sober, and supportive social network. By applying AA principles into my educational pursuits, I became a very successful student which not only allowed me to excel in my classes but participate in campus activities in a healthy manner. In 2013, I graduated from Northern Arizona University with distinction.

Currently I have over eight years of sobriety, a wife, a fulfilling career in Washington, D.C., a great social network, and the list goes on. I am grateful for all of the things in my life, but I always recognize that I didn't recover from alcoholism on my own. Without the continued guidance offered by AA, a relationship with my higher power, and commitment to helping others I know I will take a drink.

I think about JL every day. He was my best friend and will never be replaced. It is my belief that the smarter the alcoholic, the harder the road to recovery is. JL was one of the smartest guys I knew. He thought he knew all the answers. His intellect prohibited him from fully embracing a power greater than himself to help with his addictions.

"But the actual or potential alcoholic, with hardly any exception, will be absolutely unable to stop drinking on the basis of self-knowledge. This is a point we wish to emphasize and re-emphasize, to smash home upon our alcoholic readers as it has been revealed to us out of bitter experience."
—Alcoholics Anonymous, p. 39

JL is part of my story and I honor him by sharing it with those who still suffer from the disease of alcoholism.

Anne's Story

I was eleven years old when I first experienced shooting heroin. Looking back, I can hardly believe it and I am so thankful to be alive, and to be sharing my story.

My boyfriend and I watched the movies *Trainspotting* and *Requiem for a Dream* and they really piqued our interest in drugs. The way it was portrayed in those movies made me think using heroin would be an amazing dream sequence, when in actuality, it made me violently ill. My boyfriend insisted we keep trying. He became obsessed with all drugs: ecstasy, LSD, cocaine, and various pills and so I tried them all. During those first few years of using, I just went to his house to get drugs, since he was my sole provider.

My parents had no idea. I knew I was doing something they would not have wanted me to do. I was unable to ask them for help because I had a terrifying fear of their disapproval. If they knew what I was up to, I was sure they would forever view me differently and cease loving me. I also knew they would try to force me to stop. Later on, even when they did know I was on drugs, I was always lying trying to minimize what was really going on, make them think I was doing better than I was, so they would not be worried. I hated causing them anxiety.

In the beginning, the experience of euphoria and confidence kept me wanting to use. I was in a different reality—all of my insecurities did not matter. I didn't consider myself an addict right away. I assumed I was just a hard partier. But in my senior year of high school I started to get very sick and extremely uncomfortable when I didn't have drugs for any length of time. I was experiencing withdrawal. I knew I was addicted.

I think my parents assumed I was completely insulated from drug-problems of the hard-core variety. What suburban parent suspects their 12-year-old kid going to a good school could be shooting up heroin? From my perspective, there was no flaw in their parenting—they simply did not know. And how could I have asked for help? I didn't think I wanted help. I just wanted to get high and for them to somehow love me anyway. Drugs were the only thing that made me feel safe and ok—even though they put me in incredibly dangerous situations and made me insane.

I was arrested many times, each of which is its own long story. I used hard drugs, heroin and then meth, intravenously for 15 years and bounced in and out of prison, asylums, and rehab. When I was using, gone on my addiction, I was unable to answer my mother's phone calls because the sound in her voice—that worried, agonized tone, the questions I couldn't or wouldn't answer, the lies I felt I had to tell—drove me to complete insanity. What killed me was the thought that they sat there wondering what they had done wrong. Another dark spot was the anger and the lashing out. I was furious at myself and took it out on them in ways I probably still can't even fully recall or appreciate. That self-torture and the effect it had on those I loved kept me high, unable to cope, for many years.

Although my first stint in rehab perhaps didn't do much good as I wasn't ready to quit, one program did make a difference: a parole program I was sent to when I was released from prison. Was it the program or was it the timing in my life? I am not sure. But even after years of madness, complete degradation, depravity, and living in acceptance that "I'm a lifelong junkie," something clicked, and I got better. It is an impossible miracle.

I have been clean and sober for almost six years. I don't have drug cravings and I do not struggle for my sobriety: I am truly free. I have been actively involved in 12-step programs and the entire time I have been clean and maintained perfect sobriety. I attend as often as I can. I go because I like the community and I enjoy being of service to others. There are so many great people in sobriety, so many people who love life without drugs and alcohol. I was also lucky to have discovered the health-food-movement. My new addiction is health! I have found groups and communities of people who never do drugs because it decreases athletic performance and overall wellness. I worried that I would have trouble making friends with people outside of the recovery community. How could I relate to others? I don't have any interest in going to bars—will I still find people who enjoy being with me? Because of this new interest, all of my friends are safe for me, not just the ones I have in the rooms of AA/NA. Being surrounded by supportive people who bring out the good in me has been incredibly healing.

In my addiction, the destruction of my relationship with my parents was what tormented me most of all. It wasn't prison, it wasn't the breaking-down of my body, the constant sickness, the squalid living conditions, being raped and beaten up. None of that mattered because I was too high to care. But as high as I got, I could never completely crush the feelings of guilt, the total shame, and the longing to love and be loved. Today, that relationship is more joyful and whole than I ever could have imagined. This is the most important success story, for all of us. We are together and happy, and every day is a gift and a dream come true. If you have a child in active addiction and are reading this now, I want to say to you: avoiding enabling is important—but *never withhold your love*. Hold on to the image of who your child is beneath the addiction, recognize that the bad behaviors are the symptoms and not the person, and *keep on loving*: that's the key.

Why am I alive today when others are not? I don't need to understand it so much in order to be grateful for it. I know that what keeps me sober on a day to day basis is my commitment to health, exercise, and joy. I am happy, I have fun, I have my mom and dad, and I can experience euphoria and confidence in sobriety. I can be useful to others. My life is beautiful now. Maybe I can thank my addiction for the ability to truly appreciate it and be overwhelmed by it each day.

Peter's Story

My name is Peter and I'm an alcoholic and addict. This is how I introduce myself at the AA meetings I attend several times every week, as I have done for eight years. I am 29 years old, from a fairly affluent family, raised with high moral standards, and attended the best of schools. So how is it that I became an alcoholic by the time I was a senior in high school and an opioid addict and dealer by the time I was 20?

The first time I used alcohol was when I was in my junior year in high school. My family had recently moved from back east to Tucson, so I was new to the school district, I didn't play sports, so I had learned to be the comedian in order to be accepted. I felt like I didn't get the playbook for how to be a part of the group. I had been raised with really strong morals against using drugs and alcohol from my upbringing, but I wanted to fit in with the popular kids so I decided to make the decision to drink on my own.

I was at a friend's house when his parents weren't home, and I tried a capful of vodka—that was it. I hated the way it tasted and how I felt. The next day I was sick—not so much from the alcohol, but with guilt, head to toe. This would be a consistent theme in my drinking and using: I always felt guilt and the consequences of doing something soul-crushing and bending the moral line I had deep within me. My mom accused me of being drunk and I wasn't, but she knew something wasn't right. Was I drunk? No—but had I been drinking? Yes. I had such a strong belief in the lies I was telling myself and others that it was hard for anyone to convince me otherwise or to get the whole truth out of me.

From then on, it was like I had lost my drinking virginity. Once that barrier had been crossed, then anything was permissible. Initially I only drank on weekends at parties. I remember a friend having a massive "beer pong tournament" at his house and I went to help him set up. Almost everyone from our grade was going to be there, including all the popular kids, including JL. But I was so anxious, I got pretty hammered before because I didn't want to get drunk when everyone was there and then throw up. I had a pretty weak stomach. Crazy logic. Now I have a very strong stomach—which came from getting high and drinking: tolerance. During my drinking years, I could force myself to not throw up because I didn't want to lose any of the effect of the substance—it was so important for me.

At the party, everyone got drunk. Cops showed up. I jumped over a fence into a cactus trying to get away. But I just wanted to feel and look cool and fit in—it was always about the effect so that I wouldn't be the outsider. For me to be drinking was a really big thing because my group of friends were pretty bright and I looked down on them when they started drinking, and here I was doing it to an extreme. Also during this time, we would go and smoke hookah—not with pot. It was a very habitual and social thing—but it was just more of doing nothing, wasting time.

On the weekends, I would get hammered and even though I had a 1am curfew as a senior, I just couldn't show up on time. It would be 2, 3, 4 a.m. So, I'd stay over at friends' houses. Sometimes I would drink on the nights before late start mornings at school, or even drink in the morning before school. I was so against people who drank, or drank and drove, but now I had lost all shame about getting behind the wheel while drunk and had no regard for the possibility of harming someone else.

I wasn't using drugs yet and I was vehemently against people who used drugs. I was working at a restaurant and it wasn't a good environment. I wasn't treated very well. Every night when I would get off work, I would be in a rage, and drive recklessly, venting my anger. When I look back on it now, these are the telltale signs of someone who is scared, angry, frustrated. What I really needed was someone to talk to and help me deal with my feelings. But instead of doing that, I just pushed them down and poured alcohol on top of them.

I was lying more and more to my family over even trivial things. Lying had become a habit. And I was falling behind in my classes and having to catch up the last week of semester —and it worked. What I learned from this was that I could just skate by and do whatever I want. You can do this up to a certain point, but then you eventually need to do the work. Looking back on it now, my parents never groomed me for college, while other kids' parents were guiding them through the process of searching and applying for a school. I really needed more structure and encouragement, but it hadn't really worked for my sister who was older, so my parents were trying a more laid-back approach with me.

High school felt like an incredibly wasted and squandered opportunity for fun. I was mad that I hadn't been drinking earlier because I had missed out on so much fun. I barely graduated, and missed end of year parties, because I was doing an entire semester of work the last few days of school. All I cared about was going on an AP European art-history tour. We went to amazing places that I was really interested in. But I remember maybe five to ten percent of it. It was a rolling blackout. We touched down in Rome, set our bags down, got whiskey for the first time, immediately threw up, drank more and we were off and running.

One time we were walking through the streets in Switzerland and I couldn't keep my head up I was so drunk. I went into a bathroom and locked myself in. It was the women's bathroom. I was in the midst of alcohol poisoning. They called my dad to tell him and were going to fly me home, but since there were just two days left, they didn't. We went to Paris, and I had vowed I wouldn't drink again—but I drank two bottles of champagne. And we did some kind of inhalant that night, I think they are called whippets—they give you a head rush. After I got home, I felt sorry for myself because I knew that my dad now knew that I was drinking like crazy and the charade was up. If I wasn't drinking, I was restless and discontented and my skin was crawling. As soon as I got little alcohol in me, I felt like I just need a little bit more to feel like I did the first time I drank. But I would get to that tipping point and then would go until it was a blackout again.

I chose to go to the U of A, living in the off-campus apartment dorms, because my friends were all going there, and I knew I could still get alcohol when I wanted to. I got a fake ID and went to stores where they didn't check. So now I made sure I had hard liquor on hand—but also would keep beer on hand so we could be "social." The week before school, there were social events for meeting people and get to be comfortable with this new phase in life, but I was totally terrified. I drank myself out of school really fast. I remember so clearly waking up at 11 or noon, after being hammered the night before, hearing the sound of the band at the football game, but I was already late for the party. My biggest fear was missing out on something, the party. And it is exactly what happened.

Looking back on it, it was so selfish. My family was paying for my education and I was just wasting it. It was continual, repetitive drunkenness and waking up in horrible shape and feeling worse each time. So, the plan was to leave the U of A, move back home, and go to Pima Community College. But the sum of it was that I would continue to screw up, I'd somehow manipulate and convince them so they would let me get back into a situation that was really detrimental to me. As sad as it is to say, I was just continually enabled. Had I been less fortunate, had a lower income family, none of these scenarios would have come about: the free apartment, the no-consequences lifestyle. It was like being a celebrity: you don't have any responsibilities or pay your own bills, don't really have to work or go to school—just party.

I eventually figured out that I could still live like I wanted and hold a job. I didn't need my family and they didn't want to pay for my lifestyle anymore. I was a server in a restaurant, made really good money, spoke Spanish and English. I would make up stories to customers just to get really good tips, in cash. But it was gone in two days and I couldn't pay for my car or rent— and I didn't even pay for my health insurance or cell phone—my family still paid for those.

When I was just ready to turn 20, my best friend smoked weed in front of me. He and I had been so judgmental of people using drugs. And here I was, a drunk and a lush. Three days later I smoked, on my own, away from him. Then I was selling weed within a week, because I was going to do it in the most economical way. So, I could sell enough that I could smoke for free. Within a month or two, I was habitually smoking from 2-5 grams of weed a day. (A joint or blunt is about half a gram.) It was the first thing that actually calmed my ADHD way down (I had been on Adderall as a kid) and I felt like I could actually breath again, and it slowed my rapid thinking way down. It did for me what I was hoping alcohol would do for me.

But by the third time I smoked, I was drinking and smoking at the same time: "cross-fading." I had a high tolerance for alcohol at this time and would drink a fifth of hard liquor and smoke pot.

I had a good group of clients from selling weed at my work, a base to make money. Then I was regularly selling from the back of the restaurant out of my car—had my scale and baggies all hidden. I would close it all up, spray myself down with cologne, and put eye drops in, put a piece of gum in, and keep serving tables. I was making a lot of money from selling so much weed. So, I would get fronted weed and sell that, robbing Peter to pay Paul, which ended up causing me the most stress: owing some bad people lots of money.

Then a friend at the restaurant started popping Percocet or Vicodin in front of me. I tried one at my house one day and about 30 minutes later I felt like I had melted in my seat—I'd never had painkillers before. But then I was on. I'd have one or two of those when I was at work. It made me feel like I was Superman or James Bond. I had no anxiety, no problems, living in the moment every moment. I took them with alcohol and pot for over a year. I got the prescriptions from "friends"—not my close friends—who had leftovers and sold them cheap. We took them at first as a party drug—the advertised deception that they weren't addictive—but one time for them turned into needing it every day for me. Then I looked into them online and realized I was eating all this Tylenol and Advil and it's not good for me.

It is really hard for me to remember how I got into selling hard drugs, Oxy's, because I was so high and drunk all the time. I started meeting a lot of very shady people, going to places my friend and I would never have gone to in the past, but all of a sudden, we're there. Throughout this entire story, I am moving every six months because we didn't pay our bills and had all sorts of problems. Right around this time I took Xanax for the first time—it would turn drinking into being instantaneously hammered and gone. And it all escalated very rapidly.

We had already been making our own joints out of the pure parts with lots of THC, so now we did a similar thing with pills. Take one pill, then crush one up and put it in joint paper and "parachute it" so it would be broken up more thoroughly when it hit our stomachs and get a better high. The first time I snorted I was really afraid, what is called a "Perc"—but it isn't. It was a Roxicodone (blues), oxycodone, variations of the opiate part of these drugs concentrated into a circle. Each manufacturer has their own and I knew the markings. I started at first to eat half and snort the other half. I sold mostly the blues because they are a good party drug, swallowed or snorted. Girls in sororities, and guys in fraternities, liked them. So, it tailored the group of people I was involved with—the party people—not the hard-core druggies, smoking or shooting.

The first time I snorted OxyContin, this was the real thing. Usually an 80mg, and because it's pure, it's like snorting fire. But I never smoked any opiates or injected. These are all different ways of getting the drug into your body and the route you use determines how quickly you feel the effect, how long it lasts, etc. The most efficient absorption rate, other than injecting, is via the stomach. But JL would snort Roxy's with me all the time, even though he was using BT. But he wouldn't have felt comfortable pulling out a foil and smoking or a needle and shooting it in front of me, because he knew I would freak out and I would have told him he could leave. Because there was *this stigma* about heroin. Looking back now it made no difference—it was all the same thing—opioids. And it was much more efficient way to use. And JL probably felt like we were a safe group of people to be around, get high, not be sick, and not be robbed.

Because I was selling these drugs, I didn't ever have to think "I can't get my Oxy so I'll go get some BT." It is the thing that got me into trouble, but it's the thing that kept me from moving to BT. For some reason JL didn't want to deal and potentially get into trouble. The majority of buying Oxy's was from someone who had prescriptions and sold them. People who were way over prescribed—so common. Even my dad was told to take the same amount of drugs I was abusing every day just to relieve his pain.

At this point, I was using from 100-300 mg OxyContin a day, pretty consistently taking any sort of benzos I could, and drinking very heavily too—tied in with non-stop smoking weed. My mental state was in a rough spot, I was incredibly underweight and all the robbing Peter to pay Paul from dealing was starting to catch up with me. I wasn't paying my bills or car payment. Every time I had more money, I used more—I was a junkie and there was no profit. Also when you get blackout drunk every night, it's easy to give away pills here and there. You give more weed than they pay for, you're hanging out with some pretty seedy characters and people are stealing things from you—it just goes like that.

Towards the end, one of our houses got broken into at gunpoint, consequences got serious —I always had a suspended license and no license plate on my car. I have kept a photo to remind myself of those times: from one of the traffic light cameras, I was going 65-70 miles an hour as I sped thru a light, and it's me sticking my hand out the window flipping it the finger. They never found me, and I never paid the fine. I thought it made me cool—an absurd idea of bravado.

Before I'd do a line each of Adderall, Xanax, OxyContin, coke all lined up next to each other, I would even say to friends, "Well, if I don't see you again, it's been nice knowing you." There were people I used with who would say, "You need to slow down dude - something bad is going to happen." I had a lot of paranoia, I had a gun with me all the time.

I was with a friend and got pulled over by a bike cop at the University, so instead of running from them as I usually did, I didn't. I was exhausted and ready to just give up. I had stolen my step-mom's car, had a suspended license. They searched the vehicle and found weed in the trunk—they didn't breathalyzer me or drug test me—but they took me in for possession to the drunk tank overnight. They didn't find the little baggie of Oxy and Xanax in my waistband that I popped while in the back seat of the patrol car.

They contacted my dad and I got out, then we started down the long road of having to get an attorney, go to the courts, cancel my cell phone, Facebook, etc. The first two days were the really bad withdrawal—vomiting, my stomach a mess, my nerves were shot, my mental state was wrecked. But it wasn't as bad as if I had been shooting drugs and it wasn't a huge amount every day of one drug—it was a lot of different drugs. My dad was really disappointed in me because I had betrayed his trust and then a lot of fees racking up for impound fees, court fees, etc. When I stopped smoking weed, I didn't have direct withdrawal physical effects, but it affected my mental and emotional state. A year or so before this I had taken some mushrooms, hallucinogens, and it really messed up my sense of self, my inner dialogue, some of those crazy mental issues came back.

Then I started back to work, taking cabs, and I started going to AA meetings every day. My dad took me to a meeting—he didn't know what else to do with me. Every member of my family is an alcoholic—both parents' sides. My dad knew it was a possibility that I would become one too. He had been an alcoholic and sold drugs before I was born, and he had gotten clean and sober through AA.

After about two months while I was working through the steps with a sponsor, I got to the fourth step of writing out a moral inventory, but then I didn't complete it because I thought drugs were my problem and I wasn't using. I didn't think I was an alcoholic. But what I failed to realize at the time was they are not two different things: they are all "drugs," and they are all the same, because you are using them in the same way, for the effect. I thought I could just smoke some weed and drink a beer now and then, no big deal. But I didn't grasp at the time that for me, that's not an option—I can never just have one or two.

Even with all the charges and mounting consequences and debt, with no car or cell phone, emotionally and spiritually bankrupt, somehow, I convinced myself that if I just had a beer or two to calm myself it was OK. I remember a very low point for me was going to an AA meeting after this and picking up my two-month sober chip. Standing up in front of a whole room of people saying I was sober—people in AA who wouldn't have judged me if I had told them I had relapsed and who would have just loved me and encouraged me to get back up on the wagon. I couldn't even be honest with them.

I was off and running again and so my parents kicked me out of the house. But my uncle let me stay with him, although it was really hard because he lived so far away from my work. I was only drinking and not doing drugs, because I was afraid my probation officer would do a drug test. So, fear kept me clean, but it didn't keep me sober. This was the fall of 2010 and it is a bit of a fog for me because the progression was the same with my drinking getting heavier and heavier. Somehow, I managed to keep my job, regardless of all the stupid things I did, because I needed the money to drink. All of my drinking and using friends were all gone now because I didn't have anything to offer them. The people I hurt the most were my family and close friends who really loved me.

I started drinking so heavily and blacking out all the time. I went to some friends' house who were party drinkers, or so I thought. But in one room some people were smoking BT heroin—the smell was unmistakable, like burning hair. I was drunk and ended up doing a line of cocaine. I was using a variety of drugs along with the alcohol now—again. I had increasing fear and pain and the sense of impending doom every moment—with the court dates beginning and the consequences of my addictions coming down on me. I couldn't sleep due to an extreme level of anxiety and hopelessness.

In February of 2011, I met with my probation officer and I knew I had to stop drinking for the breathalyzer test, but he knew something was wrong. Every night you call in to a Task Hotline to see if you have to do a drug test the next morning. Within a couple of weeks, I had to go in after using. So, I went to a smoke shop and tried to get a detox drink to fool the test, but they wouldn't sell it to me because I told them I was going to try to fraud the State. I got someone else to buy me one, but it was the wrong one and it made me violently ill. My roommate encouraged me to just get through the test and then get clean, which I did, but I was sure the test would show dirty. I was a mess emotionally and physically—I was broken and decided I would kill myself. I got the keys to my uncle's car and decided I would drive off a cliff.

Before I did this, I had a moment of clarity and wanted to talk to my mom. She had brought me into this world, and I should tell her before I took myself out of it. And I didn't want her to feel guilty for what I had done. With the keys in my hand, I called her. She didn't try to tell me not to do it. She told me I was right, that I was going to die because I was really sick. She asked, "If you know you have a problem, do you think AA could possibly work for you? Are you willing for the first time in your life to put 100% effort into this and abandon every idea that you could ever drink or use again on the hopes that you could have a life that would be normal?" I said yes. She told me, from living out of state, that there was a meeting near my house at noon the next day. Go to it and if you still want to kill yourself, do it afterward.

Not hearing her say "I love you and it's going to be ok," but her telling me the truth is what made the difference. "No one, doctor, family member, therapist, can do this for you. You have to do it for yourself, you have to have a spiritual life-change, and the only way I know of that works is through AA." I said OK and went the next day. The meeting was nothing special, but I was completely broken and finally ready for a change. An old guy there said I'll be your sponsor. He got me some food, and we went through the first three steps, and then he drove me to a Catholic church and had me hit my knees in front of it—something you could never have gotten me to do. I'd been raised Jewish and had given up on God when I was 13. He didn't care what religion I was, and just told me to get quiet and calm, and pray. He told me to hit my knees every morning and night and thank God for my sobriety, one day at a time. Get to one or more meetings a day. If something feels wrong, don't do it and call me. It wasn't easy. I went and, having always been a loudmouth and clown, I just kept my mouth shut. The battle was just showing up. And I actually worked through the fourth step with my sponsor of "making a searching and fearless moral inventory"—things I didn't want to tell anybody.

I talked to my probation officer to try to get transferred back east so I could have a fresh start. It was supposed to take up to a year, but it took only one month. I packed up and moved.

I went to an AA meeting the day I landed. I had three months of sobriety and I started doing manual labor, but I was starting to have a bad attitude. Someone in a meeting told me I needed to change. And slowly but surely, I did. I watched others and saw how they had healthy relationships, and how to help others by sacrificing and experience joy. Then I actually did the eighth and ninth steps: making a list of people I had harmed and became willing to make amends to them, tell them I lied and cheated, and asked if there was anything I could do for them. I saved up money for a plane trip to

Arizona, where the majority of the people I had hurt lived. Some people just blew me off and others embraced me. But it was one more step in the 12-step program that I had to take. For those who think a watered down 12-step program will work, it won't. They get stuck in discussing the problems instead of focusing on the solution. As they say in AA, "half-measure avail us nothing." It's not "half measures avail us half." The program of AA is in The Big Book. Even today, with over seven years sober, I am tempted because I still can only see the dishonest part of drinking—the fun times. As an alcoholic, I can't see the consequences and where that one drink will take me. I need to stay connected and going to meetings. My sobriety is my priority.

Hope begins in the dark, the stubborn hope that if you just show up and try to do the right thing, the dawn will come. You wait and watch and work: you don't give up.
—Anne Lamott, Bird by Bird

A WORD AFTER

In order to keep our story a Memoir, we had to restrict references and statistics surrounding opioids, alcohol and addiction in general. We have learned so much in the past 15 years as we have talked with professionals, read books, and done research for the book and the blog.

I did so much research because I love trying to find the answer to the questions. There was not even basic information available if you searched for it in 2005 when we discovered JL was using Black Tar Heroin. When John Leif died in August of 2014, there had not been any national news about the Opioid Epidemic we had been living with for a decade. We knew no other families who had lost a child to a heroin overdose although we knew there were mounting deaths. We had not heard of any books written that addressed why our streets and schools were flooded with opioids.

It wasn't until 2015 that *NBC Nightly News* began their series, documenting the alarming rate of mostly young people dying from opioid overdoses. John and I looked at each other and said in exasperation, "Finally." We recorded every one of the series on my phone. *Dreamland, The Big Fix,* and *American Pain* were released, telling the story from different and important angles. Our desire is to help as many people understand what we are up against as a nation, and world, in order to work towards a common goal in whatever way each of us can. The statistics are constantly changing and new research is available almost monthly. Please head to my website, www.JudeDiMeglioTrang.com to access this information and its sources, listed by topics such as: genetics, drugs (opioids, fentanyl, cocaine, methamphetamines, marijuana, alcohol, tobacco, etc.), harm reduction, medication assisted treatment options, statistics on use and deaths, and criminalization.

A WORD OF THANKS

We have all been granted different gifts to offer to our family, friends, and the world. I have an extraordinary group of people who have shared their particular gifts with me over the past several years as I have attempted to write a book worthy of your time to read.

My husband John has been my closest friend and spiritual partner for the majority of my life on this earth. He is the voice of encouragement when I am listening to my own fearful inner dialogue and the strong hand of support when I am mired down in discouragement. He's no saint—I couldn't live with a saint—but he has been a passionate personification of God's love to me and our children. His belief in my ability to present the painful story of our life and our son's life with honesty and vulnerability gave me the confidence I needed to stick with it.

Our daughter, Johanna, overcame her discomfort at reliving the story of her brother's addiction and death in order to read the manuscript. Her encouraging words were the most important ones for me to hear and writing the opening paragraphs to our family's story brought her voice forward in such a way that reminded me of the years when John Leif was a baby and we three, together, watched over him with so much delight.

I would like to thank the three young friends have contributed their raw and honest stories to this memoir. I've called them "Stories of Hope" because they inspire me to believe that fighting addiction is not a forlorn hope. It is possible to get clean and sober and to stay that way, albeit with much dedication and determination to begin a new way of living and learning to become part of a sober community.

Linda Bale is a born enthusiast. She stood by our side through all the years of our son's battle with addiction. Linda's willingness to listen and empathize was a gift of God's love that helped us maintain a semblance of sanity when it felt that all was lost. Reading the manuscript at several points along the way and offering insights that made real improvements went above and beyond the role of friendship.

Ann Dernier has a rare ability to facilitate and support others so unpretentiously they don't realize how much she has done for them. Ann believed in the importance of hearing John's voice and my voice together, as a couple, and inspired us to proceed with confidence. As a poet and editor, she had a unique ability to ask just the right questions to draw memories and emotions out of my plain re-telling to help me create scenes that "show not tell" our most painful moments. Any parts of our story that are poetic and essential, I owe to her patient and thorough work and sacrificial love.

Kelcey Rockhold was a surprise gift who came into my life at a time when I was at a dead end and did not know where to turn. She reassured me that our story needed to be told and with youthful passion and supercharged energy, edited the manuscript with clarity of thought and attention to detail. Her ardent dedication enhanced the readability and inspired me to do my best down to the last sentence.

Greg McNamee patiently helped me take my first year of writing and weaving the backstory of our lives in with our journal entries and edit it into a workable manuscript. His belief in the value of our desire to break the silence surrounding deaths from opiate addiction was the impetus I needed to forge ahead.

Thank you to Emily Gowor for embracing our story and working with her team at Gowor International Publishing to do a beautiful job in publishing our story. Australia is our second home and Emily embodies the warmth, sincerity and friendliness of a nation of people we have come to admire and love.

Our support system of close friends and family near and far is too lengthy to list—you know who you are and how much your love, prayers, emails, texts, and visits have meant to us over the years and especially during the days, weeks, and months following JL's death. What would our lives be without you? A very sincere *Thank You* to the friends who sacrificed their time to read through our story and write encouraging reviews and insightful comments. "There is nothing on this earth more to be prized than true friendship." (Thomas Aquinas)

To all of John Leif's friends we offer you our gratitude for your love and concern for us, especially during those first dark days and months. Hearing the stories of your young adult lives together with JL, including all of the ups and downs, was a much appreciated encouragement to us and something we will away treasure. Staying in contact with us demonstrates how much you loved our son and that is consolation we cannot put into words.

May all of you be blessed as God has blessed us through you.

GIVING CREDIT: REFERENCES

A Word Before:
Trainspotting (1996), Channel Four Films, UK
Stone, Elizabeth (2002), *A Boy I Once Knew: What a Teacher Learned from her Student*, Algonquin Books

Chapter One: The Letter
Beattie, Melody (1986), *Codependent No More*, Hazelden, pg. 9
Arterburn, Stephen and Burns, Jim (1989), *Drug-Proof Your Kids: A Prevention Guide & An Intervention Plan*, W Publishing Group
Faust, James E., *quote*, American clergyman (1920-2007)

Chapter Two: The Knock at the Door
Parks, Rosa, *quote*, American activist (1913-2005)
Nietzsche, Friedrich, *quote*, German philosopher (1844-1900)

Chapter Three: Garage Mahal and The Body Bag
Heard, Mark, "I'm Cryin' Again", *Stop the Dominoes*, 2000
Substance Use Disorder (SUD), definition from: *Symptoms of Substance Use Disorder* By Johnna Medina, Ph.D., Nov.19, 2018, PsychCentral https://psychcentral.com/disorders/addictions/substance-use-disorder-symptoms/
Grant, Anne, *quote*, Scottish poet and author (1755-1838)

Chapter Four: The Urn
Keats, John, *quote from* "To Sleep", English poet (1795-1821)
Aeschylus, *quote*, ancient Greek "father of tragedy" (525-455 BC)

Chapter Five: Drug of Choice
Escher, M.C., *quote*, Dutch artist and mathematician (1898-1972)
2014 Maryland Dept. of Health and Mental Hygiene, Drug and Alcohol Related Deaths

Centers for Disease Control (CDC) 2014 Drug Overdose Data and Alcohol related deaths

Quinones, Sam (2015) *Dreamland, The True Tale of America's Opiate Epidemic*, Bloomsbury Press

Keefe, Patrick R. (October 30, 2017), The New Yorker, "The Family That Built an Empire of Pain"

CBS Evening News, June 21, 2018, Report on Purdue Pharma, interview with sales representative discussing "pseudo-addiction" and other false claims by Purdue

Centers for Disease Control (CDC) 2017 Report on life expectancy https://www.cdc.gov/media/releases/2018/s1129-US-life-expectancy.html

Nuland, Sherwin (2010), quoted in *Einstein's God: Conversations About Science and the Human Spirit*, Krista Tippett, Random House

Chapter Six: Remembering John Leif

Tennyson, Alfred Lord, *quote*, British poet (1809-1892)

Kübler-Ross, Elizabeth (1969), The Five Stages of Loss from *On Death and Dying: What the Dying Have to Teach Doctors, Nurses, Clergy, & Their Own Families*, Scribner NY

Bone Thugs N Harmony, "Tha Crossroads", *E.1999 Eternal*, 1996, Lyrics © Sony/ATV Music Publishing LLC, Kobalt Music Publishing Ltd.

Desire, "Under Your Spell", *II*, 2009, Lyrics ©Kobalt Music Publishing Ltd.

Cicero, Marcus Tullius, *quote*, Roman statesman and philosopher (106 BC-43 BC)

Chapter Seven: The Real JL

Sayers, Dorothy L., *quote*, English writer and poet (1893-1957)

Lewis, Clive Staples (1960), *The Four Loves*, Geoffrey Bles Publ. (1898-1963)

Raymond, Adam K. (June 13, 2012), The Fix, "How Brain Trauma Can Cause Addiction"

Whitehouse, Sheldon, *quote*, American lawyer & politician (b. 1955)

Chapter Eight: Grief Part 1 – Denial, Anger, Bargains

Edwards, Roger (July 2001), The Barnabas Letter, *Don't Grieve Like the Rest of Men*, pg. 4-5

Didion, Joan (2007), *The Year of Magical Thinking*, Vintage

Kübler-Ross, Elisabeth & Kessler, David (2005), *On Grief and Grieving: Finding the Meaning of Grief Through the Five Stages of Loss*, Scribner New York

Ten Boom, Corrie, *quote*, Dutch watchmaker, Nazi prisoner, and author (1892-1983)

Kübler-Ross, Elisabeth, quote, (2005) ibid

Chapter Nine: Grief, Part 2 – The Blues: Depression

Switchfoot, "The Blues", *Nothing is Sound*, 2005

Carmichael, Amy Wilson (1935) *Gold by Moonlight*, Chapter 14, pg. 154, Dohnavur Fellowship/Christian Literature Crusade (1867-1951)

London Grammar, "Sights", *Truth is a Beautiful Thing*, 2017

Isaiah 25:8, Revelation 21:4: "God will wipe away our tears and there will be no more death."

Augustine, Aurelius (400 AD), *Confessions, Book IV: My Friend Died* (354 AD-430 AD)

Ecclesiastes 7:1 "Better is the day of one's death than the days of one's birth. Vanity of vanities."

Dickinson, Emily, *quote*, American Poet (1830-1886)

Chapter Ten: The Maze

Buddha, Gautama, *quote*, Nepalese monk (c.500 BC-480 BC)

The Jesus Movement, https://www.premierchristianity.com/Past-Issues/2017/September-2017/ The-Jesus-People-Revolution-the-60s-hippies-who-changed-the-world

Carmichael, Amy (1935) *Gold Cord: The Story of a Fellowship*, Chapter 4, "Dead Babies", Dohnavur Fellowship/London Society for Promoting Christian Knowledge

Rumi, Jalal al-Din, *quote*, Persian poet, scholar, Sufi mystic (1207-1273)

Chapter Eleven: No Pain

Mandino, Augustine (Og), *quote*, American author (1923-1996)

Quinones, Sam (2015) ibid

Temple, John (2015), *American Pain: How a Young Felon and His Ring of Doctors Unleashed America's Deadliest Drug Epidemic*, Lyons Press

Mitchell, Tracey Helton (2015) *The Big Fix: Hope After Heroin*, Seal Press, San Francisco

Chapter Twelve: Secret Lives

Saint Jerome (E. S. Hieronymus), *quote*, Christian priest, theologian, historian (347-420 AD)

Substance Abuse and Mental Health Services Administration (SAMHSA) 2015 National Survey on Drug Use and Health (NSDUH)

Alcohol consumption in America:

Cook, Philip J., (2007), *Paying the Tab: The Costs and Benefits of Alcohol Control*, Princeton University Press

Ingraham, Christopher, The Washington Post, WonkBlog December 2015, Americans are drinking themselves to death at record rates: https://www.niaaa.nih.gov/alcohol-health/overview-alcohol-consumption/alcohol-facts-and-statistics

National Public Radio (NPR), June 11, 2017, *Why We Should Say Someone Is A 'Person With An Addiction,' Not An Addict* by Maia Szalavitz

https://www.npr.org/sections/health-shots/2017/06/11/531931490/change-from-addict-to-person-with-an-addiction-is-long-overdue

Tournier, Paul, *quote*, Swiss physician and author (1898-1986)

Chapter Thirteen: Community

Quinones, Sam (2015) ibid

Mumford and Sons, "The Cave", *Sigh No More*, 2009

Ornish, Dean, MD, quote, American physician & founder of nonprofit Preventative Medicine Research Institute (b. 1953)

Chapter Fourteen: Primum Non Nocere

Nightingale, Florence, *quote*, English social reformer & founder of modern nursing (1820-1920)

Medication Assisted Treatment (MAT), Lopez, German. "There's a highly successful treatment for opioid addiction. But stigma is holding it back", https://www.vox.com/science-and-health/2017/7/20/15937896/medication-assisted-treatment-methadone-buprenorphine-naltrexone

Suboxone as part of Harm Reduction/MAT, *Drugs, Brains, and Behavior: The Science of Addiction*, NIDA, https://www.drugabuse.gov/publications/drugs-brains-behavior-science-addiction/treatment-recovery

Clapton, Eric, "River of Tears", *Pilgrim*, 1998

NBC Nightly News, April 3, 2016, Gadi Schwartz and Matthew Vann, re: Heroin Safe Zones and Harm Reduction

National Public Radio, *Morning Edition*, March 1, 2016, Martha Bebinger, review of stats on supervised injection facilities

Stowe, Harriet Beecher, *quote*, American abolitionist and author, (1811-1896)

Chapter Fifteen: An Ounce of Prevention

Sun Tzu, quote from *The Art of War*, Ancient Chinese military strategist, 5th century BC

The Dalai Lama on drug addiction: Dr. Nora Volkow's blog (National Institute on Drug Abuse—NIDA) re: 2013 and meeting with the Dalai Lama at a conference in India where he convened a small group of scientists from around the world with Buddhist contemplatives and other scholars to discuss the topic of craving, desire, and addiction. https://www.drugabuse.gov/about-nida/noras-blog

Bader, Ellyn & Pearson, Peter T. (2000) *Tell Me No Lies*, Chapter 3: The Lie Invitee, St. Martin's Press, New York

"How to Make Money Selling Drugs"(2012) Documentary by Matthew Cooke, Bert Marcus, Adrian Grenier

Tubman, Harriet, *quote*, American abolitionist and political activist (c. 1822-1913)

Chapter Sixteen: Designer Genes

Lee, Harper (1960) *To Kill a Mockingbird*, quote by Atticus Finch

Marijuana and heroin addiction: www.cdc.gov/vitalsigns/heroin

Valentish, Jenny (2017), *Woman of Substances: A Journey Into Addiction and Treatment*, Black Ink, Victoria, Australia (b. 1975)

Frontline, Feb 23, 2016, Dr. Nora Volkow, Director of NIDA re: early exposure increasing genetic tendency for addiction

Mitchell, Tracey Helton (2015) ibid, pg. 195

Wheatley, Margaret J., *quote*, American writer and management consultant who studies organizational behavior (b. 1944)

Chapter Seventeen: The Secret Keepers

Perry, Tyler, *quote*, American actor and filmmaker (b. 1969)

Johnson, David & VanVonderen, Jeff (1991) *The Subtle Power of Spiritual Abuse*, Bethany House Publishers

Kubanda, Gabe, "Don't Be Lying", © 2014 Kubanda Music Publishing

Chapter 18: Hopes and Dreams

Aeschylus, quote from the play *Agamemnon (458 BC)*, ancient Greek tragedian (c. 523-456 BC)

Proverbs 13:12: "Hope deferred makes the heart sick…"

Writer, Susan D., Ph.D., "Grieving the Living" posted on the Community Alliance For Healthy Minds website: http://cahmsd.org/

Isaiah 49:15-16: "Can a nursing mother forget her own child?…"

Mumford & Sons, "Ghosts That We Knew", *Babel*, 2012

Carmichael, Amy, (1935) ibid. Chapter 4: "Dead Babies", pg. 34

Jeremiah 31:15: "A voice is heard, lamentation and bitter weeping…"

Scientific American, August 11, 2015, *It's Official: The Universe is Dying Slowly*

https://www.scientificamerican.com/article/it-s-official-the-universe-is-dying-slowly/

Didion, Joan,(2007) ibid

Lewis, C. S. (1961) *A Grief Observed*, pp. 45, 54, Faber & Faber United Kingdom

Kübler-Ross, Elisabeth & Kessler, David,(2005) ibid, pp. 52-54

Clapton, Eric, "Tears in Heaven", *Unplugged*, 1992

Smiles, Samuel, *quote*, Scottish author and government reformer (1812-1904)

Chapter Nineteen: Songs For Broken Hearts

Andersen, Hans Christian, *quote*, Danish author (1805-1875)

Clapton, Eric, (2007) *Clapton: The Autobiography*, Crown Archetype

Clapton, Eric, "Broken Hearted", *Pilgrim*, 1998

Psalm 51:17: "A broken and contrite heart God will not despise."

Herring, Annie, "I Cry for Mercy" by Annie Herring, *Waiting for My Ride to Come*, 1991

Vanauken, Sheldon (1977), *A Severe Mercy*, pg. 184, Harper & Row San Francisco

Irving, Washington, *quote*, American author (1783-1859)

Kübler-Ross, Elisabeth & Kessler, David (2005) ibid. Chpt 2, re: Tears

Dylan, Bob, "Everything is Broken", *Oh Mercy*, 1989

Switchfoot, "Head over Heels (In This Life)", *Oh! Gravity*, 2006

Joy, Vance, "We All Die Trying to Get it Right", *Dream Your Life Away*, 2014

Switchfoot, "Yesterdays", *Oh! Gravity*, 2006

Beethoven, Ludwig van, *quote*, German composer and pianist (1770-1827)

Landor, Walter Savage, *quote*, English writer, poet, activist (1775-1864)

Chapter Twenty: Shame on Who?

Beattie, Melody, (1990), The Language of Letting Go: Daily Meditations for Codependents, Hazelden

National Public Radio, October 28, 2017, 'People, Places & Things' Is A Clear-Eyed Look At Addiction by Jeff Lunden https://www.npr.org/2017/10/28/560280211/ people-places-things-is-a-clear-eyed-look-at-addiction

Hazelden-Betty Ford Institute for Recovery, *quote from web article on stigma*, https://www.hazeldenbettyford.org/ recovery-advocacy/stigma-of-addiction

Chapter Twenty-one: The Rescuers

Beattie, Melody, *quote*, American author of self-help books on codependent relationships (b. 1948)

Beattie, Melody (1986) ibid, pp. 84-85

Ephesians 4:32: "Be kind to one another tenderhearted, and forgiving one another as God ..."

Lewis, Clive Staples (1940), *The Problem of Pain*, pp. 40, 41, The Centenary Press

NBC Nightly News (2015), *The Heroin Epidemic in America* re: Narcan for parents.

Lewis, C. S. (1940) ibid, pp. 46-48

National Public Radio, August 10, 2018, Martha Bebinger, *Families Choose Empathy Over 'Tough Love' To Rescue Loved Ones From Opioids*

https://www.npr.org/sections/health-shots/2018/08/10/636556573/families-choose-empathy-over-tough-love-to-rescue-loved-ones-from-opioids

Beattie, Melody (1986 & 1990) ibid

Clapton, Eric,(2007) ibid

Beattie, Melody, *quote*, ibid

Chapter Twenty-two: Auto-Pilot

Curran, John Philpott, *quote from* "Election of Lord Mayor of Dublin" speech before the Privy Council, July 10, 1790, Irish orator, politician, judge (1750-1817)

Johnson, Samuel, *quote*, English writer, editor, literary critic, philanthropist (1709-1784)

Spektor, Regina, "Laughing With," *Far*, 2009

Mitchell, Tracey Helton,(2015) ibid, pg. 200, 145, 197

Horace, Quintus Horatius Flaccus, *quote*, Roman lyric poet (65 BC-8 BC)

Chapter Twenty-three: Shredding Your Life

Killswitch Engage, "Always," *Disarm the Descent*, 2013

Jung, Carl Gustav, *quote*, Swiss psychiatrist who founded analytical psychology (1875-1961)

Chapter Twenty-four: Time And Eternity

Seneca, Lucius Annaeus, *quote*, Roman Stoic philosopher and statesman (c. 4 BC – 65 AD)

Einstein, Albert, *quote*, German-born theoretical physicist (1879-1955)

Hill, Kim, "Mysterious Ways," *Brave Heart*, 1991

Milton, John, *quote*, English poet and civil servant under Oliver Cromwell (1608-1674)

Vanauken, Sheldon (1977) ibid, pg. 123

Lewis, Clive Staples (1950) *The Lion, The Witch, and The Wardrobe*, Geoffrey Bles Publ

Penn, William, *quote*, Founder of American colony Pennsylvania (1644-1718)

Chapter Twenty-five: Memories

Loren, Sophia, *quote*, Italian film actress (b. 1934)

National Public Radio, *Science Friday with Ira Flato*, June 2015, review of movie *Inside Out* and memoires

Carr, David Michael (2008), *The Night of the Gun*, pp.12-19, Simon & Schuster (1956-2015)

Cather, Willa Sibert, *quote*, American writer (1873-1947)

Chapter Twenty-six: Regrets

Thoreau, Henry David, *quote*, American poet, philosopher, abolitionist, surveyor (1817-1862)

Harris, Sidney J., *quote*, American journalist, from his syndicated column "Strictly Personal." (1917-1986)

Wesley, John, quoted in *War on the Saints* (abridged 1993), by Jessie Penn-Lewis, pg. 7, Christian Literature Crusade

Tozer, Aiden W. (1966), *Man: The Dwelling Place of God*, Send The Light Trust (1897-1963)

I Corinthians 15:19: "If in this life only we have hope in Christ, we of all people are most pitiful."

Kushner, Harold S., Rabbi (1981), *When Bad Things Happen to Good People*, Random House, NY(b. 1935)

Amiel, Henri-Frédéric (1896) *Journal Intime*, Swiss philosopher, poet, critic (1821-1881)

Agathon, *quote*, Greek tragic poet (448-440 BC)

Kübler-Ross, Elisabeth & Kessler, David (2005) ibid, pp. 38-40

Chapter Twenty-seven: Accepting The Mystery

Augustine, Aurelius (400 AD) ibid

U2, "Grace", *All That You Can't Leave Behind*, 2000, lyrics © Universal Music Publishing

John 11:35-36: Jesus weeps at Lazarus' death, the crowd asking why He didn't prevent it?

John 9:1-3: Jesus and the blind man: who sinned?

Burns, Robert (1759-1796), "To A Mouse": The best laid schemes o' mice an' men / Gang aft a-gley. The American Heritage® New Dictionary of Cultural Literacy, Third Edition

Carmichael, Amy (1935) ibid, Chpt. 4, "Snow"

Tolkien, J. R. R. (1954), *The Lord of the Rings*, Allen & Unwin, United Kingdom (1892-1973)

Luke 16:26: "There is a great gulf fixed between here and there..."

Dickens, Charles J. H. (1859), *A Tale of Two Cities*, Chapman & Hall, London (1812-1870)

Matthew 5:4: " Blessed are those who mourn for they will be comforted."

Karr, Mary, (1995), The Liars Club, pp. 102-104, Viking (b. 1955)

Lightfoot, Joseph B., *quote*, English Theologian (1828-1889)

Carmichael, Amy, quote, (1935) ibid, pg. 147

Carmichael, Amy, (1935) "In Acceptance," 5th stanza

Chapter Twenty-eight: Stories of Hope

Lamott, Anne (1994), *Bird by Bird*, pg. xxiii, Random House, NY (1954)

FOOD FOR THOUGHT: RESOURCES

I've listed some of the most widely acknowledged support groups
and programs, some of which we have participated in. Also a few
very helpful addiction and recovery information sites. There are
more listed on our blog and website:
www.OpiateNation.com
www.JudeDiMeglioTrang.com

GRIEF SUPPORT, USA:

Grief Share: www.griefshare.org/
Grief Anonymous: www.griefanonymous.com/
The Compassionate Friends: www.compassionatefriends.org/

RECOVERY PROGRAMS, Tucson, AZ:

The Mark Youth & Family Care Campus, Inc.: www.
themarkcounseling.com/
In Balance Continuum of Care: www.inbalancecontinuum.com/
Amity & Circle Tree Ranch: www.circletreeranch.org/
Joshua House: www.joshuahouse2415.com/

RECOVERY PROGRAMS WORLDWIDE:

The Salvation Army has more no-fee rehabilitation facilities than
any other program in America: www.salvationarmyusa.org/usn/
combat-addiction/
Alcoholics Anonymous (AA) For alcohol and substance addictions:
www.aa.org/
ICYPAA: The International Conference of Young People in
Alcoholics Anonymous: www.icypaa.org/about-icypaa

Narcotics Anonymous (NA): www.na.org

SMART Recovery (Self-Management And Recovery Training): www. smartrecovery.org

ADDICTION & RECOVERY INFORMATION:

Recovery Research Institute, John F. Kelly, Ph.D., www. recoveryanswers.org/

Community Reinforcement and Family Training (CRAFT) program: www.drugabuse.com/treatment-therapy/craft/, www. robertjmeyersphd.com/craft.html

Harm Reduction Coalition: www.harmreduction.org/

National Institute of Drug Abuse (NIDA), Dr. Nora Volkow, Director: www.drugabuse.gov

TEDMED Talk on addiction: www.tedmed.com/talks/ show?id=309096&ref=about-this-talk

The Addicts Mom: Online support for mothers with addiction in their families

https://addictsmom.com/ https://www.facebook.com/addictsmom/

AUTHOR BIO

Jude DiMeglio Trang is a landscape designer in the beautiful Sonoran Desert. She has been writing personal journals, lyrics and music for decades and most recently, maintaining a blog addressing topics related to addiction. After losing their son to a heroin overdose, she and her husband John kept a daily journal for a year as a way to hold on to their son and their sanity and as an enduring memorial to document their grief. The decision to write a memoir based on their journal and their son's life grew from her desire to help reduce the overwhelming number of lives lost to drug addiction in the 21st century.

John M Trang, Ph.D., is a pharmaceutical scientist. During his tenure in academe, he served as professor and department chairman. For the past twenty-five years John has provided independent research and consulting services to the pharmaceutical industry worldwide.

Jude and John live in Tucson, Arizona and part of the year in Melbourne, Australia with their daughter, son-in-law, and granddaughters.